A Book-by-Book Guide to New Testament Greek Vocabulary

A Book-by-Book Guide to New Testament Greek Vocabulary

Christopher J. Fresch

A Book-by-Book Guide to New Testament Greek Vocabulary

Hendrickson Publishers Marketing, LLC
P. O. Box 3473
Peabody, Massachusetts 01961-3473
www.hendrickson.com

ISBN 978-1-68307-158-7

Printed in the United States of America

First Printing — December 2019

Library of Congress Control Number: 2019946189

CONTENTS

ABBREVIATIONS

1	first person
2	second person
3	third person
acc	accusative
act	active voice
adj	adjective, adjectival
adv	adverb
Aram.	Aramaic
art	article
attr	attribute
comp	comparative
conj	conjunction
dat	dative
encl	enclitic
exclam	exclamation
fem	feminine
freq.	frequently
gen	genitive
Heb.	Hebrew
impers	impersonal
indecl	indeclinable
inf	infinitive
interj	interjection
interr	interrogative
intrans	intransitive
Lat.	Latin
masc	masculine
mid	middle voice (whether middle or middle-passive morphology)

mid-pass	middle-passive morphology
NA	*Nestle-Aland Novum Testamentum Graece*. 28th revised edition. Edited by Barbara Aland, Kurt Aland, Johannes Karavidopoulos, Carlo M. Martini, and Bruce M. Metzger. Stuttgart: Deutsche Bibelgesellschaft, 2012
neg	negator, negative
neut	neuter
NT	New Testament
obj	object
opt	optative
OT	Old Testament
pass	passive voice
pf	perfect
pl	plural
postp	postpositive
prep	preposition
pron	pronoun
ptc	participle
rel	relative
SBL	*The Greek New Testament: SBL Edition*. Edited by Michael W. Holmes. Atlanta: Society of Biblical Literature, 2010
sg	singular
subj	subjunctive
subst	substantive
superl	superlative
TH	*The Greek New Testament*. Produced at Tyndale House Cambridge. Edited by Dirk Jongkind et al. Wheaton, IL: Crossway, 2017
trans	transitive
UBS	*The Greek New Testament*. 5th revised edition. Edited by Barbara Aland, Kurt Aland, Johannes Karavidopoulos, Carlo M. Martini, and Bruce M. Metzger. Stuttgart: Deutsche Bibelgesellschaft, 2014
×	number of times

INTRODUCTION

The aim of this book is to help you memorize the vocabulary found in the Greek New Testament in a targeted and efficient way so that you can begin reading the biblical text with understanding and increasing mastery. The impetus for this volume came from the fact that, while one could attempt to memorize a seemingly endless list of all the words that occur in the NT, it is far more achievable and encouraging to memorize smaller lists of words targeted at specific reading goals. The book is structured so that you can set and achieve the goal of reading any particular book of the NT. It enables you to do so by providing the relevant vocabulary for the book in question, along with contextual glosses and any necessary grammatical and morphological information.

How This Book Is Organized

This book is composed of three sections: (1) lists of lexemes occurring 40 times or more in the NT, (2) lists of lexemes occurring 39 times or fewer in the NT, and (3) an appendix.

The first section more or less covers the vocabulary one would learn in a first-year, introductory Greek course. In order to begin reading much of anything in the NT, it is essential to know these words. The 38 lists in this section provide the 377 most common vocabulary words in the NT, in order of most frequent to least frequent. For ease of memorization, the words are grouped in lists of 10 (with 7 words in the last list). Thus, each list covers a certain frequency spectrum (e.g., List 1 contains all the words that occur from 19,865 to 1,767 times in the NT; List 2 contains all the words that occur from 1,624 to 917 times; and so on). Within each list, the lexemes are ordered alphabetically—again, to facilitate memorization.

The book's second section, which presents lexemes that occur 39 times or fewer in the NT, is divided into 27 chapters, one for each book of the NT. For the 10 largest books (Matthew, Mark, Luke, John, Acts, Romans, 1 Corinthians, 2 Corinthians, Hebrews, and Revelation), each chapter lists only the 360 lexemes that occur most frequently *within the book in question.*

(Including more words than this for these books would have made this volume too unwieldy.) Each of the remaining 17 chapters lists *all of the lexemes that occur within the book in question* (a total that never exceeds 360 words, except in the chapter for 1 Timothy, in which 366 words are listed). Similar to the lists in the book's first section (the one that presents the lexemes occurring 40 times or more in the NT), the lists in the 27 chapters of the book's second section are arranged according to descending frequency. However, in these chapters, a lexeme's frequency is determined not by its number of occurrences in the NT, but rather by its number of occurrences within the given book. For example, ἀγρός, "field," occurs 36 times in the NT, but in the Gospel of Luke it occurs only 9 times; therefore, in the chapter on Luke, this word is listed according to the latter frequency.

The book's third section, the appendix, contains additional information for certain lexemes. In most cases, the information is morphological in nature and is intended to help you recognize word forms that may not be easily understandable at first glance. More details about the appendix can be found below.

Guide to Understanding the Entries

Each entry in this book presents a Greek lexeme, glosses for it, and, in many cases, further information that provides clarification pertaining to the lexeme's meaning and usage. In addition, some entries are followed by the symbol ▻, which indicates that they have a corresponding entry in the appendix. The following comments provide details on each of these features.

The Greek Lexemes

In the entries, a Greek lexeme is often accompanied by other relevant information (e.g., genitive endings for nouns or an indication that the word is indeclinable). The entries should be straightforward, but a few details bear mentioning.

When a noun is given, I begin (in keeping with the lexicographical tradition) with its lexical form, and then present its genitive singular ending and its nominative singular article: e.g., ἑορτή, -ῆς, ἡ. If the accent shifts or changes in the genitive singular but does not fall on the ultima, or if in the genitive there is a spelling change in the stem relative to the nominative form, I provide more than the genitive ending proper: e.g., πρόβατον, -άτου, τό. At times, if I consider it to be particularly helpful (or less likely to cause confusion than other options), I provide the entire genitive singular form: e.g., ἀλέκτωρ, ἀλέκτορος, ὁ.

When an adjective is given, I provide its lexical form along with the endings or, if necessary, more fully spelled-out forms of its feminine singular (if applicable) and neuter singular. Thus, a 2-1-2 adjective (i.e., one for which the masculine and neuter have second-declension forms and the feminine has first-declension forms) may be given as follows: ἀληθινός, -ή, -όν, or σός, σή, σόν, or even ἕτοιμος, -οίμη, -ον. The same applies to a 2-2 adjective, but since for such adjectives the masculine and feminine forms are identical, a separate feminine form is not provided: e.g., ἀποσυνάγωγος, -ον. These same principles apply to 3-1-3 and 3-3 adjectives.[1]

When a pronoun is given, I provide its lexical form and, if the pronoun has gendered forms, I also give their endings (or, if necessary, more fully spelled-out forms of its feminine singular and neuter singular: e.g., αὐτός, αὐτή, αὐτό).

Changes and differences in spelling are noted when necessary. Changes are found, for example, in ἐκ and ἀπό, which in certain environments are spelled, respectively, as ἐξ and ἀπ᾽ or ἀφ᾽. For words such as these, the changes in spelling are given in parentheses next to the lexeme: e.g., ἐκ (ἐξ). Other words, such as ῥαββί and Βενιαμίν, exhibit different spellings across the NT manuscripts; for example, these particular words can also be spelled ῥαββεί and Βενιαμείν, respectively. In cases of this kind, the entry is typically presented in the following form: ῥαββ(ε)ί.[2]

The Glosses

Sources

In deciding on what glosses to use for a given word, I always consulted the actual text of the Greek New Testament (to observe the word's use in context), BDAG, LSJ, and Danker's *Concise Greek-English Lexicon of the New Testament*.[3] I often also consulted the Greek text of the Septuagint, Muraoka's

---

1. By way of reminder, 3-1-3 adjectives are those for which the masculine and neuter have third-declension forms and the feminine has first-declension forms. Likewise, 3-3 adjectives are those for which all three genders have third-declension forms and for which the masculine and feminine forms are identical.

2. These differences are especially important to note with the advent of the Tyndale House *Greek New Testament*, which does not impose standardized spellings across the Greek text.

3. Walter Bauer et al., *A Greek-English Lexicon of the New Testament and Other Early Christian Literature*, 3rd ed., rev. and ed. Frederick William Danker (Chicago:

Greek-English Lexicon of the Septuagint, Montanari's *Brill Dictionary of Ancient Greek*, Louw and Nida's *Greek-English Lexicon of the New Testament Based on Semantic Domains*, and *NIDNTTE*.[4] I also consulted and benefited from certain articles and had discussions with others with regard to a handful of words.[5] When deciding on what glosses to use in any given instance, I had three goals:

(1) To provide all the glosses I considered necessary for an informed understanding of the lexeme.

(2) To provide contextual glosses when possible.

(3) To avoid overloading the reader with glosses. (Given the priority of the first two goals, I did not always succeed at this.)

It is important to note that I provide *glosses*, not definitions, and that fuller entries on every lexeme in this book can be found in the resources cited

---

The University of Chicago Press, 2000) [= BDAG]; Henry George Liddell and Robert Scott, *A Greek-English Lexicon*, rev. Sir Henry Stuart Jones, 9th ed. (Oxford: Clarendon, 1996) [= LSJ]; Frederick William Danker, *The Concise Greek-English Lexicon of the New Testament* (Chicago: The University of Chicago Press, 2009).

4. Takamitsu Muraoka, *A Greek-English Lexicon of the Septuagint* (Louvain: Peeters, 2009); Franco Montanari, *The Brill Dictionary of Ancient Greek*, ed. Madeleine Goh and Chad Schroeder (Leiden: Brill, 2015); Johannes P. Louw and Eugene A. Nida, *Greek-English Lexicon of the New Testament Based on Semantic Domains* (New York: United Bible Societies, 1989); Moisés Silva, ed., *New International Dictionary of New Testament Theology and Exegesis*, 2nd ed. (Grand Rapids: Zondervan, 2014).

5. On ἀρσενοκοίτης and issues relating to it: a number of blog posts by Preston Sprinkle that can be found at https://www.prestonsprinkle.com/blog/category/homosexuality. On αὐθεντέω: Jamin Hübner, "Revisiting αὐθεντέω in 1 Timothy 2:12: What Do the Extant Data Really Show?" *Journal for the Study of Paul and His Letters* 5, no. 1 (2015): 41–70; Cynthia Long Westfall, "The Meaning of αὐθεντέω in 1 Timothy 2.12," *Journal of Greco-Roman Christianity and Judaism* 10 (2014): 138–73. On διακρίνω: Peter Spitaler, "Διακρίνεσθαι in Mt. 21:21, Mk. 11:23, Acts 10:20, Rom. 4:20, 14:23, Jas. 1:6, and Jude 22—The 'Semantic Shift' That Went Unnoticed by Patristic Authors," *Novum Testamentum* 49, no. 1 (2007): 1–39 (many thanks to Michael Aubrey for bringing this article to my attention). On δικαιόω: James Prothro, e-mail correspondence, January 15 and 17, 2019. On σκύβαλον: four blog posts by Michael Aubrey on the topic, all of which can be found at https://koine-greek.com/2018/06/24/the-complete-series-on-skubalon/. On ὑδροποτέω: Michael Aubrey, "Compounding and Cognitive Processes in Word Formation with ὑδροποτέω and Its Relatives: Was Anyone Ever a 'Water Drinker'?" (paper presented at the annual meeting of the Society of Biblical Literature, Denver, CO, November 18, 2018).

above. This volume is meant to be an aid to vocabulary memorization, not a definitive or comprehensive resource with regard to the semantics of Greek words.

The Syntax of the Glosses

In the chapters, glosses are sometimes separated by commas and other times by semicolons. Glosses separated by commas pertain to *a single concept* conveyed by a given Greek word. Glosses separated by semicolons, on the other hand, address *distinct concepts*. For example, the glosses for ἀρχή are "beginning; ruler, authority; rule, domain." The gloss "beginning" is given first because it represents the most central sense of the word ἀρχή. (Generally, I have attempted to place more central senses first and to put senses that extend from the prototypical core later.) No other glosses are needed to understand this concept, so "beginning" is not followed by a comma or further glosses. A second distinct concept is given after the semicolon, represented by the glosses "ruler" and "authority." Following the second semicolon is a third distinct concept, represented by the glosses "rule" and "domain."

Repeated Glosses

Occasionally, I repeat a gloss, owing both to the semantic range of the Greek lexeme and the semantic range of the English gloss. For instance, the glosses given for κληρονόμος are "heir; beneficiary, heir." The polysemy of "heir" matches up well with the polysemy of κληρονόμος. The first distinct sense of κληρονόμος is conveyed by "heir," which refers to the succession of hereditary rank (e.g., "William is heir to the throne"). The second distinct sense, which concerns the inheritance of property (e.g., "I have named fifteen heirs in my will"), can also be conveyed by "heir." For the purpose of disambiguation, I often provide one or more other glosses with a repeated term (such as "beneficiary" in the present example).

Extra Information in the Glosses

The glosses are often accompanied by extra information that is intended to help you when you see the word in context or to help you gain a fuller understanding of the word while memorizing it. Sometimes, this information elaborates on or clarifies the glosses. For example, one of the glosses I provide for μέσος is "middle [spatial or temporal]." The information in brackets here offers clarification of the term "middle." Often, the extra information I supply is grammatical in nature. For example, here is the full entry for μέσος:

middle [spatial or temporal];
(*subst*) (τὸ) μέσον middle, midst;
(*adv*) in the middle/midst (of), among;
(*prep +gen*) in the middle/midst (of), among

Since μέσος can function adjectivally, substantively, adverbially, or as a preposition, I note each of these uses separately, denoting them by means of the grammatical information that precedes each set of glosses. Two clarifications should be noted concerning how I present such information:

(1) When grammatical information is given *before* a set of glosses, it applies to *all the glosses that follow* (even if they are separated by semicolons) *until a new grammatical category is given.*

(2) When grammatical information is given *at the end of* a set of glosses separated by commas, *it applies only to the distinct sense of the Greek word that these particular glosses denote.* For example, the glosses for προσανατίθημι are "(*mid*) contribute; consult with (*+dat obj*)." The information "*+dat obj*" applies only to "consult with," since it comes after this gloss. (The former sense, "contribute," takes an accusative object, as one would assume by default.)

With regard to verbs, a few matters require explanation. First, I distinguish between transitive and intransitive uses. For example, the glosses for ἐνεργέω are "(*intrans*) be at work/active; (*trans*) work, produce." While I could have provided the glosses alone, it is important to understand that the verb's semantics and its transitivity are bound together. Consider also the glosses for κάμπτω: "(*trans*) bend; (*intrans*) bend." If only "bend" were given, the reader would be left to guess whether this refers to the bending of an object, the bending of the self, or both.

Second, I indicate distinct senses that are tied to a specific voice. For example, the glosses for κληρόω are "(*act*) appoint by lot; (*mid*) obtain by lot." It is important to understand what my terminology regarding voice—specifically "*mid-pass*," "*mid*," and "*pass*"—refers to:

(1) "*mid-pass*" refers to middle-passive *forms*, which can convey middle *or* passive voice. Every tense-form (e.g., present, aorist, imperfect) has a middle-passive form: e.g., λύομαι, ἐλύθην, ἐλυόμην, λυθήσομαι, λέλυμαι, ἐλελύμην. However, note that the aorist and future *middle* forms (e.g.,

ἐθεασάμην, θεάσομαι) are not referred to by "(*mid-pass*)," as they convey only middle, not passive, voice.[6]

(2) "*mid*" refers to middle *voice*, which *can* be conveyed by the middle-passive forms noted above and *is* conveyed by the aorist and future middle forms (e.g., ἐθεασάμην, θεάσομαι).

(3) "*pass*" refers to passive *voice*, which *can* be conveyed by the middle-passive forms noted above but is *not* conveyed by the aorist and future middle forms.

Normally, the voice designators (i.e., "*act*," "*mid*," and "*pass*") are what you will come across in the entries. They indicate whether a given gloss or set of glosses pertains to the active, middle, or passive voice (which are or can be conveyed by the active forms [for *act*], middle and middle-passive forms [for *mid*], and middle-passive forms [for *pass*]). I rarely use the *pass* designator, since the passive of a verb can usually be inferred from the active or middle. Thus, *pass* only appears when I think there is a unique need to specify a verb's meaning in the passive. The *mid-pass* designator is the least used. It only appears when I think there is a need to indicate a sense that is tied specifically to middle-passive morphology. For example, the entry for κνήθω reads "(*mid-pass*) itch" (the word does not occur outside of the middle-passive in the NT, so other voices are not given). When this word is in the active voice, it carries the sense "scratch." When it occurs in the middle voice, it carries the sense "scratch oneself, have oneself scratched." In the middle-passive forms, however, it carries the sense "itch." Given these distinctions based on voice and voice forms, it is necessary to indicate that "itch" is specifically conveyed by the middle-passive forms. Similarly, the gloss for πιστόω is "(*mid-pass*) be confident/convinced." The meaning given is linked specifically to the middle-passive form, as the active would be "make (someone) trustworthy, bind; give a proof" and the middle would be "bind to oneself, give mutual pledges of fidelity; affirm one's good faith; confirm."

A final point concerning extra information in the glosses: Given that there are a number of critical editions of the Greek New Testament that one

6. For an excellent investigation of the semantics of -(θ)η- middle-passive forms, as well as some discussion on the overlap and non-overlap of middle and middle-passive forms, see Rachel Aubrey, "Motivated Categories, Middle Voice, and Passive Morphology," in *The Greek Verb Revisited: A Fresh Approach for Biblical Exegesis*, ed. Steven E. Runge and Christopher J. Fresch (Bellingham, WA: Lexham Press, 2016).

might use, I note instances where a given lexeme occurs in some editions but not others. For example, in the chapter on 2 Peter, the gloss for σ(ε)ιρός is "pit <TH only>." The information in angle brackets indicates that this lexeme occurs in the Tyndale House *Greek New Testament* but not in the Nestle-Aland/United Bible Societies or Society of Biblical Literature editions (the other major critical editions currently in use).

The Appendix

As noted above, some entries are followed by the symbol ▻. This indicates (1) that the lexeme in question has an entry in the appendix and (2) that this entry is relevant for one or more of the lexeme's occurrences in the biblical book being studied. Thus, for example, in the 2 Thessalonians and Hebrews chapters the word αἱρέω is accompanied by the symbol ▻, because the appendix contains an entry for this word that provides the second aorist form εἱλόμην, which one needs to know in order to recognize and understand the forms of αἱρέω found in 2 Thess 2:13 (εἵλατο) and Heb 11:25 (ἑλόμενος). By contrast, in the chapter on Philippians, the entry for αἱρέω is not accompanied by the symbol ▻, since this word's form in Phil 1:22, αἱρήσομαι, is built off of the lexical form and is therefore easier to understand.

The appendix primarily contains morphological information that is intended to help you recognize forms that are irregular or that may not be immediately familiar, as the example above demonstrates. The lexical forms in the appendix are arranged alphabetically, for quick reference. For each appendix entry, I have provided a gloss of the lexeme (often shortened from what is in the vocabulary lists) and then any forms I consider relevant to the task of reading the text of the NT (the lists of forms are therefore not exhaustive).

In the appendix, the morphological information for verbs is arranged according to mood: indicative, imperative, subjunctive, optative, participle, and infinitive. Usually, I give only indicative forms (since the forms of other moods can be inferred), but there are instances when a form in another mood needs to be provided. Within each mood, the order of forms is as follows: present middle-passive, aorist active, aorist middle, aorist middle-passive, imperfect active, imperfect middle-passive, future active, future middle, future middle-passive, perfect active, perfect middle-passive, pluperfect active, pluperfect middle-passive.

As an example, consider the entry for ἐμπαίζω:

ἐμπαίζω mock, ridicule

(*aor act ind*) ἐνέπαιξα; (*aor mid-pass ind*) ἐνεπαίχθην;
(*fut act ind*) ἐμπαίξω

For this word, I have provided the aorist active, aorist middle-passive, and future active forms, since knowledge of them is necessary for reading some of the passages in which this word occurs and since these forms cannot be easily intuited from the lexical form.

In deciding what to put in the appendix, I chose to include any word that has forms associated with it that are not built off of the same root (e.g., for ἔρχομαι, I list ἦλθον, ἐλεύσομαι, and ἐλήλυθα). I also tried to put myself in the shoes of my first-year Greek students: by the end of first-year Greek, what forms would they not know, not be able to produce, or still have difficulty with? Given this, it is likely that some of the information in the appendix will be unnecessary for some readers. For others, however, there may not be as much information as they would like. My hope is that I have provided more information than will be necessary for most readers, so that those who do not need it can ignore it and those who do need it can benefit from it.

How to Use This Book

For maximum benefit, I recommend using this book according to a structured program. You may want to try the following method or something like it:

(1) Begin by memorizing the vocabulary presented in the book's first section (the lexemes that occur 40 times or more in the NT). (Hopefully, most of these words will already be familiar to most users of this book, since they are typically memorized in a first-year Greek course.)

(2) Set a reading goal, e.g., to read 1 John.

(3) Decide whether you want to:

(a) memorize every word in the book, or

(b) only memorize the words in the book down to a certain frequency (this can be a good option for bigger books in particular).

(4) Start memorizing, being careful to keep the following in mind:

(a) Work from Greek to English *and* from English to Greek.

(b) Don't try to memorize more than *ten words a day*.[7]

(5) Create a sustainable program for review:

(a) In order to memorize new words, it is important to look at them frequently. Ideally, it is best to set aside a few minutes multiple times a day to work on them. (For example, begin learning the words in List 1 around 7 a.m., then review them around noon and 7 p.m.)

(b) It is important to see words you have begun to memorize repeatedly in order to help solidify them in your memory. (For example, if you learned List 1 yesterday, in addition to starting a new list today, review the contents of List 1, perhaps for a few minutes at two or three points in the day.) If you can, try to review at least one to two old lists each day, in addition to learning a new one.

(6) Most importantly, read the Greek New Testament!

Of course, you can start reading the biblical text at any point while you are memorizing vocabulary. Learning vocabulary and reading texts is a recursive process; you will find yourself moving back and forth between this book and the Greek New Testament. You may want to put off reading the biblical text until you have mastered all of the words you intend to learn, or you may want to start reading immediately. Either way (every option in between is also possible), setting aside time to work on vocabulary to help you in your reading goal will always be beneficial.[8] Getting into the text sooner rather

---

7. Even fewer is better, with seven new words per day being the optimal cutoff point. For an excellent study of the science and application of second language vocabulary acquisition, as well as tips on how to memorize vocabulary as efficiently and effectively as possible, see Jeremy Paul Thompson, "Learning Biblical Hebrew Vocabulary: Insights from Second Language Vocabulary Acquisition" (PhD dissertation, University of Stellenbosch, 2011). Helpful insights and tips may also be found in Constantine R. Campbell, *Keep Your Greek: Strategies for Busy People* (Grand Rapids: Zondervan, 2010), 36–48; Rodney A. Whitacre, *Using and Enjoying Biblical Greek: Reading the New Testament with Fluency and Devotion* (Grand Rapids: Baker Academic, 2015), 9–22.

8. Even if you use a reader's Greek New Testament edition (something I do recommend!), expanding your vocabulary remains critical. In a reader's edition,

than later is often best, however, since—while knowing vocabulary makes reading possible—reading words in context helps cement vocabulary and expand your understanding of it.

It is my sincere hope that this book helps you to read the Greek New Testament. Reading Scripture in its original language is thrilling and is a great privilege. Moreover, it is my conviction that it benefits those who do it and that the church as a whole benefits when more of her ministers, teachers, and interested laypeople are trained and empowered to read Scripture deeply.

Acknowledgments

It has been a delight to partner with Hendrickson Publishers on this project. I am particularly grateful to my editors, Jonathan Kline and Tirzah Frank, and my typesetter, Phil Frank. Jonathan and Tirzah both possess a keen eye for detail—something that has benefited this book multiple times over. More than that, they have been invaluable dialogue partners through the process (and have been very patient with me while enduring all of my idiosyncrasies). Special thanks are due to Jonathan, as he is the one who conceived of this project and approached me for it. His passions for the biblical languages and for creating resources that aid in the learning of them are ones that I enthusiastically share. As a linguist and a teacher, I am excited to see him and Hendrickson leading the way in developing and publishing such resources.

I am also grateful to Andrew Keenan, who was an incredible help to me at a key stage in formatting this book. He saved me weeks (if not months) of work.

Of course, I would not have been able to work on this project if it were not for the support of my college, the Bible College of South Australia, and my family, Laura and Zoe. BCSA has enthusiastically given me the time to work on this book, and I am proud of the college's conviction, under the leadership of our principal, Tim Patrick, that the biblical languages are foundational to Christian academia and ministry. My wife, Laura, and daughter, Zoe, have been very gracious with me, enduring a number of late nights and busy

knowledge of Greek lexemes occurring about 25 to 30 times or more across the NT is presupposed. If you only know this group of words, however, your reading will still be interrupted by having to make frequent reference to the footnotes. The more vocabulary you learn, the more seamless your reading becomes, and, therefore, the more you are able to read.

weekends when I have locked myself in a room with my lexica. I trust they know that as much as I do love a good lexicon, I love them far more.

Finally, I wish to thank Cam Phillips, a friend and student. Cam, in his own way, convinced me of the need for this book. Perhaps now he will finally learn his Greek vocab.

HIGH-FREQUENCY NT VOCABULARY (40 × or more)

▷ List 1 — 19,865 to 1,767 ×

αὐτός, αὐτή, αὐτό	(*pron*) he, she, it; (*adj*) myself, yourself, himself/herself/itself; same	
δέ (*postp*)	but, and, now [non-temporal], [paragraph break]	▷
ἐγώ; (*pl*) ἡμεῖς	I, me; (*pl*) we, us	
εἰμί	be; there is/are	▷
εἰς	(+*acc*) into, to, in, for [indicating duration of time or the goal of an action]	
ἐν	(+*dat*) in, among, by (means of), with	
καί	(*conj*) and, but; (*adv*) also	
λέγω	say, speak	▷
ὁ, ἡ, τό	the	
σύ; (*pl*) ὑμεῖς	you	

▷ List 2 — 1,624 to 917 ×

γάρ (*postp*)	for [indicates that its host utterance strengthens or explains previous content]	
ἐκ (ἐξ)	(+*gen*) from (out of), of	
θεός, -οῦ, ὁ/ἡ	God, god; goddess	
Ἰησοῦς, -οῦ, ὁ	Jesus, Joshua	▷
μή	not, lest; εἰ/ἐὰν μή except, unless	▷
ὅς, ἥ, ὅ	who, whom, which, that; whoever, whomever, whichever [when preceding ἄν/ἐάν]	
ὅτι	because, since, that [marking direct/indirect discourse, a content clause, or an explanatory clause]	
οὐ (οὐκ, οὐχ, οὐχί)	no, not	▷
οὗτος, αὕτη, τοῦτο	this	
πᾶς, πᾶσα, πᾶν	all, whole, every, any; (*subst*) everything	

▷ List 3 890 to 632×

ἀλλά	but, rather ▶
ἀπό (ἀπ', ἀφ')	(+*gen*) (away) from; because of
γίνομαι	be(come), exist, happen, occur; be born/produced ▶
διά (δι')	(+*gen*) through, during, by [instrument/agency]; (+*acc*) because of, through; διὰ τί "why?"
ἐπί (ἐπ', ἐφ')	(+*gen*) on, over, at, before, at the time of, when, during; (+*dat*) on, on account of, to, in addition to, at; (+*acc*) on, over, onto, against, at, to
ἔρχομαι	come, go ▶
ἔχω	(*act*) have; be able [typically followed by *inf*]; ▶ (*mid ptc*) being closely associated with; next to, neighboring; next
ἵνα	in order that, (so) that [usually followed by *subj*]
κύριος, -ίου, ὁ	owner, lord, master, sir
πρός	(+*gen*) in the interest of; (+*dat*) near, in the vicinity of; in addition to; (+*acc*) toward, to; with regard to; with

▷ List 4 568 to 469×

ἄνθρωπος, -ώπου, ὁ	man, person, human being
εἰ	if; εἰ μή except, unless
κατά (κατ', καθ')	(+*gen*) down from, throughout, against; (+*acc*) according to, along, to, during
μετά (μετ', μεθ')	(+*gen*) with [association]; (+*acc*) after, behind
οὖν	so, then, now [non-temporal], anyway, therefore ▶
ποιέω	do, make, practice
τὶς, τὶ (*encl*)	(*subst*) anyone/anything, someone/something, a certain one/thing; (*adj*) any, some, a certain
τίς, τί	(*masc/fem*) who?, which?, what?; (*neut*) which?, what?, why?
Χριστός, -οῦ, ὁ	anointed one, Messiah, Christ
ὡς	as, like; about, approximately; that [content]; when

▷ **List 5**	**454 to 343×**	
ἀδελφός, -οῦ, ὁ	brother; (*pl*) brothers (and sisters)	
ἀκούω	(+*gen/acc obj*) hear, heed, obey; understand	➢
δίδωμι	give	
εἷς, μία, ἕν	one, someone, a certain (one)	➢
ἡμέρα, -ας, ἡ	day	
ὁράω	(*trans act/mid*) see, perceive; (*intrans act*) look (at); (*intrans mid*) appear	➢
πατήρ, πατρός, ὁ	father; (*pl*) parents	
πνεῦμα, πνεύματος, τό	wind, breath, spirit	
πολύς, πολλή, πολύ	much, many; [*acc* as *adv*] greatly, more	➢
υἱός, -οῦ, ὁ	son, descendant	

▷ **List 6**	**343 to 261×**	
ἐάν	if [typically collocated with *subj*]; when(ever); -ever [after a *rel pron*]; ἐὰν μή except, unless	
ἑαυτοῦ, -ῆς	himself/herself/itself/oneself; (*1pl*) ourselves; (*2pl*) yourselves; one another	
ἐκεῖνος, ἐκείνη, ἐκεῖνο	that (one)	
ἤ	or, (rather) than; ἤ . . . ἤ either . . . or; [ἤ can introduce rhetorical questions]	
λαλέω	say, speak, talk	
λόγος, -ου, ὁ	word, statement, message; matter, thing; account	
μαθητής, -οῦ, ὁ	disciple	
οἶδα	know, understand	➢
οὐρανός, -οῦ, ὁ	heaven, sky	
περί	(+*gen*) about, concerning; (+*acc*) near, around, about [temporal or physical]; with respect to	

▷ List 7 — 258 to 222×

ἅγιος, -ία, -ον	holy, consecrated; (*subst masc pl*) holy ones [angels, saints]; (*subst neut pl*) sanctuary	
ἀποκρίνομαι	answer, reply	▶
γινώσκω	know, understand, find out, realize	▶
γῆ, γῆς, ἡ	earth, land, region	
λαμβάνω	take, receive	▶
μέγας, μεγάλη, μέγα	great, large	▶
ὄνομα, ὀνόματος, τό	name, title, reputation	
οὐδείς, οὐδεμία, οὐδέν	(*adj*) no; (*subst*) no one, nobody, nothing	
πιστεύω	believe, trust, entrust (+*dat/acc obj*)	
πίστις, -εως, ἡ	faith(fulness), trust	

▷ List 8 — 220 to 195×

ἀνήρ, ἀνδρός, ὁ	man, husband	
γυνή, γυναικός, ἡ	woman, wife	
δύναμαι	be able	
ἐξέρχομαι	go/come out, go away	▶
θέλω	want, wish	▶
ἰδού	[attention-getter] look!, pay attention!	
Ἰουδαῖος, -αία, -αῖον	Judean, Jewish; (*subst*) Judean, Jew	
οὕτως (οὕτω)	in this way/manner, thus	
τέ (*encl, postp*)	and; τὲ . . . τέ both . . . and, not only . . . but, τὲ . . . καί both . . . and	
ὑπό (ὑπ᾽, ὑφ᾽)	(+*gen*) by [agency/cause]; (+*acc*) under	

▹ List 9 — 194 to 175×

ἄγγελος, -έλου, ὁ	angel, messenger, envoy
γράφω	inscribe, write, record
εἰσέρχομαι	enter, come/go into ▹
εὑρίσκω	find, discover ▹
καθώς	(just) as, to the extent that
κόσμος, -ου, ὁ	universe, world [cosmic order, planet earth, or the earth's inhabitants]
μέν (*postp*)	[anticipatory discourse marker that links its host utterance to corresponding forthcoming content (often introduced by δέ or καί)] ▹
νόμος, -ου, ὁ	law, custom, rule
παρά	(+*gen*) from (the side of); (+*dat*) near, beside, in the presence of, with; in the sight/judgment of; (+*acc*) alongside, by; more than
χείρ, χειρός, ἡ	hand

▹ List 10 — 175 to 158×

ἁμαρτία, -ας, ἡ	sin(fulness), failure
ἄν	[contingency particle (sometimes best left untranslated, though "would" or "ever" can often be added to bring out the particle's effect)]
βασιλεία, -ας, ἡ	kingship, kingdom
δόξα, -ης, ἡ	splendor, glory, renown, honor; (*pl*) transcendent beings
ἔθνος, -ους, τό	people (group), nation; (*pl*) gentiles
ἔργον, -ου, τό	work, task, action, deed
ἐσθίω	eat, consume ▹
ὄχλος, -ου, ὁ	crowd
πόλις, -εως, ἡ	city, town; inhabitants
τότε	then, at that time; then [indicating a successive event]

▷ **List 11**	**158 to 148×**	
ἄλλος, -η, -ο	other, another	
ἵστημι	(*trans*) set, place, (make) stand; establish; (*intrans*) stand (around)	▸
καλέω	call, invite, name	▸
καρδία, -ας, ἡ	heart [organ], mind, center of personhood [cognition, volition, emotion]	
Παῦλος, Παύλου, ὁ	Paul	
Πέτρος, -ου, ὁ	Peter	
πορεύομαι	go, walk, live	
πρῶτος, πρώτη, πρῶτον	first, earlier; first [in terms of prominence/importance]; (*neut adv*) firstly, especially; τὸ πρῶτον the first time, at an earlier time	
ὑπέρ	(+*gen*) for, on behalf of; because of; about, with regard to; (+*acc*) beyond, more than, over; (*adv*) even more	
χάρις, -ιτος, τό	grace, favor, goodwill, gracious deed; thanks, gratitude	

▷ **List 12**	**147 to 142×**	
ἀγαπάω	love	
ἀφίημι	send away; divorce; forgive; leave (behind)	▸
ἐγείρω	(*trans act*) wake, rouse, raise; (*intrans mid*) wake/rise up	▸
ἕως	until, while; as far as	
λαός, -οῦ, ὁ	people (group)	
νῦν	(just) now; (*adj*) present; (*subst*) present time	
ὅστις, ἥτις, ὅ τι	whoever, whatever, anyone who; who, which	
οὐδέ	and not, neither, nor, not even	
προφήτης, -ου, ὁ	prophet	
σάρξ, σαρκός, ἡ	flesh, body, human being	

▹ List 13 — 142 to 128×

ἀμήν	let it be so, amen; truly
ἀποστέλλω	send
βλέπω	see, observe, consider, perceive
δύο	two ▸
ζάω (ζῶ)	live
ζωή, -ῆς, ἡ	life
Ἰωάννης, -ου, ὁ	John
πάλιν	again, in turn, back [reversion]
σῶμα, σώματος, τό	body
φωνή, -ῆς, ἡ	voice, noise, sound

▹ List 14 — 128 to 119×

αἰών, -ῶνος, ὁ	age [a particular segment of time], the past, long ago, eternity
ἀρχιερεύς, -έως, ὁ	high/chief priest
βάλλω	throw, cast; put ▸
δοῦλος, δούλου, ὁ	slave
δύναμις, -άμεως, ἡ	power, might, capability; powerful deed
θάνατος, -άτου, ὁ	death
νεκρός, -ά, -όν	dead; (*subst*) dead person, corpse
ὅταν	when(ever)
παραδίδωμι	hand over, deliver, entrust
σύν	(+*dat*) with [association]

▹ List 15 — 118 to 114×

ἀγάπη, -ης, ἡ	love, affection	
ἀπέρχομαι	go (away), depart	▹
βασιλεύς, -έως, ὁ	king	
ἐκκλησία, -ας, ἡ	assembly, gathering, congregation, church	
ζητέω	seek, look for, consider, strive for	
ἴδιος, -ία, -ον	one's own; (*subst masc pl*) one's own people; (*subst neut pl*) home, possessions	
κρίνω	select, pass judgment, condemn, decide, consider	▹
μένω	(*intrans*) remain, stay, abide, persist; (*trans*) wait for	
μόνος, -η, -ον	only, alone	
οἶκος, οἴκου, ὁ	house(hold); descendants, nation; estate	

▹ List 16 — 111 to 105×

ἀλήθεια, -είας, ἡ	truth(fulness)	
ἀνίστημι	(*trans*) erect, raise (to life); (*intrans*) stand up, rise (from the dead)	▹
ἀποθνῄσκω	die, face death	▹
ἐκεῖ	there	
μέλλω	be about to/going to; (*adj ptc*) future, coming; (*subst*) future	▹
ὅλος, -η, -ον	whole, entire, all	
ὅσος, -η, -ον	as much as, as long as, as many as, all who	
παρακαλέω	invite, implore; comfort; encourage	▹
σῴζω	save, rescue	
ὥρα, ὥρας, ἡ	hour, time; (point of) time	

▷ List 17 — 103 to 100×

ἀγαθός, -ή, -όν	good, useful, beneficial
αἴρω	lift up, carry (along/away), take away ➤
ἀλλήλων	one another, each other
δεῖ	(*impers*) it is necessary, one must
ἐξουσία, -ας, ἡ	authority, right, power
καλός, -ή, -όν	fine, good, useful
ὁδός, -οῦ, ἡ	way, road, journey; way of life
ὅτε	when, while
πῶς	how?, in what way?
ψυχή, -ῆς, ἡ	life, person, inner self

▷ List 18 — 100 to 95×

αἷμα, αἵματος, τό	blood(shed)
ἄρτος, -ου, ὁ	bread, food
γεννάω	beget, give birth to
διδάσκω	teach, instruct ➤
ἕτερος, -έρα, -ον	other, another, different
ὀφθαλμός, -οῦ, ὁ	eye
περιπατέω	go, walk (around/about); live
τέκνον, -ου, τό	child
τίθημι	place, put, lay, set
Φαρισαῖος, -αίου, ὁ	Pharisee

▷ List 19 95 to 91 ×

δικαιοσύνη, -ης, ἡ	righteousness, justice
εἰρήνη, -ης, ἡ	peace [state of harmony or well-being]
ἐνώπιον	(+*gen*) before, in the sight/presence of
ἔτι	[expresses continuance or addition] still, yet
θάλασσα, -άσσης, ἡ	sea, lake
κάθημαι	sit; reside
οἰκία, -ας, ἡ	house(hold)
πούς, ποδός, ὁ	foot
τόπος, -ου, ὁ	place, location, space
φοβέομαι	(*intrans*) be afraid; (*trans*) fear, be afraid of; revere

▷ List 20 90 to 85 ×

ἀκολουθέω	follow (+*dat obj*)	
ἀπόλλυμι	(*trans act*) destroy, lose; (*intrans mid*) perish, be ruined/lost	▸
ἄρχω	(*act +gen obj*) rule; (*mid*) begin	
ἑπτά (*indecl*)	seven	
καιρός, -οῦ, ὁ	time [an exact time or a period of time judged to be significant], period, season	
μηδείς, μηδεμία, μηδέν	(*adj*) no; (*subst*) nobody, nothing	
οὔτε	and not, neither; οὔτε . . . οὔτε neither . . . nor	
πίπτω	fall, perish	▸
πληρόω	fill, complete, fulfill	
προσέρχομαι	come/go to, approach	▸

▹ List 21 — 85 to 81×

ἀναβαίνω	go up	▸
ἀπόστολος, -όλου, ὁ	apostle, messenger, ambassador	
ἕκαστος, ἑκάστη, ἕκαστον	each, every	
ἐκβάλλω	expel, throw/send out	▸
καταβαίνω	come/go down	▸
μᾶλλον	more; rather	
μήτηρ, μητρός, ἡ	mother	
ὅπου	where; whereas; ὅπου ἐάν/ἄν wherever (+*subj*)	
προσεύχομαι	pray	
ὥστε	therefore; so that	

▹ List 22 — 80 to 77×

ἀνοίγω	(*trans*) open; (*intrans*) be open	▸
βαπτίζω	wash, purify, baptize, immerse	
δίκαιος, -αία, -ον	just, (up)right, fair	
κἀγώ [< καὶ ἐγώ]	and/but I; I also	
Ἰερουσαλήμ, ἡ (*indecl*)	Jerusalem	
Μωϋσῆς, -έως, ὁ	Moses	
πέμπω	send	
πονηρός, -ά, -όν	bad, evil	
στόμα, -ατος, τό	mouth	
ὑπάγω	leave, go	

▹ List 23 — 77 to 74×

ἀποκτείνω	kill
δώδεκα (*indecl*)	twelve
ἐμός, ἐμή, ἐμόν	my; (*subst*) my property, what belongs to me
εὐαγγέλιον, -ίου, τό	good news, gospel
κεφαλή, -ῆς, ἡ	head, top
μαρτυρέω	bear witness, testify, attest; approve (of) [+*dat* of person]
πρόσωπον, -ώπου, τό	face [sometimes with a focus on personal presence], person
σημεῖον, σημείου, τό	sign
Σίμων, -ωνος, ὁ	Simon
ὕδωρ, ὕδατος, τό	water

▹ List 24 — 74 to 68×

Ἀβραάμ, ὁ (*indecl*)	Abraham
αἰτέω	ask, request
αἰώνιος, -ία, -ον	long ago, eternal ▸
ἱερόν, -οῦ, τό	temple [often the whole temple complex], sanctuary
Ἰσραήλ, ὁ (*indecl*)	Israel
πίνω	drink ▸
πῦρ, πυρός, τό	fire
τηρέω	keep, maintain, guard; observe
φῶς, φωτός, τό	light; [that which emits light] torch, lamp, fire
χαίρω	rejoice, be happy; (*impv, inf*) greetings

▷ List 25 — 68 to 66×

ἄγω	(*trans*) lead, bring, carry; (*intrans*) go	➢
ἀπολύω	set free, release; dismiss; divorce	
ἐντολή, -ῆς, ἡ	command(ment)	
καρπός, -οῦ, ὁ	fruit, produce, yield	
πιστός, -ή, -όν	faithful, trustworthy; trusting, believing	
πλοῖον, πλοίου, τό	ship, boat	
πρεσβύτερος, -έρα, -ον	old(er); (*subst*) elder	
ῥῆμα, ῥήματος, τό	word, saying, statement; thing, matter	
σάββατον, -άτου, τό	Sabbath, week	➢
τρεῖς, τρία	three	➢

▷ List 26 — 66 to 62×

γραμματεύς, -έως, ὁ	expert in the law, scholar, scribe; clerk	
δαιμόνιον, -ίου, τό	divine being, daemon; evil spirit, demon	
δοκέω	(*trans*) think, suppose; (*intrans*) seem, appear, have the appearance of	
εἴτε	whether, if; [typically] εἴτε . . . εἴτε if . . . if, whether . . . or	
ἔξω	(*adv*) out(side); (*prep +gen*) out(side); (*adj*) outside, outer; (*subst +pl art*) outsiders	
ἐρωτάω	ask; request	
θέλημα, -ήματος, τό	will, wish, desire	
ὄρος, ὄρους, τό	mountain, hill	
φέρω	bring, take along, bear	➢
φημί	say; mean	

▷ List 27 — 62 to 60×

ἀγαπητός, -ή, -όν	beloved, dear
Γαλιλαία, -ας, ἡ	Galilee
δοξάζω	praise, glorify
ἤδη	now, already
θρόνος, -ου, ὁ	chair, seat, throne
Ἱεροσόλυμα, -ύμων, τά/ἡ	Jerusalem
ἱμάτιον, -ίου, τό	clothing; cloak
κηρύσσω	proclaim, announce ▸
νύξ, νυκτός, ἡ	night
ὧδε	here (to/in this place); in this case

▷ List 28 — 60 to 58×

ἀσπάζομαι	greet, welcome; take leave of
Δαυίδ, ὁ (*indecl*)	David
διδάσκαλος, -άλου, ὁ	teacher
θεωρέω	see, observe, watch; perceive
λίθος, -ου, ὁ	stone
μέσος, -η, -ον	middle [spatial or temporal]; (*subst*) (τὸ) μέσον middle, midst; (*adv*) in the middle/midst (of), among; (*prep +gen*) in the middle/midst (of), among
προσκυνέω	worship, do obeisance to [typically with a gesture of prostration]
συνάγω	gather, bring together ▸
ὑπάρχω	exist, be (present); (*subst ptc*) property
χαρά, -ᾶς, ἡ	joy

▹ LIST 29 — 57 TO 55×

ἀρχή, -ῆς, ἡ	beginning; ruler, authority; rule, domain
δέχομαι	receive, take; welcome
ἐπερωτάω	ask; request
κράζω	cry out, scream; call out
λοιπός, -ή, -όν	remaining, rest; other; (*subst +pl art*) the rest, the others, the survivors; (*adv*) from now on; finally
μηδέ	and/but not, nor; not even
Πιλᾶτος, Πιλάτου, ὁ	Pilate
συναγωγή, -ῆς, ἡ	place of assembly, synagogue
τοιοῦτος, τοιαύτη, τοιοῦτο(ν)	of such a kind, such (as this)
τρίτος, -η, -ον	third; (*adv*) τὸ τρίτον (for) the third time; (*subst*) a third, the third part

▹ LIST 30 — 54 TO 52×

δεξιός, -ά, -όν	right [directional frame of reference]; true
διό	therefore, for this reason
ἐλπίς, -ίδος, ἡ	hope, expectation; basis for hope; something hoped for
ἐπαγγελία, -ας, ἡ	promise
ἔσχατος, -άτη, -ον	last; (*subst*) last, end
εὐαγγελίζω	bring/announce good news, proclaim the gospel
ὅπως	(*adv*) how; (*conj*) in order that
παιδίον, -ου, τό	child [normally prepubescent]
πείθω	(*act*) convince, persuade; (*mid*) obey, follow (*+dat obj*); be sure/convinced; (*pf act +dat obj*) trust; (*pf act/mid-pass*) be certain ▹
χρόνος, -ου, ὁ	(period of) time; moment in time, occasion

▷ List 31 — 52 to 49×

ἄρα	so, then; as a result
γλῶσσα, γλώσσης, ἡ	tongue; language; ecstatic speech
γραφή, -ῆς, ἡ	writing; scripture
εὐθύς	immediately; then
κακός, -ή, -όν	bad, evil
μακάριος, -ία, -ον	fortunate, happy, blessed
παραβολή, -ῆς, ἡ	parable; symbol
τυφλός, -ή, -όν	blind
σοφία, -ας, ἡ	wisdom
σπείρω	sow (seed)

▷ List 32 — 49 to 47×

ἁμαρτωλός, -όν	sinful; (*subst*) sinner
ἀποδίδωμι	pay, give back, return
ἄχρι(ς)	(+*gen*) until, as far as; (*conj*) until [typically +*rel pron* οὗ]
ἔμπροσθεν	in front; (*subst*) what is ahead, εἰς τὸ ἔμπροσθεν forward; (*prep* +*gen*) before, in front of
ἔρημος, -ον	desolate, deserted; (*subst*) wilderness, desert
ἔτος, -ους, τό	year
κρατέω	seize, grasp; hold
παραλαμβάνω	take (with/along), receive ▷
φανερόω	(*trans act*) reveal; make known; (*intrans mid*) appear; become known
χρεία, -ας, ἡ	need, lack, want

▷ List 33 — 47 to 46×

θηρίον, -ου, τό	animal; beast
καθίζω	(*trans*) seat, set; (*intrans*) sit down
κρίσις, κρίσεως, ἡ	judgment
μικρός, -ά, -όν	small, short, little
οὐκέτι	no longer/more
ποῦ	where?
πρό	(+*gen*) before [spatial or temporal], in front of, earlier
προσφέρω	bring (to); offer ▶
φόβος, -ου, ὁ	fear; reverence
φυλακή, -ῆς, ἡ	prison; watch of the night

▷ List 34 — 46 to 44×

ἀπαγγέλλω	report (back); declare, proclaim
δεύτερος, -έρα, -ον	second; [*neut* as *adv*] second time
διώκω	persecute; pursue; run after
ἐπιγινώσκω	know; learn; recognize ▶
θλῖψις, θλίψεως, ἡ	affliction; distress
ναός, -οῦ, ὁ	temple
ὅμοιος, ὁμοία, ὅμοιον	similar (to), like
οὐαί	woe!, alas!, (*subst*) woe
σταυρόω	crucify
σωτηρία, -ας, ἡ	deliverance, salvation

▷ List 35	44 to 43 ×
ἁμαρτάνω	do wrong, sin
γενεά, -ᾶς, ἡ	generation [people linked as contemporaries]; age [time of a generation]
δέω	bind, tie
Ἡρῴδης, -ου, ὁ	Herod
θαυμάζω	(*intrans*) be amazed, wonder; (*trans*) admire, wonder at
θεραπεύω	heal
Ἰάκωβος, -ώβου, ὁ	James
Ἰουδαία, -ας, ἡ	Judea
Ἰούδας, -α, ὁ	Judas, Judah, Jude
κατοικέω	live, dwell

▷ List 36	43 to 41 ×
ἀνάστασις, ἀναστάσεως, ἡ	rising; resurrection
ἄξιος, ἀξία, ἄξιον	comparable, corresponding, deserving; worthy
ἐγγίζω	approach, draw/come near [spatially or temporally]
καινός, -ή, -όν	new
λύω	untie, loose; set free; destroy; abolish
μέρος, -ους, τό	part; share
πάσχω	suffer, endure
σεαυτοῦ	yourself
σπέρμα, -ατος, τό	seed; descendant
φωνέω	call, cry out, proclaim; summon

➤

▹ List 37 — 41 to 40×

διέρχομαι	come/go through	▸
ἐργάζομαι	(*intrans*) work; (*trans*) do, accomplish, effect	
ἑτοιμάζω	prepare, make ready	
εὐλογέω	bless	
κλαίω	weep	▸
πάντοτε	always	
παρίστημι	(*trans*) put at one's disposal; present; (*intrans*) be present; come to	▸
σήμερον	today	
τιμή, -ῆς, ἡ	honor; value, price	
χωρίς	(+*gen*) without, apart from; (*adv*) apart, separately, by itself	

▹ List 38 — 40×

λογίζομαι	reckon, calculate; consider
μισέω	hate
μνημεῖον, -είου, τό	monument, memorial; tomb, grave
οἰκοδομέω	build; build up
ὀλίγος, -η, -ον	few; little, small [amount, duration, or distance]; [*neut* as *adv*] short time/distance
τέλος, -ους, τό	end; outcome; goal; [*acc* as *adv*] finally
τέσσαρες, -α	four

MATTHEW

▷ List 1 — 17 to 12×

ἀγρός, -οῦ, ὁ	field, land, countryside, tilled land
δένδρον, -ου, τό	tree
ἐκεῖθεν	from there
εὐθέως	immediately
ὀμνύω	make an oath, swear
πέντε (*indecl*)	five
σκανδαλίζω	cause (someone) to sin; shock, offend
τάλαντον, -άντου, τό	talent [monetary unit]
ὑποκριτής, -οῦ, ὁ	pretender, hypocrite
φαίνω	(*act*) shine; (*mid*) appear

▷ List 2 — 11 to 9×

ἀμπελών, -ῶνος, ὁ	vineyard
ἀναχωρέω	depart, leave, withdraw
ἄνεμος, ἀνέμου, ὁ	wind
ἅπτω	(*act*) light, kindle; (*mid +gen obj*) touch, hold, cling to
ἀργύριον, -ίου, τό	silver, silver coin [drachma or shekel]; money
ἡγεμών, ἡγεμόνος, ὁ	leader; governor
Ἰωσήφ, ὁ (*indecl*)	Joseph
μισθός, -οῦ, ὁ	pay, wages; recompense, reward
πρόβατον, -άτου, τό	sheep
ὥσπερ	(just) as

▹ List 3 — 9 to 8×

γάμος, -ου, ὁ	wedding celebration; marriage
δῶρον, δώρου, τό	gift [general or votive]
ἐλεέω	have compassion (on), show mercy to
ἔξεστιν	(*impers*) it is right/permitted [*3sg* of ἔξειμι] ▹
Ἠλίας, Ἠλίου, ὁ	Elijah
θησαυρός, -οῦ, ὁ	repository, container, chest; treasure
ναί	yes
παρέρχομαι	pass by; pass [of time]; pass away, disappear ▹
πεινάω	hunger, be hungry [physically or metaphorically]
συνίημι/συνίω	understand, comprehend ▹

▹ List 4 — 8×

ἐπάνω	(*adv*) above, over; more than; (*prep +gen*) above, over
ζιζάνιον, -ίου, τό	darnel [troublesome weed in grain fields]
θυγάτηρ, θυγατρός, ἡ	daughter
Μαρία, -ας, ἡ	Mary
μήποτε	(*conj*) so that . . . not
νηστεύω	fast [from food]
ὀδούς, ὀδόντος, ὁ	tooth
ὁμοιόω	(*intrans mid*) be like, become like; (*trans act*) compare
παῖς, παιδός, ὁ/ἡ	child [boy or girl]; child [son or daughter]; slave; servant
πλανάω	(*act*) lead astray, deceive; (*mid*) wander, go astray, be misled

▷ List 5 — 8 to 7×

ἀγοράζω	buy	
ἀναγινώσκω	read (aloud)	▶
ἄρτι	(just) now <TH ἀπάρτι "just now; from now" instead of ἀπ᾽ ἄρτι>	
βαπτιστής, -οῦ, ὁ	Baptizer	
γαμέω	marry	▶
γέεννα, γεέννης, ἡ	Gehenna, Valley of Hinnom	
δαιμονίζομαι	be demon possessed	
πόσος, -η, -ον	[*interr* or *exclam*] how much?, how great?; how much?, how many?	
σός, σή, σόν	your, yours; (*subst neut sg*) what is yours	
τελώνης, -ου, ὁ	tax collector	

▷ List 6 — 7×

ἔνδυμα, -ύματος, τό	garment, clothing	
ἕνεκα/ἕνεκεν	(+*gen*) because of, for the sake of	
ἐπιτίθημι	lay/put upon	
ἐχθρός, -ά, -όν	hated; hostile; (*subst*) enemy	
καθαρίζω	cleanse, make clean	
καθεύδω	be sleeping/asleep	
κακῶς	badly, ill; wrongly, wickedly	
κελεύω	command, order	
κλαυθμός, -οῦ, ὁ	weeping	
κρύπτω	(*trans act*) hide (something); (*intrans mid*) hide (oneself), be hidden	▶

▹ List 7 — 7×

κωφός, -ή, -όν	mute; deaf
μάχαιρα, -αίρης, ἡ	dagger, short sword
μεριμνάω	worry (about), be anxious; care for, be concerned about
οἰκοδεσπότης, -ου, ὁ	master of the house
οὐράνιος, -ον	heavenly
οὖς, ὠτός, τό	ear; hearing, understanding
ὀψία, -ας, ἡ	evening
πέραν	on the other side; (*subst* +*art*) the other side; (*prep* +*gen*) on the other side of
ποῖος, ποία, ποῖον	of what kind?; which?, what?
πότε	when?

▹ List 8 — 7 to 6×

βρυγμός, -οῦ, ὁ	grinding, gnashing [of teeth]
γεωργός, -οῦ, ὁ	farmer, cultivator
ποτήριον, -ίου, τό	cup
Σαδδουκαῖος, -αίου, ὁ	Sadducee
συλλέγω	collect, gather ▹
σφόδρα	very much, greatly, extremely
τελέω	complete, finish; carry out (completely), accomplish; pay
ὕστερος, -έρα, -ον	latter, last; [*neut* as *adv*] (*comp*) later, (*superl*) finally
φεύγω	flee; escape; avoid ▹
φρόνιμος, -ον	prudent, sensible, thoughtful, wise

▷ List 9	6×
γρηγορέω	be (fully) awake/alert; be watchful/on the alert
δεῦτε	come!, come here!, come on! ➤
δηνάριον, -ίου, τό	denarius
διάβολος, -ον	slanderous; (*subst*) adversary; devil
διακονέω	(+*dat obj*) serve; care for; wait on
ἐκτείνω	stretch (something) out
ἐπιτιμάω	(+*dat obj*) rebuke; sternly warn
ἐργάτης, -ου, ὁ	worker, laborer; doer
Ζεβεδαῖος, -αίου, ὁ	Zebedee
Ἠσαΐας, Ἠσαΐου, ὁ	Isaiah

▷ List 10	6×
θερισμός, -οῦ, ὁ	time of harvesting; harvest
θυσιαστήριον, -ίου, τό	altar
Ἰακώβ, ὁ (*indecl*)	Jacob
Ἰορδάνης, -ου, ὁ	Jordan (River)
κερδαίνω	gain ➤
λυπέω	(*act*) cause grief/sorrow; (*mid*) grieve, be sad/distressed
μεταβαίνω	go, move ➤
μήτε	[continuing a previous *neg*] and not, neither, nor
μωρός, -ά, -όν	foolish, stupid
νυμφίος, -ου, ὁ	bridegroom

▷ List 11 — 6×

ὄναρ, τό	dream, κατ᾽ ὄναρ in a dream	▷
ὀπίσω	behind, back; (*prep +gen*) behind; after [temporal or spatial]	
ὅριον, -ίου, τό	boundary; (*pl*) region, district	
ὀφείλω	owe, be indebted to; be obligated, ought; have to	
πειράζω	test; tempt	
προάγω	(*trans*) lead/bring out; (*intrans +acc* of person) go before, precede [spatially or temporally]	▷
προσέχω	look after, pay attention/attend to (*+dat obj*); [with ἀπό] watch out for, beware of	
προσκαλέω	(*mid*) invite, call to, summon	
πωλέω	sell	
σκότος, -ους, τό	darkness [literal or figurative]	

▷ List 12 — 6 to 5×

ἄκανθα, ἀκάνθης, ἡ	thorn; thornbush	
ἀνάκειμαι	recline at table, dine	
ἀνατολή, -ῆς, ἡ	rising [of a celestial body]; east	
ἀντί	(*+gen*) instead of, in place of	
ἀπάγω	lead off, take away; bring (before a magistrate/court) [legal terminology]	▷
ἀπέχω	(*trans act*) receive in full; (*intrans act*) be far away/distant	
ἄρχων, ἄρχοντος, ὁ	ruler; official	
στρέφω	(*trans act*) turn; return; change; (*intrans mid*) turn (around); change	▷
τάφος, -ου, ὁ	tomb, grave	
τιμάω	honor; set a price	

▷ List 13 5×

ἀστήρ, -έρος, ὁ	(luminous) celestial body, star
Βαραββᾶς, Βαραββᾶ, ὁ	Barabbas
Βηθλέεμ, ἡ (*indecl*)	Bethlehem
διψάω	be thirsty
ἐκπορεύομαι	go/come out
ἐλάχιστος, -ίστη, -ον	least, smallest [in status, value, or size]
ἐμβαίνω	embark ▸
ἐμπαίζω	(*act +dat obj*) mock, ridicule; (*pass*) be mocked; be deceived/tricked ▸
ἔνοχος, -ον	subject to, held in; (held) liable (for), guilty (of), deserving of
εὐώνυμος, -ον	left [as opposed to right]

▷ List 14 5×

ἥλιος, -ίου, ὁ	sun
ἰχθύς, -ύος, ὁ	fish
Ἰωνᾶς, Ἰωνᾶ, ὁ	Jonah
κάλαμος, -άμου, ὁ	reed, stalk
καταλύω	(*trans*) tear down, destroy; abolish, bring to an end
κλέπτω	steal
κοινόω	make common/impure, defile
κρυπτός, -ή, -όν	hidden, secret
λαμπάς, λαμπάδος, ἡ	torch; lamp
μετανοέω	repent

▷ LIST 15 5×

νόσος, -ου, ἡ	sickness, disease
ξένος, -η, -ον	strange, foreign; (*subst*) stranger, foreigner
οὐδέποτε	never
παραλυτικός, -ή, -όν	paralyzed; (*subst*) paralytic
περιβάλλω	(*trans act*) clothe, put on; (*trans mid*) clothe/put on oneself; (*intrans mid*) be wearing/clothed
περισσεύω	(*intrans*) abound (in), overflow; be left over
πέτρα, -ας, ἡ	rock [formation or piece]
πλήν	nevertheless, but, only; (*prep +gen*) except ▷
πόθεν	from where?, how is it that?
ποτίζω	give to drink

▷ LIST 16 5×

πτωχός, -ή, -όν	poor
σαπρός, -ά, -όν	bad, rotten
σκάνδαλον, -άλου, τό	trap; cause of sin ["stumbling block"]; offense
Σολομών, -ῶνος, ὁ	Solomon
σπλαγχνίζομαι	have compassion, feel sympathy
σταυρός, -οῦ, ὁ	cross
συκῆ, -ῆς, ἡ	fig tree
συμβούλιον, -ίου, τό	plan, plot, counsel
σύνδουλος, -ούλου, ὁ	fellow slave
συντέλεια, -είας, ἡ	completion, end

▹ List 17 — 5 to 4×

Αἴγυπτος, -ύπτου, ἡ	Egypt
ἀκοή, -ῆς, ἡ	hearing, listening; ear; news, rumor, report, message
ἀνομία, -ας, ἡ	lawlessness [condition or action]
ἀπαρνέομαι	deny, reject
ἀποκαλύπτω	reveal, disclose
τριάκοντα (*indecl*)	thirty
φιλέω	love, like; kiss
φονεύω	murder
χρυσός, -οῦ, ὁ	gold; objects of gold [e.g., jewelry, money]
χωλός, -ή, -όν	crippled, lame

▹ List 18 — 4×

ἀρνέομαι	deny; refuse; disown
ἀσκός, -οῦ, ὁ	wineskin
Βαβυλών, -ῶνος, ἡ	Babylon
βλασφημία, -ας, ἡ	slander, defamation, reviling
γέ (*encl*)	indeed, even; yet, at least, though
γυμνός, -ή, -όν	naked, bare, [figurative] uncovered; inadequately dressed; lightly dressed
ἑκατόν (*indecl*)	one hundred
ἑκατοντάρχης, -ου, ὁ	centurion [commander of approximately one hundred men]
ἐκκόπτω	cut off/down; do away with
ἐκλεκτός, -ή, -όν	chosen, elect

▹ List 19 4×

ἐκπλήσσω	(*mid*) be amazed/astounded	
ἐντέλλω	(*mid*) command, instruct	
ἐπιστρέφω	(*intrans act/mid*) return, go/come back; turn (around); change (one's thinking or behavior)	▸
ἔσωθεν	(from) within, (from) inside	
ἕτοιμος, -οίμη, -ον	ready	
ζύμη, -ης, ἡ	fermented dough, leaven	
ἥκω	be present, have come	
θεάομαι	see, look at	
θύρα, -ας, ἡ	door; entrance	
ἰάομαι	heal; restore	

▹ List 20 4×

ἴδε	[attention-getter] look!, pay attention!	
Ἰσαάκ, ὁ (*indecl*)	Isaac	
ἰσχυρός, -ά, -όν	strong, mighty [of living beings]; strong, powerful, violent [pertaining to strength or impact]; (*comp*) ἰσχυρότερος	
ἰσχύω	be strong/powerful/able; prevail	
καθίστημι/καθιστάνω	appoint, put in charge; make, cause to be	▸
Καῖσαρ, Καίσαρος, ὁ	Caesar	
κατακρίνω	condemn	▸
καταλείπω	leave (behind)	▸
Καφαρναούμ, ἡ (*indecl*)	Capernaum	
κώμη, -ης, ἡ	village	

▷ List 21 4×

λεπρός, -ά, -όν	having a skin disease; (*subst*) leper
λῃστής, -οῦ, ὁ	robber; revolutionary
λίαν	very (much), exceedingly
μάγος, -ου, ὁ	Magus [wise man and priest]
μετοικεσία, -ας, ἡ	deportation
μήτι	not
μοιχεύω	commit adultery
νεφέλη, -ης, ἡ	cloud
νοέω	understand; consider, think about
ὅθεν	from where; as a result of which, consequently

▷ List 22 4×

οἶνος, οἴνου, ὁ	wine
ὀλιγόπιστος, -ον	of little faith
ὁμολογέω	acknowledge; declare, confess; promise
ὅρκος, -ου, ὁ	oath
παρθένος, -ου, ἡ	virgin; young woman [of marriageable age]
παρουσία, -ας, ἡ	presence; arrival, coming
πάσχα, τό (*indecl*)	Passover (festival); Passover lamb; Passover meal
πετεινόν, -οῦ, τό	bird
προφητεύω	prophesy [disclose divine will]; foretell; reveal
πύλη, -ης, ἡ	gate

▷ List 23	4×
ῥαββ(ε)ί	[Heb.] Rabbi; (my) master
σατανᾶς, σατανᾶ, ὁ	[Heb.] Satan
σεισμός, -οῦ, ὁ	shaking, shock, commotion [earthquake, storm]
σῖτος, σίτου, ὁ	wheat, grain
συμφέρω	(*impers*) it is beneficial/of advantage; it is better
τελευτάω	die
τίκτω	give birth to, bear, [inanimate] produce ➢
τροφή, -ῆς, ἡ	nourishment, food
χοῖρος, χοίρου, ὁ	pig
χορτάζω	(*trans act*) fill, feed; (*intrans mid*) eat one's fill; be satisfied

▷ List 24	4 to 3×
ἀγανακτέω	be angry/indignant
ἀγέλη, -ης, ἡ	herd
ἁγιάζω	consecrate, make holy; regard as holy
ἀγορά, -ᾶς, ἡ	marketplace
ἀδελφή, -ῆς, ἡ	sister
αἰτία, -ας, ἡ	cause, reason; case, circumstance; accusation, charge
ἀλέκτωρ, ἀλέκτορος, ὁ	rooster
ἀληθῶς	truly, actually
χωρέω	hold, have room for, [extended sense] accept; go, reach
ὡσαύτως	in the same way, likewise

▹ List 25 3×

ἀμφότεροι, -αι, -α	both
ἀνά	each, apiece; ἀνὰ μέσον in the midst/middle
ἀναβλέπω	look up; receive sight
ἀνατέλλω	(*trans*) cause to rise; (*intrans*) rise, come up
ἀνεκτός, -όν	(*comp*) ἀνεκτότερος more bearable/endurable
ἅπας, ἅπασα, ἅπαν	whole, all; (*subst*) everyone, all, everything
ἀποδημέω	go on a journey, take a trip
ἀποθήκη, -ης, ἡ	storehouse, barn
ἀργός, -ή, -όν	idle, having nothing to do; lazy; useless
ἁρπάζω	seize; take away, snatch

▹ List 26 3×

ἀσθενέω	be sick; be weak
ἀσθενής, -ές	weak; sick, ill
ἀσφαλίζω	(*mid*) secure, make secure
αὐλή, -ῆς, ἡ	enclosed open space: courtyard; dwelling complex: house, palace
αὔριον	next day, tomorrow; soon, shortly
ἀφανίζω	destroy; disfigure
ἀφορίζω	separate; set apart
βασανίζω	torment, torture
βαστάζω	pick up; carry, bear
Βεελζεβούλ, ὁ (*indecl*)	Beelzebul

▹

▷ List 27 3×

βλασφημέω	slander, speak disrespectfully about, revile
γαστήρ, γαστρός, ἡ	belly; womb
γέννημα, -ήματος, τό	that which is produced, offspring
δέκα (*indecl*)	ten
δεκατέσσαρες, -α	fourteen
διάκονος, -όνου, ὁ/ἡ	servant, helper
διαλογίζομαι	consider, reason; discuss, debate, argue
διασκορπίζω	scatter, disperse
διαφέρω	differ in worth, surpass, be worth more (than)
διδαχή, -ῆς, ἡ	teaching [activity or content]

▷ List 28 3×

διορύσσω	dig through, break in ▷
δοκός, -οῦ, ὁ	beam (of wood)
δυνατός, -ή, -όν	able, capable, strong, powerful; possible
ἐγγύς	near [spatial or temporal]
ἐθνικός, -ή, -όν	gentile, (*subst*) gentile
ἐλαία, -ας, ἡ	olive tree
ἔλαιον, ἐλαίου, τό	olive oil
ἐλεημοσύνη, -ης, ἡ	charitable giving; alms
ἔλεος, ἐλέους, τό	compassion, mercy
ἔνατος, ἐνάτη, ἔνατον	ninth

▷ List 29 3×

ἐνδύω	(*act*) dress/clothe (someone); (*mid*) put on, wear
ἔξωθεν	(from) outside; (*prep* +*gen*) outside
ἐξώτερος, -έρα, -ον	farthest, outer
ἐπεί	since, because
ἐπιδείκνυμι	show
ἐπιζητέω	seek after, search for; seek, want
ἐπισυνάγω	(*trans act*) gather together; (*intrans mid*) assemble, gather together
ἑταῖρος, ἑταίρου, ὁ	companion, ἑταῖρε friend [general form of address not necessarily indicating affection]
εὐδοκέω	be well pleased; determine, resolve
εὐνοῦχος, -ούχου, ὁ	eunuch

▷ List 30 3×

ἔχιδνα, ἐχίδνης, ἡ	snake [of a poisonous variety]
θανατόω	put to death
θάπτω	bury
θαρσέω	have courage
θερίζω	reap, harvest
θρίξ, τριχός, ἡ	hair
Ἰερεμίας, Ἰερεμίου, ὁ	Jeremiah
ἱερεύς, -έως, ὁ	priest
ἱκανός, -ή, -όν	sufficient; able, qualified, worthy
καθαρός, -ά, -όν	clean; pure; innocent

▷ List 31 3×

κάμηλος, -ήλου, ὁ	camel
κάρφος, -ους, τό	small stick, twig, chip of wood
κεῖμαι	be lying/reclining/resting
κῆνσος, κήνσου, ὁ	poll tax
κλάδος, -ου, τό	branch
κλάω	break
κλείω	shut, close
κλέπτης, -ου, ὁ	thief
κληρονομέω	(*intrans*) be an heir; (*trans*) inherit; acquire, obtain
κοιλία, -ας, ἡ	stomach; womb

▷ List 32 3×

κόπτω	(*trans act*) cut off; (*intrans mid*) beat one's breast in mourning, mourn
κοράσιον, -ίου, τό	girl
κοσμέω	put in order, arrange, prepare; adorn, make attractive
κουστωδία, -ας, ἡ	group of soldiers on guard duty, guard
κράσπεδον, -έδου, τό	edge, hem [of a garment]; tassel
κριτής, -οῦ, ὁ	judge
κυλλός, -ή, -όν	crippled, deformed
λάμπω	give light, shine
λευκός, -ή, -όν	white; bright, shining
Μαγδαληνή, -ῆς, ἡ	Magdalene

▷ List 33 3×

μαθητεύω	(*trans act*) make a disciple, instruct; (*intrans act*) be a disciple
Μαθθαῖος, -αίου, ὁ	Matthew
μαλακία, -ας, ἡ	weakness, sickness
μανθάνω	learn ➢
μαργαρίτης, -ου, ὁ	pearl
Μαριάμ, ἡ (*indecl*)	Miriam, Mary
μαρτύριον, -ίου, τό	testimony, witness, proof
μαστιγόω	flog, whip
μερίζω	(*trans act*) divide; distribute, allot; (*intrans mid-pass*) be divided [with regard to oneself]
μεταμέλομαι	regret; change one's mind

▷ List 34 3×

μέχρι	(*conj*) until; (*prep +gen*) until; as far as; to the point of
μιμνήσκομαι/ μιμνῄσκομαι	(*+gen obj*) remember; be mindful of ➢
μοιχάω	(*mid*) commit adultery
Ναζαρά/Ναζαρέθ/ Ναζαρέτ, ἡ (*indecl*)	Nazareth
νομίζω	think, suppose, believe
ξηραίνω	(*mid*) become dry; wither
ὁδηγός, -οῦ, ὁ	guide, leader
ὁμοίως	likewise, in the same way
ὀνειδίζω	revile, mock, insult; reprimand, reproach
ὄνος, -ου, ὁ/ἡ	donkey

▹ List 35 3×

ὀργίζω	(*mid*) be(come) angry
οὗ	(to) where
ὄφις, -εως, ὁ	snake, serpent
παλαιός, -ά, -όν	old
παραγίνομαι	come, arrive, be present ▹
παράγω	go along, pass by; go away
παράδοσις, -όσεως, ἡ	tradition
περιάγω	go around/about
περιστερά, -ᾶς, ἡ	pigeon, dove
περιτίθημι	put/place around/on

▹ List 36 3×

πιπράσκω	sell ▹
πλησίον	(+*gen*) near; (*subst*) neighbor
πλούσιος, -ία, -ον	rich, wealthy; rich (in), abounding (in)
ποιμήν, ποιμένος, ὁ	shepherd
πορνεία, -ας, ἡ	sexual immorality, fornication
ποταμός, -οῦ, ὁ	river, stream
πραΰς, πραεῖα, πραΰ	gentle, meek
πρίν	before
πρωΐ	early in the morning
πῶλος, πώλου, ὁ	foal, colt

MARK

▷ List 1	11 to 8×
ἀγρός, -οῦ, ὁ	field, land, countryside, tilled land
ἀκάθαρτος, -ον	impure, unclean [cultic or moral]
ἅπτω	(*act*) light, kindle; (*mid +gen obj*) touch, hold, cling to
εἰσπορεύομαι	go into, enter
ἐκπορεύομαι	go/come out
ἐπιτίθημι	lay/put upon
ἐπιτιμάω	rebuke, warn, strictly charge (+*dat obj*)
Ἠλίας, Ἠλίου, ὁ	Elijah
ἴδε	[attention-getter] look!, pay attention!
προσκαλέω	(*mid*) invite, call to, summon

▷ List 2	8 to 6×
ἀναβλέπω	look up; receive sight
ἄνεμος, ἀνέμου, ὁ	wind
γρηγορέω	be (fully) awake/alert; be watchful/on the alert
διαλογίζομαι	consider, reason; discuss, debate, argue
ἐκεῖθεν	from there
καθεύδω	be sleeping/asleep
κώμη, -ης, ἡ	village
Μαρία, -ας, ἡ	Mary
πέραν	on the other side; (*subst +art*) the other side; (*prep +gen*) on the other side of
σκανδαλίζω	cause (someone) to sin; shock, offend

▹ LIST 3 6×

ἔξεστιν	(*impers*) it is right/permitted [*3sg* of ἔξειμι]
θύρα, -ας, ἡ	door; entrance
καλῶς	well, appropriately, effectively; correctly
νηστεύω	fast [from food]
ξηραίνω	(*mid*) become dry; wither
ὀπίσω	behind, back; (*prep* +*gen*) behind; after [temporal or spatial]
ὀψία, -ας, ἡ	evening; (*adj*) late
περιβλέπω	(*mid*) look around (at)
πόσος, -η, -ον	[*interr* or *exclam*] how much?, how great?; how much?, how many?
ποτήριον, -ίου, τό	cup

▹ LIST 4 6 TO 5×

ἀγοράζω	buy
ἀμπελών, -ῶνος, ὁ	vineyard
γεωργός, -οῦ, ὁ	farmer, cultivator
διακονέω	(+*dat obj*) serve; care for; wait on; administer
διαστέλλω	(*mid*) order, instruct
διδαχή, -ῆς, ἡ	teaching [activity or content]
δυνατός, -ή, -όν	able, capable, strong, powerful; possible
πρωΐ	early in the morning
σατανᾶς, σατανᾶ, ὁ	[Heb.] Satan
συ(ν)ζητέω	discuss; dispute, argue, debate

▷ List 5 5×

ἐκπλήσσω	(*mid*) be amazed/astounded
ἐμβαίνω	embark ▷
ἕνεκα/ἕνεκεν	(+*gen*) because of, for the sake of
θυγάτηρ, θυγατρός, ἡ	daughter
κοινόω	make common/impure, defile
κοράσιον, -ίου, τό	girl
κράβαττος, -άττου, ὁ	mat, pallet
μακρόθεν	from far away, from a distance
οἶνος, οἴνου, ὁ	wine
ὅριον, -ίου, τό	boundary; (*pl*) region, district

▷ List 6 5×

οὔπω	not yet
παράδοσις, -όσεως, ἡ	tradition
παραλυτικός, -ή, -όν	(*subst*) paralytic
παρέρχομαι	pass by; pass [of time]; pass away, disappear ▷
πάσχα, τό (*indecl*)	Passover (festival); Passover lamb; Passover meal
πότε	when?
προάγω	(*trans*) lead/bring out; (*intrans* +*acc* of person) go before, precede [spatially or temporally]
πτωχός, -ή, -όν	poor
σιωπάω	be/keep silent; become silent
συνίημι/συνίω	understand, comprehend ▷

▷ List 7 — 5 to 4×

ἀδελφή, -ῆς, ἡ	sister	
ἀλέκτωρ, ἀλέκτορος, ὁ	rooster	
ἀναγινώσκω	read (aloud)	➤
Ἀνδρέας, -ου, ὁ	Andrew	
ἀπαρνέομαι	deny, reject	
ἅπας, ἅπασα, ἅπαν	whole, all; (*subst*) everyone, all, everything	
ἀρχισυνάγωγος, -ώγου, ὁ	ruler/leader of a synagogue	
ἀσκός, -οῦ, ὁ	wineskin	
βάπτισμα, -ίσματος, τό	baptism, (ceremonial) plunging/washing	
φεύγω	flee; escape; avoid	➤

▷ List 8 — 4×

Βηθανία, -ας, ἡ	Bethany	
βλασφημέω	slander, speak disrespectfully about, revile	
γαμέω	marry	
δαιμονίζομαι	be demon possessed	
εἶτα	then, next; furthermore	
ἐκθαμβέω	(*mid*) be amazed/astonished; be very excited; be distressed; be alarmed	
ἐμβλέπω	look at (intently) (+*dat obj*)	
ἐξίστημι/ἐξιστάνω	(*intrans*) be amazed; be out of one's mind	➤
ἐπιβάλλω	(*trans*) lay/put on; (*intrans*) throw oneself; fall to, belong to	
ἐπιστρέφω	(*intrans act/mid*) return, go/come back; turn (around); change (one's thinking or behavior)	➤

▷ List 9 4×

ἐπιτάσσω	command, order (+*dat obj*)
Ζεβεδαῖος, -αίου, ὁ	Zebedee
ἥλιος, -ίου, ὁ	sun
Ἰορδάνης, -ου, ὁ	Jordan (River)
ἰσχύω	be strong/powerful/able; prevail
ἰχθύς, -ύος, ὁ	fish
καθαρίζω	cleanse, make clean
Καῖσαρ, Καίσαρος, ὁ	Caesar
κακῶς	badly, [with ἔχω] be sick; wrongly, wickedly
κατάκειμαι	be lying down; recline (for a meal), dine

▷ List 10 4×

καταλείπω	leave (behind); cause to be left over ▷
κλάσμα, -ατος, τό	fragment, piece
λίαν	very (much), exceedingly
Μαγδαληνή, -ῆς, ἡ	Magdalene
μερίζω	(*trans act*) divide; distribute, allot; (*intrans mid-pass*) be divided [with regard to oneself]
μηκέτι	no longer
Ναζαρηνός, -ή, -όν	from Nazareth, (*subst*) Nazarene
νεφέλη, -ης, ἡ	cloud
οὖς, ὠτός, τό	ear; hearing, understanding
παραπορεύομαι	pass by, go through

▷ List 11 4×

παρατίθημι	(*act*) set/put before; (*mid*) demonstrate; commend, entrust
πειράζω	test; tempt
πλανάω	(*act*) lead astray, deceive; (*mid*) wander, go astray, be misled
ποῖος, ποία, ποῖον	of what kind?; which?, what?
πῶλος, πώλου, ὁ	foal, colt
σινδών, σινδόνος, ὁ	linen cloth; light garment
σπλαγχνίζομαι	have compassion, feel sympathy
σταυρός, -οῦ, ὁ	cross
συκῆ, -ῆς, ἡ	fig tree
χοῖρος, χοίρου, ὁ	pig

▷ List 12 4 to 3×

ἀγανακτέω	be angry/indignant; express indignation
ἀγορά, -ᾶς, ἡ	marketplace
ἄκανθα, ἀκάνθης, ἡ	thorn; thornbush
ἀκοή, -ῆς, ἡ	hearing, listening; ear; news, rumor, report, message
ἄλαλος, -ον	mute, unable to speak
ἅλας, -ατος, τό	salt
ἅλυσις, ἁλύσεως, ἡ	chain, [extended sense] imprisonment
ἀνάκειμαι	recline at table, dine
χορτάζω	(*trans act*) fill, feed; (*intrans mid*) eat one's fill; be satisfied
χώρα, -ας, ἡ	land; region; country

➤

▷ List 13 3×

ἀπάγω	lead off, take away; bring (before a magistrate/ court) [legal terminology]	➤
ἀπιστία, -ας, ἡ	unbelief; unfaithfulness	
ἀποκαθίστημι/ ἀποκαθιστάνω	restore, reestablish	
ἄρρωστος, -ον	ill, sick	
αὐλή, -ῆς, ἡ	enclosed open space: courtyard, sheepfold; dwelling complex: house, farm, palace	
Βαραββᾶς, Βαραββᾶ, ὁ	Barabbas	
βλασφημία, -ας, ἡ	slander, defamation, reviling	
γαζοφυλάκιον, -ίου, τό	treasury	
γέεννα, γεέννης, ἡ	Gehenna, Valley of Hinnom	
δέρω	violently mistreat, beat	➤

▷ List 14 3×

δεῦτε	come!, come here!, come on!	➤
δηνάριον, -ίου, τό	denarius	
ἑκατόν (*indecl*)	one hundred	
ἐκλεκτός, -ή, -όν	chosen, elect	
ἐκτείνω	stretch (something) out	
ἐλαία, -ας, ἡ	olive tree	
ἐλεέω	have compassion (on), show mercy to	
ἐμπαίζω	mock, ridicule (+*dat obj*)	➤
ἐμπτύω	spit (on/at)	
ἐνδύω	(*act*) dress/clothe (someone); (*mid*) put on, wear	

▷ List 15 3×

Ἡρῳδιάς, Ἡρῳδιάδος, ἡ	Herodias
θαμβέω	(*mid*) be astounded/amazed
ἱκανός, -ή, -όν	sufficient; qualified, worthy; considerable
ἰσχυρός, -ά, -όν	strong, mighty; (*comp*) ἰσχυρότερος, -έρα, -ον more powerful, stronger
Ἰωσῆς, -ῆ/ῆτος, ὁ	Joses
κατακρίνω	condemn
καταλύω	(*trans*) tear down, destroy; abolish, bring to an end
κατέναντι	(+*gen*) ahead/in front of, opposite; in the sight of, before
κατηγορέω	accuse
Καφαρναούμ, ἡ (*indecl*)	Capernaum

▷

▷ List 16 3×

κεντυρίων, -ωνος, ὁ	centurion [commander of approximately one hundred men]
κλάω	break
κλίνη, -ῆς, ἡ	couch, bed, stretcher
κτίσις, -εως, τό	creation [act or product]
κύκλῳ	in a circle; around, round about; in a circuit
κωλύω	hinder, prevent
κωφός, -ή, -όν	mute; deaf
λῃστής, -οῦ, ὁ	robber; revolutionary
μαρτυρία, -ας, ἡ	[the act of giving] testimony; evidence
μαρτύριον, -ίου, τό	testimony, witness, proof

▹ List 17 3 ×

μάστιξ, μάστιγος, ἡ	whip, lash; affliction, suffering, disease
μάχαιρα, -αίρης, ἡ	dagger, short sword
μεθερμηνεύω	translate
μύρον, -ου, τό	fragrant ointment
νοέω	understand; consider, think about
νυμφίος, -ου, ὁ	bridegroom
παλαιός, -ά, -όν	old
παραγγέλλω	command, instruct, give orders
παράγω	go along, pass by; go away
πέντε (*indecl*)	five

▹ List 18 3 ×

περιτίθημι	put/place around/on
πλήρωμα, -ώματος, τό	that which fills, content; that which completes; fullness
πόθεν	from where?, how is it that?
προσπίπτω	fall down before/at the feet of; fall upon, strike against ▸
πωλέω	sell
ῥαββ(ε)ί	[Heb.] Rabbi; (my) master
ῥίζα, -ης, ἡ	root; shoot [from a root]
στάχυς, -υος, ὁ	head/ear of grain
συνέδριον, -ίου, τό	council; Sanhedrin
τελώνης, -ου, ὁ	tax collector

▷ List 19 — 3 to 2×

ἀγέλη, -ης, ἡ	herd
τιμάω	honor; set a price
Τύρος, -ου, ἡ	Tyre
ὑποκάτω	under, below, beneath
φανερός, -ά, -όν	visible, plain, evident, known; (*subst*) the open
Φίλιππος, -ίππου, ὁ	Philip
φύλλον, -ου, τό	leaf
χήρα, -ας, ἡ	widow
ψευδομαρτυρέω	bear false witness, give false testimony
ὠφελέω	help, benefit, be of use to (+*dat/acc obj*); accomplish

▷ List 20 — 2×

ἄζυμος, -ον	unleavened, (*subst*) unleavened bread; Feast of Unleavened Bread
ἀθετέω	nullify, invalidate; reject
ἄκρον, -ου, τό	high point, top; extreme limit, end
ἀλάβαστρος, -άστρου, ὁ/ἡ / ἀλάβαστρον, -άστρου, τό	alabaster vase
ἀλείφω	anoint
ἀληθῶς	truly, actually
ἁλιεύς, -έως, ὁ	fisher
Ἁλφαῖος, -αίου, ὁ	Alphaeus
ἁμάρτημα, -ήματος, τό	sin, sinful act
ἀνακράζω	cry out, shout

▷

▷ List 21 2×

ἀναμιμνῄσκω	(*trans act*) remind; (*intrans mid*) remember	▶
ἀναπαύω	(*trans act*) give rest, refresh; (*intrans mid*) rest	
ἀναπίπτω	recline, lean back	▶
ἀνατέλλω	(*trans*) cause to rise; (*intrans*) rise, come up	
ἀπέχω	(*trans act*) receive in full; (*intrans act*) be far away/distant; (*impers*) it is enough	
ἀπιστέω	not believe; be unfaithful	
ἀποδοκιμάζω	reject as unworthy/unfit	
ἀποκεφαλίζω	behead	
ἀποκόπτω	cut off/away	
ἀποκυλίω	roll away	

▷ List 22 2×

ἀρνέομαι	deny; refuse; disown
ἄφεσις, ἀφέσεως, ἡ	release; forgiveness (of)
ἀφρίζω	foam (at the mouth)
βαπτιστής, -οῦ, ὁ	Baptizer
βασανίζω	torment, torture
Βηθσαϊδά(ν), ἡ (*indecl*)	Bethsaida
βοάω	call/cry out, shout
βοηθέω	help, come to the aid of (+*dat obj*)
βόσκω	(*trans act*) tend, feed; (*intrans mid*) graze, feed
γεμίζω	fill

▷ List 23 2×

γένος, -ους, τό	people group, family; offspring, descendant; kind, class
γονυπετέω	kneel down (before), fall on one's knees (before) (*+acc obj*)
γυμνός, -ή, -όν	naked, bare, [figurative] uncovered; inadequately dressed; lightly dressed
δείκνυμι	show, make known; explain ➢
δεῖπνον, δείπνου, τό	dinner; feast, banquet
Δεκάπολις, -όλεως, ἡ	Decapolis
διάκονος, -όνου, ὁ/ἡ	servant, helper; ministerial attendant
διαπεράω	cross over, go across
διαρπάζω	rob (thoroughly), plunder
διηγέομαι	recount in detail, relate, describe

▷ List 24 2×

δίκτυον, -ύου, τό	(fish)net
δίς	twice
διωγμός, -οῦ, ὁ	persecution
δόλος, -ου, ὁ	deceit, cunning, craftiness
ἐγγύς	near [spatial or temporal]
ἐκπνέω	breathe one's last
ἔκστασις, -άσεως, ἡ	entrancement, astonishment, amazement
ἐλωΐ/ελωι	[Aram.] my God
ἐμβριμάομαι	(*trans +dat obj*) sternly warn; speak angrily to; (*intrans*) be distressed
ἐναγκαλίζομαι	take into one's arms

▹ List 25 2×

ἐναντίος, -α, -ον	opposite, facing; opposed, contrary
ἔνατος, ἐνάτη, ἔνατον	ninth
ἔνοχος, -ον	subject to, held in; (held) liable (for), guilty (of), deserving of
ἐντέλλω	(*mid*) command, instruct
ἑξήκοντα (*indecl*)	sixty
ἔξωθεν	(from) outside; (*prep +gen*) outside
ἑορτή, -ῆς, ἡ	festival; feast
ἐπαισχύνομαι	be ashamed (of)
ἐπιγραφή, -ῆς, ἡ	inscription
ἐπισυνάγω	(*trans act*) gather together; (*intrans mid*) assemble, gather together

▹ List 26 2×

ἐπιτρέπω	permit, give permission, allow (+*dat obj*)
ἔσω	inside, within
ἔσωθεν	(from) within, (from) inside
εὔκοπος, -ον	(*comp*) εὐκοπώτερος easier
εὐχαριστέω	thank, give thanks, be thankful
εὐώνυμος, -ον	left [as opposed to right]
ζύμη, -ης, ἡ	fermented dough, leaven
ζώνη, -ης, ἡ	belt
ἡδέως	gladly; (*superl*) ἥδιστα most/very gladly
Ἡρῳδιανοί, -ῶν, οἱ	Herodians

▷ List 27 2×

Ἠσαΐας, Ἠσαΐου, ὁ	Isaiah
θανατόω	put to death
θαρσέω	have courage
θεάομαι	see, look at
θερμαίνω	(*mid*) warm oneself
θόρυβος, -ύβου, ὁ	uproar, turmoil, tumult, (noisy) disturbance
θυγάτριον, -ίου, τό	(little) daughter
ἰατρός, -οῦ, ὁ	physician
ἱερεύς, -έως, ὁ	priest
Ἰεριχώ, ἡ (*indecl*)	Jericho

▷ List 28 2×

Ἰσκαριώθ, ὁ (*indecl*) / Ἰσκαριώτης, -ου, ὁ	Iscariot	
ἴσος, -η, -ον	equal, same	
ἰσχύς, -ύος, ἡ	strength	
Ἰωσήφ, ὁ (*indecl*)	Joseph	
καθαιρέω	take/bring down; tear down, [extended sense] destroy	▷
κακολογέω	speak badly of, revile	
κάλαμος, -άμου, ὁ	reed, stalk	
κάμηλος, -ήλου, ὁ	camel	
καρποφορέω	bear fruit	
κατεσθίω	devour, consume	▷

▹ List 29 2×

κάτω	down(ward); below
κλάδος, -ου, τό	branch
κοινός, -ή, -όν	common, shared; common, ordinary; impure, unclean
κολοβόω	curtail, cut short
κοπάζω	abate, cease
κόφινος, -ίνου, ὁ	basket
κυνάριον, -ίου, τό	(house) dog
λεγιών, -ῶνος, ὁ	[Lat. loanword] legion [approximately six thousand soldiers]
λεπρός, -ά, -όν	having a skin disease; (*subst*) leper
λευκός, -ή, -όν	white; bright, shining

▹ List 30 2×

λυπέω	(*act*) cause grief/sorrow; (*mid*) grieve, be sad/distressed
μέλει	(*impers*) it is a concern to/of interest to [*3sg* of μέλω]
μετανοέω	repent
μετρέω	measure; measure out, apportion
μήποτε	(*conj*) so that . . . not
μήτι	not
μνῆμα, μνήματος, τό	tomb
μοιχάω	(*mid*) commit adultery
νεανίσκος, -ου, ὁ	young man
νέος, -α, -ον	new; young

▹

▷ **List 31**	**2×**
ξύλον, -ου, τό	wood; object made of wood [e.g., club, stocks, cross]; tree
οἰκοδομή, -ῆς, ἡ	building, structure; construction, building up
οἷος, οἵα, οἷον	such as, of what sort
ὁμοίως	likewise, in the same way
ὀνειδίζω	revile, mock, insult; reprimand, reproach
οὐδέποτε	never
ὀψέ	late (+*gen*); in the evening (+*gen*), (*subst*) evening
παιδίσκη, -ης, ἡ	female slave
πανταχοῦ	everywhere
πατρίς, -ίδος, ἡ	fatherland, homeland; hometown

▷ **List 32**	**2×**
πέδη, -ης, ἡ	shackle
πεινάω	hunger, be hungry [physically or metaphorically]
πεντακισχίλιοι, -αι, -α	five thousand
περιβάλλω	(*intrans mid*) be wearing/clothed ▷
περίλυπος, -ον	deeply grieved
περισσός, -ή, -όν	extraordinary, remarkable; abundant, superfluous; (*comp*) περισσότερος, -έρα, -ον greater, better, excessive
περισσῶς	exceedingly; even more
περιστερά, -ᾶς, ἡ	pigeon, dove
πετεινόν, -οῦ, τό	bird
πετρώδης, -ες	(*subst*) rocky ground

▷ List 33 2×

πίναξ, -ακος, ὁ	dish, platter
πλῆθος, πλήθους, τό	multitude, a great quantity
πλήρης, -ες (freq. *indecl*)	full, filled; full, complete
πλησίον	(+*gen*) near; (*subst*) neighbor
πλούσιος, -ία, -ον	rich, wealthy; rich (in), abounding (in)
ποιμήν, ποιμένος, ὁ	shepherd
πόλεμος, -έμου, ὁ	war; battle, fight
πολλάκις	often, many times
πορφύρα, -ας, ἡ	purple garment/cloth
ποταπός, -ή, -όν	of what sort/kind, how great

▷ List 34 2×

ποτίζω	give to drink
πρασιά, -ᾶς, ἡ	garden plot; πρασιαὶ πρασιαί group by group, in groups
πρίν	before
πρόβατον, -άτου, τό	sheep
προέρχομαι	go forward, advance; go ahead ▷
προσευχή, -ῆς, ἡ	prayer
προστρέχω	run to(ward) ▷
προφητεύω	prophesy [disclose divine will]; foretell; reveal
πτύω	spit
πτῶμα, πτώματος, τό	dead body, corpse

▷ List 35 2×

πωρόω	(*trans act*) harden, make callous; (*intrans mid*) become hard/callous/insensitive
Σαλώμη, -ης, ἡ	Salome
Σιδών, -ῶνος, ἡ	Sidon
σκεῦος, σκεύους, τό	object, thing; vessel, container
σκληροκαρδία, -ας, ἡ	stubbornness
σός, σή, σόν	your, yours; (*subst masc*) your own people
σπαράσσω	throw into convulsions, shake to and fro
σπόρος, -ου, ὁ	seed
σπυρίς, -ίδος, ἡ	basket
στήκω	stand; stand firm

▷ List 36 2×

στολή, -ῆς, ἡ	long robe
στρωννύω/στρώννυμι	spread/lay (something) out [over a surface]; equip, furnish ▷
συμβούλιον, -ίου, τό	plan, plot
συμπνίγω	choke
συμπόσιον, -ίου, τό	συμπόσια συμπόσια in parties/groups
συνακολουθέω	(+*dat obj*) accompany; follow
συνανάκειμαι	recline/eat with (+*dat obj*), (*subst pl ptc*) fellow guests/diners
συνέρχομαι	come together with, gather; go/come with, travel together with
συνθλίβω	press upon, crowd around
συντρίβω	crush, shatter, break ▷

LUKE

▷ LIST 1 — 21 TO 11×

ἅπας, ἅπασα, ἅπαν	whole, all; (*subst*) everyone, all, everything
ἅπτω	(*act*) light, kindle; (*mid +gen obj*) touch, hold, cling to
δέκα (*indecl*)	ten
ἐπιτιμάω	rebuke, sternly warn (+*dat obj*)
κώμη, -ης, ἡ	village
Μαριάμ, ἡ (*indecl*)	Miriam, Mary
πίμπλημι	fill, fulfill, complete ▸
πλήν	nevertheless, but, only; (*prep +gen*) except ▸
ὑποστρέφω	return, turn back
φίλος, -η, -ον	friendly; (*subst*) friend

▷ LIST 2 — 11 TO 9×

ἀγρός, -οῦ, ὁ	field, land, countryside, tilled land
Ἐλισάβετ, ἡ (*indecl*)	Elizabeth
Ζαχαρίας, Ζαχαρίου, ὁ	Zechariah, Zacharias
θυγάτηρ, θυγατρός, ἡ	daughter
ἰάομαι	heal; restore
ὁμοίως	likewise, in the same way
παραχρῆμα	at once, immediately
πλούσιος, -ία, -ον	rich, wealthy; rich (in), abounding (in)
πτωχός, -ή, -όν	poor
τελώνης, -ου, ὁ	tax collector

▷ List 3	9 to 8×
ἄρχων, ἄρχοντος, ὁ	ruler; official
ἱκανός, -ή, -όν	sufficient; qualified, worthy; considerable, large
μετανοέω	repent
μνᾶ, μνᾶς, ἡ	mina [monetary unit = one hundred drachmas]
παῖς, παιδός, ὁ/ἡ	child [boy or girl]; child [son or daughter]; slave; servant
παρέρχομαι	pass by; pass [of time]; come by/alongside; pass away, disappear; neglect, transgress ▷
πέντε (*indecl*)	five
χήρα, -ας, ἡ	widow
χώρα, -ας, ἡ	land; region; country
ὡσεί	as, like; about, approximately

▷ List 4	8 to 7×
ἀμπελών, -ῶνος, ὁ	vineyard
γέ (*encl*)	indeed, even; yet, at least, though
δέομαι	ask, petition, pray [+*gen* of person(s) petitioned]
διακονέω	(+*dat obj*) serve; care for; wait on; administer
ἐχθρός, -ά, -όν	hated; hostile; (*subst*) enemy
ἰσχύω	be strong/powerful/able; prevail
Ἰωσήφ, ὁ (*indecl*)	Joseph
παραγίνομαι	come, arrive, be present ▷
πλῆθος, πλήθους, τό	multitude, a great quantity
ποῖος, ποία, ποῖον	of what kind?; which?, what?

▷ List 5 — 7×

ἀναβλέπω	look up; receive sight
δένδρον, -ου, τό	tree
ἐπιστάτης, -ου, ὁ	master
ἐπιστρέφω	(*intrans act/mid*) return, go/come back; turn (around); change (one's thinking or behavior); (*trans act*) turn, redirect
ἐφίστημι	stand by/near; [with reference to events] come/spring upon ▸
Ἠλίας, Ἠλίου, ὁ	Elijah
ἰχθύς, -ύος, ὁ	fish
καθαρίζω	cleanse, make clean
Καῖσαρ, Καίσαρος, ὁ	Caesar
κοιλία, -ας, ἡ	stomach; womb; heart [figurative, representing one's inner desires and feelings]

▷ List 6 — 7 to 6×

ἀκάθαρτος, -ον	impure, unclean [cultic or moral]
μήποτε	(*conj*) so that . . . not; (*interr*) whether (perhaps)
νέος, -α, -ον	new; young ▸
ὀπίσω	behind, back; (*prep +gen*) behind; after [temporal or spatial]
οὖς, ὠτός, τό	ear; hearing, understanding
πάσχα, τό (*indecl*)	Passover (festival); Passover lamb; Passover meal
προστίθημι	add on/to; continue (to), do again [indicates the repetition of another verb's action]
στρέφω	(*trans act*) turn; return; change; (*intrans mid*) turn (around); change ▸
συλλαμβάνω	(*act*) arrest; conceive; catch (*+dat obj*); (*mid +dat obj*) assist, help; (*fut mid*) will conceive ▸
ὕψιστος, -ίστη, -ον	highest, (*subst*) Most High

▷ List 7 6×

γαμέω	marry	▷
γονεύς, -έως, ὁ	parent	
διαλογίζομαι	consider, reason; discuss, debate, argue	
διαλογισμός, -οῦ, ὁ	reasoning, thought	
διαμερίζω	divide, separate; distribute, apportion	
ἔλεος, ἐλέους, τό	compassion, mercy	
ἐπαίρω	lift up	▷
εὐθέως	immediately	
εὐφραίνω	(*trans act*) make glad; (*intrans mid*) be glad, enjoy oneself, rejoice	
κεῖμαι	be lying/reclining/resting; exist for, be set for	

▷ List 8 6×

κριτής, -οῦ, ὁ	judge	
κωλύω	hinder, prevent; withhold	
λύχνος, -ου, ὁ	lamp	
μήτε	[continuing a previous *neg*] and not, neither, nor	
μιμνήσκομαι/ μιμνῄσκομαι	(+*gen obj*) remember; be mindful of	▷
νομικός, -οῦ, ὁ	relating to/about law(s); (*subst*) legal expert, lawyer	
οἶνος, οἴνου, ὁ	wine	
πειρασμός, -οῦ, ὁ	test, trial; temptation	
πόσος, -η, -ον	[*interr* or *exclam*] how much?, how great?; how much?, how many?	
πράσσω	do, accomplish, perform	▷

▷ List 9 — 6 to 5×

ἀγοράζω	buy	
ἀθετέω	nullify, invalidate; reject	
ἀμφότεροι, -αι, -α	both	
ἀποκαλύπτω	reveal, disclose	▸
ἀπολαμβάνω	receive; recover, get back	▸
προσδοκάω	wait (for), expect	
πωλέω	sell	
συνέχω	(*act*) enclose, surround; hold, confine; constrain, affect; [additional *pass* senses] be afflicted, seized	▸
ὑψόω	lift up; exalt	
φυλάσσω	observe, follow; guard, protect, keep watch	

▷ List 10 — 5×

ἀσπασμός, -οῦ, ὁ	greeting	
ἄφεσις, ἀφέσεως, ἡ	release; forgiveness (of)	
βαστάζω	pick up; carry, bear	
βίος, -ου, ὁ	life, manner of living; livelihood, means of living	
βρέφος, -ους, τό	infant, baby	
Γαλιλαῖος, -αία, -ον	Galilean	
γεωργός, -οῦ, ὁ	farmer, cultivator	
δείκνυμι	show, make known; explain	▸
δεῖπνον, δείπνου, τό	dinner; feast, banquet	
δέρω	violently mistreat, beat	▸

▷ List 11 5×

διάβολος, -ον	slanderous; (*subst*) adversary; devil
δικαιόω	justify, consider right/righteous, make righteous; vindicate, put in the right
εἰσπορεύομαι	go into, enter
ἐμπαίζω	mock, ridicule (+*dat obj*) ▷
ἔξεστιν	(*impers*) it is right/permitted [*3sg* of ἔξειμι]
ἐπάνω	(*adv*) above, over; more than; (*prep +gen*) above, over
ἐπιβάλλω	(*trans*) lay/put on; (*intrans*) throw oneself; fall to, belong to
ἐπιδίδωμι	give, hand over
ἐπιλαμβάνομαι	take/lay hold of (+*gen obj*); catch, arrest
ἐπιτίθημι	lay/put upon

▷ List 12 5×

ἥκω	be present, have come
ἱερεύς, -έως, ὁ	priest
κατακλίνω	(*trans act*) cause to recline/sit [for dining]; (*intrans mid*) recline [for dining] ▷
λίμνη, -ης, ἡ	lake
μάχαιρα, -αίρης, ἡ	dagger, short sword
μεριμνάω	worry (about), be anxious; care for, be concerned about
μετάνοια, -οίας, ἡ	change of mind and heart, repentance
μήν, μηνός, ὁ	month
Ναζαρά/Ναζαρέθ/ Ναζαρέτ, ἡ (*indecl*)	Nazareth
νεφέλη, -ης, ἡ	cloud

▹ **List 13**	**5×**
οὗ	(to) where
ὀφείλω	owe, be indebted to; be obligated, ought; have to
παλαιός, -ά, -όν	old
παρατίθημι	(*act*) set/put before; (*mid*) demonstrate; commend, entrust
πεινάω	hunger, be hungry [physically or metaphorically]
περίχωρος, -ον	neighboring
ποτήριον, -ίου, τό	cup
προσδέχομαι	receive, welcome; wait for, await, expect
σατανᾶς, σατανᾶ, ὁ	[Heb.] Satan
ταπεινόω	bring low; humble [positive], humiliate [negative]

▹ **List 14**	**5 to 4×**
ἀγαθοποιέω	do good to [+*acc* of person]; do good/what is right
ἀδικία, -ας, ἡ	injustice, unrighteousness; wrongdoing, misdeed
ἄδικος, -ον	unjust, unrighteous
ἄκανθα, ἀκάνθης, ἡ	thorn; thornbush
ἀναπίπτω	recline, lean back ▸
ἄνεμος, ἀνέμου, ὁ	wind
ἀντί	(+*gen*) instead of, in place of; ἀνθ’ ὧν because
ἀπάγω	lead off, take away; bring (before a magistrate/ court) [legal terminology] ▸
ἀπέχω	(*trans act*) receive in full; (*intrans act*) be far away/distant
τίκτω	give birth to, bear, [inanimate] produce ▸

▷ List 15 4×

ἀργύριον, -ίου, τό	silver; money
ἀρνέομαι	deny; refuse; disown
ἀσθένεια, -είας, ἡ	sickness, disease; weakness
ἀσκός, -οῦ, ὁ	wineskin
αὐξάνω/αὔξω	(*trans*) make grow/increase; (*intrans*) grow, increase
αὔριον	next day, tomorrow; soon, shortly
ἀφαιρέω	(*act*) remove, take away; (*mid*) take away, do away with ▷
ἀφίστημι	(*trans*) draw away, incite; (*intrans*) withdraw, depart; keep away ▷
βαλλάντιον, -ίου, τό	money bag, purse
βάπτισμα, -ίσματος, τό	baptism, (ceremonial) plunging/washing

▷ List 16 4×

βοάω	call/cry out, shout
διανοίγω	open; explain
διατάσσω	(*act/mid*) instruct, direct ▷
δίκτυον, -ύου, τό	(fish)net
δυνατός, -ή, -όν	able, capable, strong, powerful; possible
εἰσφέρω	lead/bring in ▷
ἐκεῖθεν	from there
ἐκλέγομαι	choose; select
ἐλαία, -ας, ἡ	olive tree
ἐλάχιστος, -ίστη, -ον	least, smallest [in status, value, or size]

▷ List 17 4×

ἐλεέω	have compassion (on), show mercy to
ἐνδύω	(*act*) dress/clothe (someone); (*mid*) put on, wear
ἕνεκα/ἕνεκεν	(+*gen*) because of, for the sake of
ἐξαποστέλλω	send out/off, dispatch; send away, dismiss
ἐπιθυμέω	long for, desire (+*gen/acc obj*)
ἐπιτάσσω	command, order (+*dat obj*)
ἐπιτρέπω	permit, give permission, allow (+*dat obj*)
ἐργάτης, -ου, ὁ	worker, laborer; doer
εὐχαριστέω	thank, give thanks, be thankful
θησαυρός, -οῦ, ὁ	repository, container, chest; treasure

▷ List 18 4×

θρίξ, τριχός, ἡ	hair
θύρα, -ας, ἡ	door; entrance
θύω	sacrifice; slaughter, kill
Ἰακώβ, ὁ (*indecl*)	Jacob
ἰσχυρός, -ά, -όν	strong, mighty [of living beings]; strong, powerful [pertaining to strength or impact]; (*comp*) ἰσχυρότερος, -έρα, -ον more powerful, stronger
Ἰωνᾶς, Ἰωνᾶ, ὁ	Jonah
καλῶς	well, appropriately, effectively; correctly
καταλείπω	leave (behind); cause to be left over
κατανοέω	look at, observe; consider [something one is looking at]; think about, contemplate
κατηγορέω	accuse

▸

▷ List 19 4×

Καφαρναούμ, ἡ (*indecl*)	Capernaum
κλ(ε)ίνω	(*trans act*) lay; bend, bow; (*intrans act*) decline, come to an end ▷
κρούω	knock
κωφός, -ή, -όν	mute; deaf
Λάζαρος, -άρου, ὁ	Lazarus
Λευ(ε)ί(ς), Λευ(ε)ί, ὁ (freq. *indecl*)	Levi
λῃστής, -οῦ, ὁ	robber; revolutionary
λιμός, -οῦ, ὁ/ἡ	hunger; famine
μακρόθεν	from far away, from a distance
Μάρθα, -ας, ἡ	Martha

▷ List 20 4×

Μαρία, -ας, ἡ	Mary
μύρον, -ου, τό	fragrant ointment
ναί	yes
νηστεύω	fast [from food]
νόσος, -ου, ἡ	sickness, disease
οἰκοδεσπότης, -ου, ὁ	master of the house
οἰκονόμος, -ου, ὁ	household manager/steward; administrator, manager
παραγγέλλω	command, instruct, give orders
παρέχω	(*act*) bring about, make happen; present, provide; (*mid*) show oneself to be; grant [something from one's own means]
περισσεύω	(*intrans*) abound (in), overflow, be left over

▷ List 21 4×

πετεινόν, -οῦ, τό	bird
πήρα, -ας, ἡ	leather bag, travel bag
πόθεν	from where?, how is it that?
ποιμήν, ποιμένος, ὁ	shepherd
πότε	when?
προσέχω	look after, pay attention/attend to (+*dat obj*); [with ἀπό] watch out for, beware of
προσκαλέω	(*mid*) invite, call to, summon
προσφωνέω	call out to, address (+*dat obj*); call for, summon
πῶλος, πώλου, ὁ	foal, colt
σαλεύω	shake; disturb, upset

▷ List 22 4×

σῖτος, σίτου, ὁ	wheat, grain
σκότος, -ους, τό	darkness [literal or figurative]
σός, σή, σόν	your, yours; (*subst*) your own people (*masc*), what is yours (*neut*)
συγγενής, -ές	(*subst*) relative; (*pl*) relatives, kin, countrymen
συγκαλέω	(*act*) call together, summon; (*mid*) call to one's side, summon
συνίημι/συνίω	understand, comprehend
τελέω	complete, finish; carry out (completely), accomplish; pay
τράπεζα, -έζης, ἡ	table, [extended sense] meal
τύπτω	beat, strike, wound
ὑπόδημα, -ήματος, τό	sandal

➤

▷ List 23 — 4 to 3×

ἀγορά, -ᾶς, ἡ	marketplace
ἀδελφή, -ῆς, ἡ	sister
αἰνέω	praise
αἴτιος, -ία, -ον	(*subst*) cause, reason; ground [for legal action]
ἀλείφω	anoint
ἀλέκτωρ, ἀλέκτορος, ὁ	rooster
φάτνη, -ης, ἡ	manger
φυτεύω	plant
χοῖρος, χοίρου, ὁ	pig
χορτάζω	(*trans act*) fill, feed; (*intrans mid*) eat one's fill; be satisfied

▷ List 24 — 3×

ἀληθῶς	truly, actually	
ἀνά	each, apiece	
ἀναγινώσκω	read (aloud)	➢
ἀνάγω	lead/bring up; [additional *mid* sense] put out to sea, set sail	
ἀνακλίνω	(*act*) lay down, cause to lie down; cause to recline (at a meal); (*mid*) recline (at a meal)	➢
ἀνακράζω	cry out, shout	➢
ἀναπέμπω	send up (to one in a higher position); send back	
ἀπαρνέομαι	deny, reject	
ἀπογράφω	(*mid*) register, enter oneself into a list	
ἀποδοκιμάζω	reject as unworthy/unfit	

▷ List 25 3×

ἀποθήκη, -ης, ἡ	storehouse, barn
ἀστραπή, -ῆς, ἡ	lightning
βαπτιστής, -οῦ, ὁ	Baptizer
βασιλεύω	reign, rule, be king
Βεελζεβούλ, ὁ (*indecl*)	Beelzebul
βιβλίον, -ου, τό	scroll; document
βλασφημέω	slander, speak disrespectfully about, revile
βόσκω	(*trans act*) tend, feed; (*intrans mid*) graze, feed
βοῦς, βοός, ὁ	ox
βρέχω	wet; send rain; (*impers*) it rains

▷ List 26 3×

γείτων, -ονος, ὁ/ἡ	neighbor
δάκτυλος, -ύλου, ὁ	finger
δανίζω	(*act*) lend; (*mid*) borrow
δέησις, δεήσεως, ἡ	entreaty; prayer, petition
δηνάριον, -ίου, τό	denarius
διαπορεύομαι	go/pass through
διασκορπίζω	scatter, disperse; squander
διότι	because, since; for; because of this
δοκιμάζω	examine, evaluate; determine, put to the test; approve
δοκός, -οῦ, ὁ	beam (of wood)

▷ List 27 3×

δουλεύω	be a slave; slave (for), serve (+*dat obj*)
δραχμή, -ῆς, ἡ	drachma
δῶμα, δώματος, τό	roof
ἐγγύς	near [spatial or temporal]
ἔθος, -ους, τό	custom; habit
εἰσάγω	lead/bring in(to) ▷
ἑκατόν (*indecl*)	one hundred
ἑκατοντάρχης, -ου, ὁ	centurion [commander of approximately one hundred men]
ἐκδίκησις, -ήσεως, ἡ	carrying out of justice; vengeance; punishment
ἐκκόπτω	cut off/down; do away with

▷ List 28 3×

ἐκλείπω	fail, give out, be wanting; cease, stop
ἐκπλήσσω	(*mid*) be amazed/astounded
ἐκπορεύομαι	go/come out
ἐκτείνω	stretch (something) out
ἕκτος, -η, -ον	sixth
ἐκχέω/ἐκχύν(ν)ω	pour out ▷
ἔλαιον, ἐλαίου, τό	olive oil
ἐλπίζω	hope (for); expect
ἐμβαίνω	embark ▷
ἐναντίον	(+*gen*) in front of, before, [extended sense] in the sight/judgment of

▹ List 29 3×

ἐννέα (*indecl*)	nine
ἐντρέπω	(*mid*) be ashamed; have regard for, respect ➢
ἐξίστημι/ἐξιστάνω	(*trans*) amaze; (*intrans*) be amazed ➢
ἑορτή, -ῆς, ἡ	festival; feast
ἐπέρχομαι	come (up)on, approach ➢
ἐπισκέπτομαι	inspect, observe; visit; look after
ἐπισυνάγω	(*trans act*) gather together; (*intrans mid*) assemble, gather together
ἔσωθεν	(from) within, (from) inside
ἕτοιμος, -οίμη, -ον	ready
εὔκοπος, -ον	(*comp*) εὐκοπώτερος easier

▹ List 30 3×

Ζακχαῖος, -αίου, ὁ	Zacchaeus
ἡλικία, -ας, ἡ	maturity; stature [physical]
ἥλιος, -ίου, ὁ	sun
θάπτω	bury
θεάομαι	see, look at
θεμέλιος, -ίου, ὁ	foundation
θερίζω	reap, harvest
θερισμός, -οῦ, ὁ	time of harvesting; harvest
ἰατρός, -οῦ, ὁ	physician
Ἰεριχώ, ἡ (*indecl*)	Jericho

▷ List 31 3×

Ἰσαάκ, ὁ (*indecl*)	Isaac	
καθαιρέω	take/bring down; tear down, [extended sense] destroy	➢
καθίστημι/καθιστάνω	appoint, put in charge; make, cause to be	➢
κακοῦργος, -ον	(*subst*) criminal	
κάρφος, -ους, τό	small stick, twig, chip of wood	
κατάκειμαι	be lying down; recline (for a meal), dine	
καταλύω	(*trans*) tear/throw down; (*intrans*) lodge, find lodging	
καταφιλέω	kiss	
κατεσθίω	devour, consume	➢
κατέχω	hold fast/to; hold back, restrain, suppress; possess; occupy	

▷ List 32 3×

κενός, -ή, -όν	empty(-handed); empty, fruitless; in vain, for nothing
κλίνη, -ῆς, ἡ	couch, bed, stretcher
κόλπος, -ου, ὁ	chest, bosom; fold of a garment, lap; bay
κρίμα, -ατος, τό	judgment [process of evaluation]; judgment [end result], judicial verdict
λατρεύω	serve, worship [the carrying out of religious duties] (+*dat obj*)
λεπρός, -ά, -όν	having a skin disease; (*subst*) leper
Λώτ, ὁ (*indecl*)	Lot
μακρός, -ά, -όν	far away, distant; [*neut* as *adv*] for a long time
μαμωνᾶς, μαμωνᾶ, ὁ	[Aram.] wealth
μαρτύριον, -ίου, τό	testimony, witness, proof

▹ List 33 3×

μισθός, -οῦ, ὁ	pay, wages; recompense, reward
μνῆμα, μνήματος, τό	tomb
μοιχεύω	commit adultery
μονογενής, -ές	only; unique
μόσχος, -ου, ὁ	calf, young bull
νότος, -ου, ὁ	south(west) wind; south [direction or area]
Νῶε, ὁ (*indecl*)	Noah
ξηρός, -ά, -όν	dry; withered, paralyzed
ὀδυνάω	(*mid*) suffer pain; be distressed/pained
οἰκονομία, -ας, ἡ	management, administration; arrangement, plan

▹ List 34 3×

οἰκουμένη, -ης, ἡ	the inhabited world; the (Roman) empire
ὀκτώ (*indecl*)	eight
ὁμοιόω	(*intrans mid*) be(come) like; (*trans act*) compare
ὀρθῶς	rightly, correctly
παραιτέομαι	request; excuse oneself; reject, refuse
παρατηρέω	watch closely, keep an eye on
παύω	(*trans act*) make stop/cease; (*intrans mid*) stop, cease
πενθερά, -ᾶς, ἡ	mother-in-law
πεντήκοντα (*indecl*)	fifty
περιζώννυμι/ περιζωννύω	(*act*) gird about; (*mid*) gird oneself

▸

▹ List 35 3×

περισσός, -ή, -όν	extraordinary, remarkable; abundant, superfluous; (*comp*) περισσότερος, -έρα, -ον greater, better, excessive	
πέτρα, -ας, ἡ	rock [formation or piece]	
πλατεῖα, -είας, ἡ	(wide) road, street	
πλησίον	(+*gen*) near; (*subst*) neighbor	
προβαίνω	move forward, advance, [extended sense] advance (in time/age)	▹
προσευχή, -ῆς, ἡ	prayer	
προσπίπτω	fall down before/at the feet of; fall upon, strike against	▹
πρωτοκλισία, -ας, ἡ	the place of honor [at a dinner]	
Σαμαρίτης, -ου, ὁ	Samaritan	
σιγάω	be/keep silent	

▹ List 36 3×

Σιδών, -ῶνος, ἡ	Sidon	
σιτευτός, -ή, -όν	fattened	
σκάπτω	dig	
σκιρτάω	leap, bound [exuberantly]	
Σολομών, -ῶνος, ὁ	Solomon	
σπεύδω	(*intrans*) hurry; (*trans*) make hurry, hasten	
σπλαγχνίζομαι	have compassion, feel sympathy	
σταυρός, -οῦ, ὁ	cross	
στεῖρα, στείρας, ἡ	barren woman	
στηρίζω	set, establish; strengthen/make more firm [inwardly]	▹

JOHN

▷ List 1	19 to 12×
ἀληθής, -ές	true, trustworthy; real
ἄρτι	(just) now <TH ἀπάρτι “just now; from now” instead of ἀπ’ ἄρτι>
ἐμαυτοῦ, -ῆς	myself, my (own) [when *gen*]
ἑορτή, -ῆς, ἡ	festival; feast
ἴδε	[attention-getter] look!, pay attention!
μαρτυρία, -ας, ἡ	[the act of giving] testimony; evidence
νίπτω	(*act*) wash (something); (*mid*) wash (oneself)
πόθεν	from where?, how is it that?
πρόβατον, -άτου, τό	sheep
φιλέω	love, like; kiss

▷ List 2	12 to 9×
ἀληθινός, -ή, -όν	true, trustworthy; real
ἐγγύς	near [spatial or temporal]; (*prep +gen/dat*) near
Λάζαρος, -άρου, ὁ	Lazarus
Μάρθα, -ας, ἡ	Martha
Μαριάμ, ἡ (*indecl*)	Miriam, Mary
οὔπω	not yet
παρρησία, -ας, ἡ	plainness; openness; boldness; (*adv*) plainly, openly, boldly
πάσχα, τό (*indecl*)	Passover (festival); Passover lamb; Passover meal
ὑπηρέτης, -ου, ὁ	helper, server, attendant
Φίλιππος, -ίππου, ὁ	Philip

▷ LIST 3 — 8 TO 7×

ἀληθῶς	truly, actually
ἄρχων, ἄρχοντος, ὁ	ruler; official
ἀσθενέω	be sick; be weak
θύρα, -ας, ἡ	door; entrance
Θωμᾶς, Θωμᾶ, ὁ	Thomas
κεῖμαι	be lying/reclining/resting; exist for, be set for
πέραν	on the other side; (*subst* +*art*) the other side; (*prep* +*gen*) on the other side of
πιάζω	grasp; seize, arrest
ῥαββ(ε)ί	[Heb.] Rabbi; (my) master
σκοτία, -ας, ἡ	darkness [literal or figurative]

▷ LIST 4 — 7 TO 6×

ἀδελφή, -ῆς, ἡ	sister
γονεύς, -έως, ὁ	parent
δείκνυμι	show, make known; explain ▶
διψάω	be thirsty
ἐντεῦθεν	from here
θεάομαι	see, look at
κραυγάζω	cry out, shout
Ναθαναήλ, ὁ (*indecl*)	Nathanael
οἶνος, οἴνου, ὁ	wine
ὀπίσω	behind; (*subst*) back, that which is behind; (*prep* +*gen*) after, behind [spatial or temporal]

▷ List 5 — 6 to 5 ×

ἀναγγέλλω	report; disclose, announce
ἀναπίπτω	recline, lean back ▶
Ἀνδρέας, -ου, ὁ	Andrew
ἄνωθεν	from above; again [usually with πάλιν]
ποιμήν, ποιμένος, ὁ	shepherd
στρατιώτης, -ου, ὁ	soldier
ταράσσω	agitate, disturb [physically, mentally, or spiritually] ▶
τιμάω	honor; set a price
ὑγιής, -ές	whole, healthy; wholesome, sound
φίλος, -η, -ον	friendly; (*subst*) friend

▷ List 6 — 5 ×

βαστάζω	pick up; carry, bear
Ἑβραϊστί	in Hebrew/Aramaic
ἐκλέγομαι	choose; select
ἕλκω	draw, pull; draw, attract ▶
ἐπαύριον	tomorrow; (*subst*) the next day
Ἰσκαριώθ, ὁ (*indecl*) / Ἰσκαριώτης, -ου, ὁ	Iscariot
Καϊάφας, -α, ὁ	Caiaphas
Καφαρναούμ, ἡ (*indecl*)	Capernaum
Μαρία, -ας, ἡ	Mary
μέντοι (*postp*)	nevertheless, however

▷ List 7 — 5 to 4×

ἁγιάζω	consecrate, make holy; regard as holy
ἀναβλέπω	look up; receive sight
Νικόδημος, -ήμου, ὁ	Nicodemus
ὀψάριον, ὀψαρίου, τό	fish
πέντε (*indecl*)	five
πηλός, -οῦ, ὁ	mud, clay
σός, σή, σόν	your, yours; (*subst neut*) what is yours
τελειόω	complete, finish; bring (something) to its goal/conclusion; perfect
τρώγω	eat
ὑψόω	lift up; exalt

▷ List 8 — 4×

ἀνάκειμαι	recline at table, dine
ἀντλέω	draw [liquid, generally water]
ἀρνέομαι	deny; refuse; disown
ἁρπάζω	seize; take away, snatch
Βηθανία, -ας, ἡ	Bethany
βρῶσις, βρώσεως, ὁ	food; eating, consumption
γογγύζω	grumble, complain; whisper, murmur
δεῖπνον, δείπνου, τό	dinner; feast, banquet
δίκτυον, -ύου, τό	(fish)net
ἐντέλλω	(*mid*) command, instruct

▷ List 9 4×

ἐπαίρω	lift up	➤
ἥκω	be present, have come	
Ἠσαΐας, Ἠσαΐου, ὁ	Isaiah	
θερίζω	reap, harvest	
Ἰωσήφ, ὁ (*indecl*)	Joseph	
καθαρός, -ά, -όν	clean; pure; innocent	
καλῶς	well, appropriately, effectively; correctly	
Κανά/Κανᾶ, ἡ (*indecl*)	Cana	
καταλαμβάνω	grasp; seize; catch; understand	➤
κῆπος, κήπου, ὁ	orchard, garden	

▷ List 10 4×

κλέπτης, -ου, ὁ	thief
κλῆμα, κλήματος, τό	branch
κράβαττος, -άττου, ὁ	mat, pallet
λιθάζω	stone (someone)
λύπη, -ης, ἡ	grief, sadness; pain
μονογενής, -ές	only; unique
μύρον, -ου, τό	fragrant ointment
νυμφίος, -ου, ὁ	bridegroom
ὀθόνιον, -ίου, τό	linen cloth
ὁμολογέω	acknowledge; declare, confess

▷ List 11	4×
παράκλητος, -ήτου, ὁ	helper, intercessor, advocate
παροιμία, -ας, ἡ	illustration, figure of speech; proverb
πλευρά, -ᾶς, ἡ	side [in NT, side of the human body]
πλοιάριον, -ίου, τό	small boat
ποῖος, ποία, ποῖον	of what kind?; which?, what?
πραιτώριον, -ίου, τό	the praetorium
πτωχός, -ή, -όν	poor
πώποτε	at any time, ever
Σαμαρίτης, -ου, ὁ	Samaritan
σταυρός, -οῦ, ὁ	cross

▷ List 12	4 to 3×
ἀγοράζω	buy
αἰτία, -ας, ἡ	cause, reason; accusation, charge
ἄμπελος, -έλου, ἡ	vine, grapevine
ἄν	if [in place of ἐάν]
ἄνω	above; up(ward)
ἀποσυνάγωγος, -ον	expelled from the synagogue
στρέφω	(*trans act*) turn; return; change; (*intrans mid*) turn (around); change ▷
τοσοῦτος, -αύτη, -οῦτο(ν)	so many; so much/great; such
ὑπαντάω	meet (+*dat obj*)
ψωμίον, -ου, τό	piece of bread

▷ **List 13**	3×
ἀρχιτρίκλινος, -ίνου, ὁ	head steward
αὐλή, -ῆς, ἡ	enclosed open space: courtyard, sheepfold; dwelling complex: house, farm, palace
γεμίζω	fill
γνωρίζω	make known, inform; know
δάκτυλος, -ύλου, ὁ	finger
διάβολος, -ον	slanderous; (*subst*) adversary; devil
διαζώννυμι	tie around ▸
διακονέω	(+*dat obj*) serve; care for; wait on; administer
διάκονος, -όνου, ὁ/ἡ	servant, helper; ministerial attendant
διδαχή, -ῆς, ἡ	teaching [activity or content]

▷ **List 14**	3×
Δίδυμος, -ύμου, ὁ	Didymus; twin
εἶτα	then, next; furthermore
ἐκμάσσω	wipe (dry)
ἐλέγχω	expose; reprove; convict, accuse
Ἕλλην, -ηνος, ὁ	Greek (person); a person of Hellenic culture, gentile
ἐμβαίνω	embark ▸
ἐνιαυτός, -οῦ, ὁ	year
ἕξ (*indecl*)	six
εὐθέως	immediately
εὐχαριστέω	thank, give thanks, be thankful

▷ List 15 3×

ζωοποιέω/ζῳοποιέω	give life to, make alive
θερμαίνω	(*mid*) warm oneself
θυρωρός, -οῦ, ὁ	gatekeeper, doorkeeper
Ἰακώβ, ὁ (*indecl*)	Jacob
ἰάομαι	heal; restore
Ἰορδάνης, -ου, ὁ	Jordan (River)
ἰχθύς, -ύος, ὁ	fish
καθέζομαι	be sitting; sit
Καῖσαρ, Καίσαρος, ὁ	Caesar
κατάγνυμι	break, shatter ▷

▷ List 16 3×

κατηγορέω	accuse
κολυμβήθρα, -ας, ἡ	pool
κοπιάω	be weary/tired; labor, toil
κρυπτός, -ή, -όν	hidden, secret
κρύπτω	(*trans act*) hide (something); (*intrans mid*) hide (oneself), be hidden ▷
κώμη, -ης, ἡ	village
λῃστής, -οῦ, ὁ	robber; revolutionary
Μαγδαληνή, -ῆς, ἡ	Magdalene
μεστός, -ή, -όν	full
μεταβαίνω	go, move ▷

▹ List 17 3×

μήτι	not	▸
μιμνήσκομαι/ μιμνῄσκομαι	(+*gen obj*) remember; be mindful of	▸
μνημονεύω	remember (+*gen/acc obj*)	
Ναζωραῖος, -αίου, ὁ	Nazarene	
ναί	yes	
ὁμοίως	likewise, in the same way	
ὁμοῦ	together	
ὄξος, -ους, τό	wine vinegar	
οὐδέπω	not yet	
παρασκευή, -ῆς, ἡ	preparation [in the NT, this word refers to a day of preparation for a festival]	

▹ List 18 3×

περιστερά, -ᾶς, ἡ	pigeon, dove
πηγή, -ῆς, ἡ	spring; well
πρίν	before
πρότερος, -έρα, -ον	former, earlier; [*neut sg* as *adv*] before, formerly
Σαμάρεια, -είας, ἡ	Samaria
σημαίνω	indicate; report, reveal
σκέλος, -ους, τό	leg
συμφέρω	(*impers*) it is beneficial/of advantage; it is better; (*subst ptc*) benefit, profit
σχίσμα, -ατος, τό	division, dissension; tear, crack
ταχέως	quickly, without delay; soon; (*comp*) τάχιον more quickly

▷ List 19 — 3 to 2×

ἀγαλλιάω	exult, rejoice; be overjoyed
ἀλείφω	anoint
ἀλέκτωρ, ἀλέκτορος, ὁ	rooster
ἀλλότριος, -ία, -ον	another's; foreign; (*subst*) another's property; stranger
Τιβεριάς, -άδος, ἡ	Tiberias
ὑδρία, -ας, ἡ	water jar
ὑμέτερος, -έρα, -ον	your, yours, (*subst neut*) what belongs to you
φυλάσσω	observe, follow; guard, protect
χώρα, -ας, ἡ	land; region; country
χωρέω	hold, have room for; go, reach

▷ List 20 — 2×

ἀμνός, -οῦ, ὁ	lamb
ἀνακύπτω	stand up (straight)
ἀνθρακιά, -ᾶς, ἡ	charcoal fire
Ἅννας, Ἅννα, ὁ	Hannas, Annas
ἀποκόπτω	cut off/away
ἀπόκρισις, -ίσεως, ἡ	answer
ἀριστάω	eat breakfast; eat a meal
ἀρκέω	(*act*) be enough/sufficient; (*mid*) be content/satisfied
ἀσθένεια, -είας, ἡ	sickness, disease; weakness
βάπτω	dip

▷ **List 21**	**2×**
Βαραββᾶς, Βαραββᾶ, ὁ	Barabbas
βασιλικός, -ή, -όν	royal
Βηθσαϊδά(ν), ἡ (*indecl*)	Bethsaida
βιβλίον, -ου, τό	scroll; document
βόσκω	tend, feed
βουλεύω	(*mid*) deliberate; decide
βοῦς, βοός, ὁ	ox
γάμος, -ου, ὁ	wedding celebration; marriage
γεύομαι	taste, partake (+*gen/acc obj*)
γλωσσόκομον, -όμου, τό	money box

▷ **List 22**	**2×**
γνωστός, -ή, -όν	known; capable of being known
γράμμα, -ατος, τό	letter [of the alphabet]; document, writing, letter
δεῦτε	come!, come here!, come on!
δηνάριον, -ίου, τό	denarius
διακόσιοι, -αι, -α	two hundred
ἑκατόν (*indecl*)	one hundred
ἐκεῖθεν	from there
ἐκπορεύομαι	go/come out
ἕκτος, -η, -ον	sixth
ἐλεύθερος, -έρα, -ον	free

▸

▷ List 23	2×
ἐλευθερόω	set free
ἐμβλέπω	look at (intently) (+*dat obj*)
ἐμβριμάομαι	(*trans* +*dat obj*) sternly warn; speak angrily to; (*intrans*) be distressed
ἐμφανίζω	(*trans act*) make visible; inform, make known; (*intrans mid*) appear
ἐνθάδε	here
ἔξεστιν	(*impers*) it is right/permitted [*3sg* of ἔξειμι]
ἐπάνω	(*adv*) above, over; more than; (*prep* +*gen*) above, over
ἐπεί	since, because; for otherwise
ἐπιβάλλω	(*trans*) lay/put on; (*intrans*) throw oneself; fall to, belong to
ἐπίκειμαι	lie upon; press upon [+*dat* of person]; impose [+*dat* of person]

▷ List 24	2×
ἐπιτίθημι	lay/put upon
ἐπιχρίω	anoint, smear on
ἐραυνάω	search, examine
ἑρμηνεύω	interpret, explain; translate, mean
ζώννυμι/ζωννύω	gird ▷
Ἠλίας, Ἠλίου, ὁ	Elijah
ἡλικία, -ας, ἡ	maturity; stature [physical]
ἧλος, ἥλου, ὁ	nail
θερισμός, -οῦ, ὁ	time of harvesting; harvest
θνήσκω	die ▷

▷ **List 25**	**2×**
θρίξ, τριχός, ἡ	hair
καθαρισμός, -οῦ, ὁ	cleansing
καίω	kindle, light; burn (up)
κατάκειμαι	be lying down; recline (for a meal), dine
κατακρίνω	condemn
κάτω	down(ward); below
κλάσμα, -ατος, τό	fragment, piece
κλείω	shut, close
κοιλία, -ας, ἡ	stomach; womb; heart [figurative, representing one's inner desires and feelings]
κοιμάω	(*mid*) sleep, fall asleep; die

▷ **List 26**	**2×**
κόλπος, -ου, ὁ	chest, bosom; fold of a garment, lap; bay
κρίθινος, -ίνη, -ον	made of barley flour
λαλιά, -ᾶς, ἡ	speech [content]; way of speaking
λέντιον, -ίου, τό	linen towel
λευκός, -ή, -όν	white; bright, shining
λίτρα, -ας, ἡ	(Roman) pound
λύκος, -ου, ὁ	wolf
λυπέω	(*act*) cause grief/sorrow; (*mid*) grieve, be sad/distressed
μανθάνω	learn
μάννα, τό (*indecl*)	manna

▸

▹ **List 27**	**2×**
μάχαιρα, -αίρης, ἡ	dagger, short sword
μεθερμηνεύω	translate
μέλει	(*impers*) it is a concern to/of interest to [*3sg* of μέλω]
Μεσσίας, -ου, ὁ	Messiah
μηκέτι	no longer
μισθωτός, -οῦ, ὁ	hired laborer
μονή, -ῆς, ἡ	abiding, staying; room, dwelling place
Ναζαρά/Ναζαρέθ/ Ναζαρέτ, ἡ (*indecl*)	Nazareth
ὀκτώ (*indecl*)	eight
ὀφείλω	owe, be indebted to; be obligated, ought; have to

▹ **List 28**	**2×**
ὀψία, -ας, ἡ	evening
ὄψις, -εως, ἡ	face; outward appearance
παραγίνομαι	come, arrive, be present ▹
παρακύπτω	stoop down (and look); look into [figuratively]
παραμυθέομαι	console, comfort
πάρειμι	be present/here, have come
πειράζω	test; tempt
πεντήκοντα (*indecl*)	fifty
περισσεύω	(*intrans*) abound (in), overflow, be left over ▹
περιτομή, -ῆς, ἡ	circumcision; one who is circumcised

▹ List 29 2×

πλανάω	(*act*) lead astray, deceive; (*mid*) wander, go astray, be misled
πλῆθος, πλήθους, τό	multitude, a great quantity
πνέω	blow [of wind]
πορφυροῦς, πορφυρᾶ, πορφυροῦν	purple
πότε	when?
πράσσω	do, accomplish, perform
προσκόπτω	(*trans*) cause to strike against; (*intrans*) stumble
πρωΐ	early in the morning
πυνθάνομαι	inquire, ask
πωλέω	sell

▹ List 30 2×

ῥάπισμα, ῥαπίσματος, τό	strike, blow; slap in the face
Σαμαρῖτις, -ίτιδος, ἡ	Samaritan
Σιλωάμ, ὁ (*indecl*)	Siloam
σκανδαλίζω	cause (someone) to sin; shock, offend
σκορπίζω	scatter, disperse; distribute
σουδάριον, -ίου, τό	cloth
σπεῖρα, σπείρης, ἡ	military unit [a cohort, though the number varied]
στάδιον, -ίου, τό	stade [one-eighth mile]; stadium
στέφανος, -άνου, ὁ	wreath, crown
στῆθος, στήθους, ἡ	chest

▷ **List 31**		2×
στοά, -ᾶς, ἡ	portico	
συκῆ, -ῆς, ἡ	fig tree	
συνεισέρχομαι	enter/go into with	➤
συνέρχομαι	come together with, gather; go/come with, travel together with	➤
σφραγίζω	seal; seal up; mark with a seal; certify	
σχίζω	tear, divide, split; cause division	
τελέω	complete, finish; carry out (completely), accomplish; pay	
τέσσαρες, -α	four	
τίτλος, -ου, ὁ	inscription	
τρέχω	run	

▷ **List 32**		2×
τριάκοντα (*indecl*)	thirty	
τύπος, -ου, ὁ	mark	
φαίνω	(*act*) shine; (*mid*) appear	
φαῦλος, φαύλη, φαῦλον	bad; low-grade	
φεύγω	flee; escape; avoid	
φρέαρ, -ατος, τό	well [for water]; pit	
χαμαί	to/on the ground	
χιτών, -ῶνος, τό	tunic	
ψεύστης, -ου, ὁ	liar	
ὥσπερ	(just) as	

▷ List 33	2 to 1×
ἀγγέλλω	report, announce
ἁγνίζω	purify
ἀγωνίζομαι	exert effort, strive; struggle, fight
ἀδικία, -ας, ἡ	injustice, unrighteousness; wrongdoing, misdeed
ἀθετέω	nullify, invalidate; reject
αἰγιαλός, -οῦ, ὁ	beach, seashore
Αἰνών, ἡ (*indecl*)	Aenon
ἄκανθα, ἀκάνθης, ἡ	thorn; thornbush
ἀκάνθινος, -ίνη, -ον	made of thorns, thorny
ὠφελέω	help, benefit, be of use to (*+dat/acc obj*); accomplish

▷ List 34	1×
ἀκοή, -ῆς, ἡ	hearing, listening; ear; news, rumor, report, message
ἁλιεύω	fish
ἀλλαχόθεν	from elsewhere
ἅλλομαι	leap, spring up; bubble/well up (of water)
ἀλόη, -ης, ἡ	aloes
ἀνά	each, apiece
ἀναγινώσκω	read (aloud)
ἀναμάρτητος, -ον	without sin, blameless
ἀνατρέπω	overturn; ruin, subvert
ἀναχωρέω	depart, leave, withdraw

▶

▹ List 35 1×

ἄνεμος, ἀνέμου, ὁ	wind	
ἀνέρχομαι	go/come up	▸
ἀνθρωποκτόνος, -ου, ὁ	murderer	
ἀντί	(+*gen*) instead of, in place of	
ἀντιλέγω	[+*dat* of person] argue (against), contradict; oppose	
ἄντλημα, -ήματος, τό	bucket	
ἅπας, ἅπασα, ἅπαν	whole, all; (*subst*) everyone, all, everything	
ἀπειθέω	disobey, be disobedient, resist (+*dat obj*)	
ἄπιστος, -ον	unbelieving; unbelievable	
ἀποβαίνω	move off, disembark	▸

▹ List 36 1×

ἀποκαλύπτω	reveal, disclose	▸
ἀπορέω	be perplexed/at a loss	
ἅπτω	(*mid* +*gen obj*) touch, hold, cling to	
ἀπώλεια, -είας, ἡ	destruction; waste	
ἄραφος, -ον	seamless	
ἀρεστός, -ή, -όν	pleasing	
ἀριθμός, -οῦ, ὁ	number, total	
Ἁριμαθαία/Ἀριμαθαία, -ας, ἡ	Arimathea	
ἀρνίον, -ου, τό	lamb, sheep	
ἄρωμα, ἀρώματος, τό	aromatic spice	

ACTS

▷ LIST 1	23 TO 16×
ἀνάγω	lead/bring up; bring (before) [for judicial examination]; [additional *mid* sense] put out to sea, set sail
ἀναιρέω	(*act*) do away with, destroy, kill; (*mid*) take/pick up for oneself, claim ▸
Ἀντιόχεια, -είας, ἡ	Antioch
Βαρναβᾶς, Βαρναβᾶ, ὁ	Barnabas
ἐπικαλέω	(*act*) call, name; (*mid*) call upon, invoke, appeal ▸
ἱκανός, -ή, -όν	sufficient, (*subst*) bail, security; to a considerable degree, large, many, great
κελεύω	command, order
παραγίνομαι	come, arrive, be present ▸
πλῆθος, πλήθους, τό	multitude, a great quantity
χιλίαρχος, -άρχου, ὁ	commander, captain [of approximately six hundred soldiers]

▷ LIST 2	16 TO 13×
Αἴγυπτος, -ύπτου, ἡ	Egypt
βούλομαι	want, desire; intend, plan
Δαμασκός, -οῦ, ἡ	Damascus
ἑκατοντάρχης, -ου, ὁ	centurion [commander of approximately one hundred men]
ἐπιτίθημι	(*act*) lay/put upon; attack; (*mid*) give; attack
Καισάρεια, -είας, ἡ	Caesarea
Σαῦλος, Σαύλου, ὁ	Saul
συνέδριον, -ίου, τό	council; Sanhedrin
συνέρχομαι	come together with, gather; go/come with, travel together with ▸
Φίλιππος, -ίππου, ὁ	Philip

▷ List 3 — 13 to 11×

Ἀγρίππας, Ἀγρίππα, ὁ	Agrippa
ἅπας, ἅπασα, ἅπαν	whole, all; (*subst*) everyone, all, everything
Ἀσία, -ας, ἡ	Asia
ἐκεῖθεν	from there
κατέρχομαι	come/go down; arrive, put in [nautical term] ▸
μάρτυς, μάρτυρος, ὁ	witness
πράσσω	(*trans*) do, accomplish, perform; (*intrans*) act, behave ▸
Σιλᾶς, Σιλᾶ, ὁ / Σίλας, Σίλα, ὁ	Silas
στρατιώτης, -ου, ὁ	soldier
Φῆστος, Φήστου, ὁ	Festus

▷ List 4 — 11 to 10×

Ἁνανίας, -ου, ὁ	Ananias
ἄρχων, ἄρχοντος, ὁ	ruler; official
ἀτενίζω	look intently (at), stare (at) [+*dat* or εἰς]
ἐπιστρέφω	(*intrans act/mid*) return, go/come back; turn (around); change (one's thinking or behavior); (*trans act*) turn, redirect
ἐφίστημι	stand by/near; attack (+*dat obj*); [with reference to events] (*pf*) be at hand/impending ▸
καταγγέλλω	announce, proclaim, declare
ὅραμα, -άματος, τό	sight [that which is seen]; vision [that which is seen in a transcendent or revelatory experience]
παραγγέλλω	command, instruct, give orders
Ῥωμαῖος, -αία, -ον	Roman
ὑποστρέφω	return, turn back

▷ List 5 — 10 to 9×

γένος, -ους, τό	people group, family; offspring, descendant; kind, class
γνωστός, -ή, -όν	known; notable; capable of being known
διαλέγομαι	converse, address, discuss; dispute, argue
διαμαρτύρομαι	[generally more emphatic than similar words] bear witness, attest; warn, exhort (+*dat obj*)
Ἕλλην, -ηνος, ὁ	Greek (person); a person of Hellenic culture, gentile
ἐπαύριον	tomorrow; (*subst*) the next day
θύρα, -ας, ἡ	door; entrance
Ἰόππη, -ης, ἡ	Joppa
Καῖσαρ, Καίσαρος, ὁ	Caesar
ὁμοθυμαδόν	with one mind/accord

▷ List 6 — 9×

ἐπίσταμαι	understand; know
εὐθέως	immediately
καταντάω	come (to), arrive (at), [extended sense] attain (to)
κατηγορέω	accuse
μεταπέμπω	(*mid*) send for, summon
πίμπλημι	fill, fulfill, complete
προσευχή, -ῆς, ἡ	prayer; place of prayer
προσκαλέω	(*mid*) invite, call to, summon
Σαούλ, ὁ (*indecl*)	Saul
τέρας, -ατος, τό	wonder, marvel, portent

▷

▷ List 7 — 9 to 8×

αἰτία, -ας, ἡ	cause, reason; accusation, charge
ἀναγινώσκω	read (aloud) ▷
ἀναλαμβάνω	lift up; take up/along ▷
βῆμα, βήματος, τό	step [as a measure of length]; platform; judicial bench, judgment seat
διακονία, -ας, ἡ	service, serving; (ministerial) service, ministry
διατρίβω	remain/stay [in a place], spend (time)
ἐλεημοσύνη, -ης, ἡ	charitable giving; alms
ἐξάγω	lead/bring out ▷
ἐξίστημι/ἐξιστάνω	(*trans*) amaze; (*intrans*) be amazed ▷
Φῆλιξ, Φήλικος, ὁ	Felix

▷ List 8 — 8×

Ἔφεσος, -έσου, ἡ	Ephesus
Ἰακώβ, ὁ (*indecl*)	Jacob
Κορνήλιος, -ίου, ὁ	Cornelius
Μακεδονία, -ας, ἡ	Macedonia
μήτε	[continuing a previous *neg*] and not, neither, nor
οὗ	(to) where
πλήρης, -ες (freq. *indecl*)	full, filled; full, complete
σέβω	(*mid*) worship, revere
στρατηγός, -οῦ, ὁ	chief (Roman) magistrate [of a city]; captain [of the temple guard in Jerusalem]
τεσσεράκοντα/τεσσαράκοντα (*indecl*)	forty

▷ List 9 — 8 to 7×

βουλή, -ῆς, ἡ	intention, motive; decision, plan, purpose
δέομαι	ask, petition, pray [+*gen* of person(s) petitioned]
ἐάω	allow, permit, let ▸
ἔθος, -ους, τό	custom; habit
ἐκλέγομαι	choose; select
ἐξαποστέλλω	send out/off, dispatch
ἐπιλαμβάνομαι	take/lay hold of (+*gen obj*); catch, arrest
Ἰωσήφ, ὁ (*indecl*)	Joseph
φυλάσσω	(*act*) observe, follow; guard, protect; (*mid*) be on guard against, avoid
χώρα, -ας, ἡ	land; region; country

▷ List 10 — 7×

κατάγω	(*act*) lead/bring down; (*mid*) put in, land [nautical term] ▸
Κιλικία, -ας, ἡ	Cilicia
Ναζωραῖος, -αίου, ὁ	Nazarene
νομίζω	think, suppose, believe
ξενίζω	(*trans act*) receive/entertain as a guest; astonish, surprise; (*intrans mid*) lodge/stay as a guest
παρρησιάζομαι	speak freely/boldly
πυνθάνομαι	inquire, ask; learn [via inquiry] ▸
Σαμάρεια, -είας, ἡ	Samaria
Στέφανος, -άνου, ὁ	Stephen
τροφή, -ῆς, ἡ	nourishment, food

▷ List 11 — 7 to 6×

αἵρεσις, -έσεως, ἡ	faction, sect
ἀπολογέομαι	speak in one's defense, defend oneself
ἀφίστημι	(*trans*) draw away, incite; (*intrans*) withdraw, depart; keep away ▸
βάπτισμα, -ίσματος, τό	baptism, (ceremonial) plunging/washing
δέσμιος, -ίου, ὁ	prisoner
διάλεκτος, -έκτου, ὁ	language; dialect
διαφθορά, -ῆς, ἡ	decay
δυνατός, -ή, -όν	able, capable, strong, powerful; possible
ἐγκαλέω	accuse, bring charges against ▸
χωρίον, -ου, τό	piece of land, field

▷ List 12 — 6×

εἰσάγω	lead/bring in(to) ▸
ἐπιμένω	remain, stay; persist, continue
ἐπιπίπτω	fall upon ▸
ἡγεμών, ἡγεμόνος, ὁ	leader; governor
ἰσχύω	be strong/powerful/able; prevail
κωλύω	hinder, prevent; withhold
μετάνοια, -οίας, ἡ	change of mind and heart, repentance
νῆσος, νήσου, ἡ	island
παῖς, παιδός, ὁ/ἡ	child [boy or girl]; child [son or daughter]; slave; servant
παραχρῆμα	at once, immediately

▹ List 13 — 6 to 5×

ἀδικέω	(*intrans*) do wrong, be in the wrong; (*trans*) wrong; injure
ἀκάθαρτος, -ον	impure, unclean [cultic or moral]
ἀκριβῶς	diligently, carefully, well
παρεμβολή, -ῆς, ἡ	(fortified) camp; barracks
παύω	(*trans act*) make stop/cease; (*intrans mid*) stop, cease
προσέχω	look after, pay attention/attend to (+*dat obj*)
προσκαρτερέω	hold fast to, be devoted to [+*dat* of thing or person]
προστίθημι	add on/to; continue (to), do again [indicates the repetition of another verb's action]
τέσσαρες, -α	four
Τιμόθεος, -έου, ὁ	Timothy

▹ List 14 — 5×

ἀναβλέπω	look up; receive sight
ἀναγγέλλω	report; disclose, announce
ἀνακρίνω	examine closely, inquire into; hear a case, put on trial, investigate
ἀνθύπατος, -άτου, ὁ	proconsul
ἀποδέχομαι	welcome, receive; accept
ἀργύριον, -ίου, τό	silver, silver coin [drachma or shekel]; money
ἀριθμός, -οῦ, ὁ	number, total
Ἄρτεμις, -έμιδος, ἡ	Artemis
ἄφεσις, ἀφέσεως, ἡ	release; forgiveness (of)
δεσμός, -οῦ, ὁ	(*sg*) binding, impediment; (*pl*) bonds, chains, [extended sense] imprisonment

▷ List 15 5×

διασῴζω	bring safely through, preserve; save, rescue	➢
διατάσσω	(*act*) instruct, direct; (*mid*) instruct, direct; make arrangements	➢
διότι	because, since; for; because of this	
ἐκπίπτω	fall off; run aground [nautical term]	➢
ἐμφανίζω	inform, make known; present evidence (against)	
ἐνθάδε	here	
ἐξαιρέω	(*act*) take out; (*mid*) rescue, deliver, set free	➢
ἐπαίρω	lift up	➢
ἔπειμι	come upon/near; (*attr ptc*) next, following	
ἐπιβαίνω	board (a ship); set foot in	➢

▷ List 16 5×

ἐπιστολή, -ῆς, ἡ	letter	
ἐπιτρέπω	permit, give permission, allow (+*dat obj*)	➢
εὐνοῦχος, -ούχου, ὁ	eunuch	
Ἐφέσιος, -ία, -ον	Ephesian	
ζήτημα, ζητήματος, τό	point of disagreement, controversial issue	
Ἰκόνιον, -ίου, τό	Iconium	
Ἰσραηλίτης, -ου, ὁ	Israelite	
καθίστημι/καθιστάνω	appoint, put in charge; bring	➢
κακόω	harm, mistreat; spoil, corrupt	
καταλείπω	leave (behind); cause to be left over	➢

▷ List 17 5×

κλῆρος, κλήρου, ὁ	lot; allotment, share
κοινός, -ή, -όν	common, shared; common, ordinary; impure, unclean
κολλάω	(*intrans mid*) cling (to), join (with), join oneself (to)
Κύπρος, -ου, ἡ	Cyprus
λατρεύω	serve, worship [the carrying out of religious duties] (*+dat obj*)
Λύστρα, -ας, ἡ/τά	Lystra ▷
μετανοέω	repent
μήν, μηνός, ὁ	month
οἰκουμένη, -ης, ἡ	the inhabited world; the (Roman) empire
ὁρίζω	determine, set, fix; [of persons] appoint, designate

▷ List 18 5×

οὖς, ὠτός, τό	ear; hearing, understanding
Παμφυλία, -ας, ἡ	Pamphylia
πάρειμι	be present/here, have come
παρέχω	(*act*) bring about, furnish; present, provide; (*mid*) grant, show [something from one's own means] ▷
παρρησία, -ας, ἡ	plainness; openness; boldness; (*adv*) plainly, openly, boldly
πειράζω	test; tempt; attempt, try
πέντε (*indecl*)	five
περιτέμνω	circumcise ▷
πληθύνω	(*intrans act/mid*) increase in number, grow, multiply
προσδοκάω	wait (for), expect

▷ List 19 5×

προσλαμβάνω	(*mid*) take to oneself; receive, welcome; take aside; take, partake ➢
πυλών, -ῶνος, ὁ	gateway
Ῥώμη, -ης, ἡ	Rome
Σαδδουκαῖος, -αίου, ὁ	Sadducee
σκεῦος, σκεύους, τό	object, thing; vessel, container; instrument, vessel
στάσις, -εως, ἡ	uprising, revolt; discord, dissension, dispute
συγχέω/συγχύν(ν)ω	(*trans act*) confuse, confound; stir up; (*intrans mid*) be confounded/confused ➢
Συρία, -ας, ἡ	Syria
τυγχάνω	(*trans +gen obj*) experience, obtain; (*intrans adj ptc +neg*) uncommon, extraordinary ➢
τύπτω	beat, strike, wound

▷ List 20 5 to 4×

Αἰγύπτιος, -ία, -ον	(*subst*) Egyptian
ἅλυσις, ἁλύσεως, ἡ	chain, [extended sense] imprisonment
ἄνεμος, ἀνέμου, ὁ	wind
ἀντιλέγω	[+*dat* of person] argue (against), contradict; oppose ➢
ἀποπλέω	sail away/off ➢
ἀρνέομαι	deny; refuse; disown
αὐξάνω/αὔξω	(*trans*) make grow/increase; (*intrans*) grow, increase
αὔριον	next day, tomorrow; soon, shortly
βαστάζω	pick up; carry, bear
ὡσεί	as, like; about, approximately

▷ List 21 4×

βλασφημέω	slander, speak disrespectfully about, revile
γέ (*encl*)	indeed, even; yet, at least, though
γόνυ, γόνατος, τό	knee
δῆμος, δήμου, ὁ	people, crowd; popular assembly
δημόσιος, -ία, -ον	public; (*adv*) δημοσίᾳ publicly
διακρίνω	(*act*) make a distinction; (*mid*) dispute, contest, contend (with)
διδαχή, -ῆς, ἡ	teaching [activity or content]
δωρεά, -ᾶς, ἡ	gift
εἰσπορεύομαι	go into, enter
ἔκστασις, -άσεως, ἡ	entrancement, astonishment, amazement; trance

▷ List 22 4×

ἐκτίθημι	(*act*) abandon, expose; (*mid*) explain, expound	
ἐκφέρω	carry/bring out; produce	➤
ἐμαυτοῦ, -ῆς	myself, my (own) [when *gen*]	
ἐξαυτῆς	immediately, at once	
ἔξειμι	go out, leave	➤
ἔξεστιν	(*impers*) it is right/permitted [*3sg* of ἔξειμι]	➤
ἐξηγέομαι	report, describe; explain, expound	
ἐπέρχομαι	come (up)on, approach	➤
ἐπιβάλλω	(*trans*) lay/put on; (*intrans*) throw oneself; fall to, belong to	
ἐπιβουλή, -ῆς, ἡ	plot, scheme	

▹ List 23 4×

ἐπισκέπτομαι	inspect, observe; visit; look after
ἐργασία, -ας, ἡ	work, labor, activity, [extended sense] business, trade; profit
ἡγέομαι	consider; lead, (*subst pres ptc*) leader, ruler
ἥλιος, -ίου, ὁ	sun
θάπτω	bury
θύω	sacrifice; slaughter, kill
ἰάομαι	heal; restore
Ἰάσων, Ἰάσονος, ὁ	Jason
Ἰσαάκ, ὁ (*indecl*)	Isaac
καθότι	because; [with ἄν] insofar as

▹ List 24 4×

κατανοέω	look at, observe; consider [something one is looking at]; think about, contemplate
κατασείω	shake, wave [+τὴν χεῖρα (one's) hand]; motion, gesture [+τῇ χειρί with (one's) hand]
καταφέρω	bring/weigh down; bring against ▹
κατήγορος, -όρου, ὁ	accuser
κλάω	break
Κρήτη, -ης, ἡ	Crete
κριτής, -οῦ, ὁ	judge
Μᾶρκος, Μάρκου, ὁ	Mark
μετακαλέω	(*mid*) summon, call to oneself
μεταλαμβάνω	have/receive a share, partake (+*gen obj*); καιρὸν δὲ μεταλαβών when one has time ▹

▷ List 25 4×

μόλις	scarcely, barely, with difficulty; rarely
νεανίσκος, -ου, ὁ	young man
ξύλον, -ου, τό	wood; object made of wood [e.g., club, stocks, cross]; tree
παράκλησις, -ήσεως, ἡ	encouragement, exhortation; comfort, consolation
παρατίθημι	(*act*) set/put before; (*mid*) demonstrate; commend, entrust
πλέω	sail
πλήν	nevertheless, but, only; (*prep* +*gen*) except ▶
ποῖος, ποία, ποῖον	of what kind?; which?, what?
προάγω	lead/bring out ▶
προφητεύω	prophesy [disclose divine will]; foretell; reveal

▷ List 26 4×

πύλη, -ης, ἡ	gate
σαλεύω	shake; disturb, upset
συλλαμβάνω	(*act*) capture, seize, arrest; (*mid*) arrest ▶
συμβάλλω	(*act*) confer, converse; meet; (*mid*) assist, help ▶
συνίημι/συνίω	understand, comprehend ▶
τάσσω	(*act*) order, arrange; appoint, determine, designate; (*mid*) agree upon, settle ▶
τρόπος, -ου, ὁ	manner, way, ὃν τρόπον in the manner in which, (just) as
Τρῳάς, -άδος, ἡ	Troas
ὑπερῷον/ὑπερῶον, -ῴου/ώου, τό	upstairs room
ὑπηρέτης, -ου, ὁ	helper, server, attendant

▷ List 27 4 to 3×

ἄγκυρα, -ύρας, ἡ	anchor
ἁγνίζω	purify
Ἀθῆναι, -ῶν, αἱ	Athens
αἰγιαλός, -οῦ, ὁ	beach, seashore
αἰνέω	praise
Ἀκύλας, Ἀκύλα, ὁ	Aquila
Ἀλέξανδρος, -άνδρου, ὁ	Alexander
χαρίζομαι	give graciously/freely; forgive
χρῆμα, χρήματος, τό	money
ὦ	(*interj*) O [address]; oh!

▷ List 28 3×

ἀμφότεροι, -αι, -α	both; all
ἀναθεματίζω	put under a curse [invoking consequences should someone break an oath]
ἀνατρέφω	bring up, care for, raise, rear ▷
ἀποφθέγγομαι	speak out, declare
ἀπωθέω	(*mid*) push back; reject
Ἀρίσταρχος, -άρχου, ὁ	Aristarchus
ἅρμα, -ατος, τό	chariot [for traveling or military use]
ἀρχαῖος, -αία, -ον	old, ancient; early, of earliest times
ἀρχισυνάγωγος, -ώγου, ὁ	ruler/leader of a synagogue
ἀσθενέω	be sick; be weak

▹ List 29 3×

ἀσθενής, -ές	weak; sick, ill
ἀσφαλής, -ές	certain, sure, dependable, safe
ἄφνω	suddenly
Ἀχαΐα, -ας, ἡ	Achaia
Βερνίκη, -ης, ἡ	Bernice
βία, βίας, ἡ	force [brought to bear on someone/something], violence
βίβλος, -ου, ἡ	written account, book
βοάω	call/cry out, shout
βυρσεύς, -έως, ὁ	tanner
Γαλιλαῖος, -αία, -ον	Galilean

▹ List 30 3×

Γαλλίων, -ωνος, ὁ	Gallio
γεύομαι	taste, partake (+*gen/acc obj*)
Δέρβη, -ης, ἡ	Derbe
δέρω	violently mistreat, beat
δεσμοφύλαξ, -ακος, ὁ	jailer
δεσμωτήριον, -ίου, τό	prison
διακόσιοι, -αι, -α	two hundred
διανοίγω	open; explain
διαπορέω	be very perplexed/at a loss
διασπείρω	(*pass*) be scattered

▸

▷ List 31 3×

διαστρέφω	turn aside, mislead; make crooked, distort	➢
διηγέομαι	recount in detail, relate, describe	
ἑβδομήκοντα (*indecl*)	seventy	
Ἑβραΐς, -ΐδος, ἡ	Hebrew [language]	
ἐγγύς	near [spatial or temporal]; (*prep +gen/dat*) near	
εἴσειμι	go in(to), enter	➢
ἐκπλέω	sail out/away	➢
ἐκπορεύομαι	go/come out	
ἐκτείνω	stretch (something) out	
ἐκχέω/ἐκχύν(ν)ω	pour out	➢

▷ List 32 3×

ἐκψύχω	die	
Ἑλληνιστής, -οῦ, ὁ	Hellenist [one who adopts various aspects of Hellenic culture]	
ἐναντίος, -α, -ον	opposite, facing; opposed, contrary	
ἔνατος, ἐνάτη, ἔνατον	ninth	
ἕνεκα/ἕνεκεν	(+*gen*) because of, for the sake of	
ἕξ (*indecl*)	six	
ἑξῆς	next, on the next (day)	
ἐπειδή	when, after; since, because	
ἐπιζητέω	seek after, search for; seek, want	
ἐπιστηρίζω	support, firm up, strengthen	➢

▹ List 33 3×

ἐπιφωνέω	shout, cry out	
ἐσθής, -ῆτος, ἡ	clothing	▸
εὐθύς, -εῖα, -ύ	straight; proper, right	
εὐλαβής, -ές	devout	
ζηλωτής, -οῦ, ὁ	enthusiast, loyalist; zealot	
ζήτησις, -ήσεως, ἡ	investigation; discussion; controversy	
Ἠσαΐας, Ἠσαΐου, ὁ	Isaiah	
θεάομαι	see, look at	
Θεσσαλονίκη, -ης, ἡ	Thessalonica	
θόρυβος, -ύβου, ὁ	uproar, turmoil, tumult, (noisy) disturbance	

▹ List 34 3×

θυγάτηρ, θυγατρός, ἡ	daughter	
ἱερεύς, -έως, ὁ	priest	
Ἰταλία, -ας, ἡ	Italy	
καθαιρέω	take/bring down; tear down, [extended sense] destroy	▸
καθαρίζω	cleanse, make clean	
καθεξῆς	in sequence, in order, οἱ καθεξῆς those following, successors	
καθίημι	let down, lower	▸
καλῶς	well, appropriately, effectively; correctly	
καταλαμβάνω	grasp; seize; understand, realize	▸
καταλύω	(*trans*) tear down, destroy; abolish, bring to an end	

▹ List 35 3×

κατηχέω	report, inform; teach, instruct
κ(ε)ινέω	(*trans act*) move, remove; disturb, incite; (*intrans mid*) move
Κλαύδιος, -ίου, ὁ	Claudius
κοιμάω	(*mid*) sleep, fall asleep; die
κοινόω	make common/impure, defile; consider ritually unclean
κράτιστος, -ίστη, -ον	most excellent
κρεμάννυμι	(*trans act*) make (something) hang; (*intrans mid*) hang ▸
κτάομαι	procure for oneself, get, acquire
Κύπριος, -ίου, ὁ	Cypriot
Κυρηναῖος, -αίου, ὁ	Cyrenian

▹ List 36 3×

λιθοβολέω	throw stones (at someone); stone (to death)
Λύδδα, -ας/ης, ἡ	Lydda ▸
μαίνομαι	rave, be out of one's mind
Μακεδών, Μακεδόνος, ὁ	Macedonian
μακράν	far off/away [spatial or temporal]
μάλιστα	most of all, especially
μεγαλύνω	make large/great; magnify, exalt, glorify
μεταξύ	(+*gen*) between [spatial or social distinction]; (*adv*) next
μηκέτι	no longer
νεανίας, -ου, ὁ	young man

ROMANS

▷ List 1	15 to 7×
ἀδικία, -ας, ἡ	injustice, unrighteousness; wrongdoing, misdeed
ἀκροβυστία, -ας, ἡ	foreskin; uncircumcision; one who is uncircumcised
δικαιόω	justify, consider right/righteous, make righteous; vindicate, put in the right
κατεργάζομαι	do; produce, bring about ➤
μέλος, -ους, τό	member [of the human body], limb; member [of a group]
ὀργή, -ῆς, ἡ	anger; wrath
παράπτωμα, -ώματος, τό	transgression
περιτομή, -ῆς, ἡ	circumcision; one who is circumcised
πράσσω	do, accomplish, perform
φρονέω	think

▷ List 2	7 to 6×
ἀγνοέω	not know, be uninformed/ignorant; not understand; ignore, disregard
βασιλεύω	reign, rule, be king
δουλεύω	be a slave; slave (for), serve (+*dat obj*)
ἐγκεντρίζω	graft (in)
ἐλεέω	have compassion (on), show mercy to
Ἕλλην, -ηνος, ὁ	Greek (person); a person of Hellenic culture, gentile
καταργέω	make useless; make ineffective, nullify; [+ἀπό] separate, set free
κτίσις, -εως, τό	creation [act or product]
ὑπακοή, -ῆς, ἡ	obedience
φύσις, -εως, τό	nature [inherent/basic qualities, features, or character]

▷ List 3 — 6 to 5×

ἀπειθέω	disobey, be disobedient, resist (+*dat obj*)	
ἀσθενέω	be sick; be weak	
δικαίωμα, -ώματος, τό	ordinance, requirement; righteous/just act	
κρίμα, -ατος, τό	judgment [process of evaluation]; judgment [end result], judicial verdict	
νοῦς, νοός, ὁ	mind; understanding, intellect; thought	▷
νυνί	now, at this time	
ὑπομονή, -ῆς, ἡ	endurance, perseverance, steadfastness	
ὑποτάσσω	subject, subordinate	▷
χάρισμα, -ίσματος, τό	(gracious) gift	
ὥσπερ	(just) as	

▷ List 4 — 5×

δυνατός, -ή, -όν	able, capable, strong, powerful; possible	
ἐπιθυμία, -ας, ἡ	desire, longing; lust, craving	
εὐχαριστέω	thank, give thanks, be thankful	
Ἠσαΐας, Ἠσαΐου, ὁ	Isaiah	
καυχάομαι	boast (about)	▷
κλάδος, -ου, τό	branch	
οἰκέω	(*intrans*) dwell, live; (*trans*) inhabit	
πλοῦτος, πλούτου, ὁ/τό	wealth, riches; abundance	
ῥίζα, -ης, ἡ	root; shoot [from a root]	
χρηστότης, -ητος, ἡ	kindness, goodness	

▷ List 5 4×

ἀπιστία, -ας, ἡ	unbelief; unfaithfulness	
ἀρέσκω	please (+*dat obj*)	➤
διακονία, -ας, ἡ	service, serving; (ministerial) service, ministry	
διάκονος, -όνου, ὁ/ἡ	servant, helper; ministerial attendant ["deacon(ess)"]	
διότι	because, since; for; because of this	
δοκιμάζω	examine, evaluate; determine, put to the test; approve	
ἐκλογή, -ῆς, ἡ	choice, election; chosen, elect	
ἐλευθερόω	set free	
ἐλπίζω	hope (for); expect	➤
κατακρίνω	condemn	

▷ List 6 4×

κληρονόμος, -ου, ὁ	heir; beneficiary, heir	
κλητός, -ή, -όν	called, invited	
κυριεύω	lord over, rule (over) (+*gen obj*)	
ὁμοίωμα, -ώματος, τό	likeness	
πλήρωμα, -ώματος, τό	that which fills, content; that which completes, complement; fullness, full number	
πρόσκομμα, -κόμματος, τό	stumbling; obstacle	
προσλαμβάνω	(*mid*) take to oneself; receive, welcome	➤
σκάνδαλον, -άλου, τό	trap; cause of sin ["stumbling block"]; offense	
σοφός, -ή, -όν	wise; skillful	
συγγενής, -ές	(*subst*) relative; (*pl*) relatives, kin, countrymen	

▷ List 7 — 4 to 3×

ἀκοή, -ῆς, ἡ	hearing, listening; ear; news, rumor, report, message
ἀνθίστημι	resist, oppose, withstand (+*dat obj*) ➢
ἀνομία, -ας, ἡ	lawlessness [condition or action]
ἀπαρχή, -ῆς, ἡ	firstfruits
ἀπεκδέχομαι	await
ἀποκαλύπτω	reveal, disclose ➢
ἀποκάλυψις, -ύψεως, ἡ	revelation, disclosure
ὑπακούω	obey
φρόνημα, -ήματος, τό	mind-set, mind, aim
ὦ	(*interj*) O [address]; oh!

▷ List 8 — 3×

ἄρσην, -εν	male ➢
ἀσύνετος, -ον	without understanding, foolish
βλασφημέω	slander, speak disrespectfully about, revile
βρῶμα, βρώματος, τό	food
γνωρίζω	make known, inform; know
γνῶσις, γνώσεως, ἡ	knowledge [understanding/comprehension or that which is known]
γράμμα, -ατος, τό	letter [of the alphabet]; document, writing, letter
εἴπερ	if indeed; since
ἐκκλάω	break off
ἔλεος, ἐλέους, τό	compassion, mercy

▷ List 9 3×

ἐνδείκνυμι	(*mid*) show, demonstrate, exhibit ➤
ἐντυγχάνω	appeal (+*dat obj*)
ἐπεί	since, because; for otherwise
ἐπίγνωσις, -ώσεως, ἡ	knowledge
ἐπικαλέω	(*act*) call, name; (*mid*) call upon, invoke, appeal
ἐπιμένω	remain, stay; persist, continue
εὐάρεστος, -ον	pleasing
ἐχθρός, -ά, -όν	hated; hostile; (*subst*) enemy
θανατόω	put to death
καταισχύνω	put to shame

▷ List 10 3×

κατάκριμα, -ίματος, τό	condemnation, punishment
κλέπτω	steal
κοινός, -ή, -όν	common, shared; common, ordinary; impure, unclean
κοπιάω	be weary/tired; labor, toil
μηκέτι	no longer
μοιχεύω	commit adultery
νικάω	(*trans*) overcome, defeat, conquer; (*intrans*) prevail, be victorious
ὅπλον, -ου, τό	tool, weapon
οὗ	(to) where
ὀφειλέτης, -ου, ὁ	debtor

▷ List 11 3×

ὀφείλω	owe, be indebted to; be obligated, ought; have to
παράβασις, -άσεως, ἡ	transgression, violation
παραζηλόω	make jealous
παράκλησις, -ήσεως, ἡ	encouragement, exhortation; comfort, consolation
περισσεύω	(*intrans*) abound (in), overflow; (*trans*) cause (something) to abound, increase ➤
πλεονάζω	(*intrans*) increase, abound; (*trans*) (cause to) increase
πλησίον	(+*gen*) near; (*subst*) neighbor
πνευματικός, -ή, -όν	spiritual
ποτέ (*encl*)	when, at some time; formerly, once; [+ἤδη] at last
προσευχή, -ῆς, ἡ	prayer

▷ List 12 3×

πώς (*encl*)	somehow, perhaps, in any way, at all
ῥύομαι	save, rescue, deliver ➤
σκεῦος, σκεύους, τό	object, thing; vessel, container
συμμαρτυρέω/ συνμαρτυρέω	confirm
συνείδησις, -ήσεως, ἡ	consciousness, awareness; conscience
συνεργός, -όν	helpful, contributing; [only *subst* in NT] fellow worker
συνίστημι/συνιστάνω/ συνιστάω	(*trans pres/aor*) recommend, commend; establish, prove
υἱοθεσία, -ας, ἡ	adoption
φανερός, -ά, -όν	visible, plain, evident, known; (*subst*) the open
φείδομαι	spare (+*gen obj*); refrain (from)

▷ List 13 — 3 to 2×

ἁγιασμός, -οῦ, ὁ	holiness, consecration
ἀγριέλαιος, -ον	from a wild olive tree; (*subst*) wild olive tree
Ἀδάμ, ὁ (*indecl*)	Adam
ἀδελφή, -ῆς, ἡ	sister
ἀδύνατος, -ον	powerless, disabled; impossible
ἀκαθαρσία, -ας, ἡ	uncleanness, filth; immorality
ἀλλότριος, -ία, -ον	another's
ἀναπολόγητος, -ον	without excuse/defense
ἀνόμως	without law
φόρος, -ου, ὁ	tax, tribute

▷ List 14 — 2×

ἀνοχή, -ῆς, ἡ	relief; forbearance, leniency
ἀνταποδίδωμι	give/pay back [favorable or unfavorable actions]
ἀπείθεια, -είας, ἡ	disobedience
ἀπολύτρωσις, -ώσεως, ἡ	release, liberation, deliverance, redemption
ἀποτομία, -ας, ἡ	severity
ἀπωθέω	(*mid*) push back; reject
ἀσέβεια, -είας, ἡ	ungodliness
ἀσεβής, -ές	ungodly
ἀσθένεια, -είας, ἡ	sickness, disease; weakness
ἀτιμάζω	dishonor, shame

▷ List 15 2×

ἀτιμία, -ας, ἡ	dishonor, disgrace
ἀφορμή, -ῆς, ἡ	opportunity
βάθος, -ους, τό	depth
βαστάζω	pick up; carry, bear
γόνυ, γόνατος, τό	knee
διαθήκη, -ης, ἡ	will, testament; covenant
διακρίνω	(*act*) evaluate; make a distinction; (*mid*) dispute, contest, contend (with) ▷
διαλογισμός, -οῦ, ὁ	reasoning, thought
διαστολή, -ῆς, ἡ	distinction, difference
διδασκαλία, -ας, ἡ	teaching, instruction [activity or content]

▷ List 16 2×

διδαχή, -ῆς, ἡ	teaching [activity or content]
δικαίωσις, -ώσεως, ἡ	justification
δοκιμή, -ῆς, ἡ	testing; (proven) character; proof
δόκιμος, -ον	approved
δουλεία, -ας, ἡ	slavery
δουλόω	enslave
δωρεά, -ᾶς, ἡ	gift
ἐγγύς	near [spatial or temporal]; (*prep +gen/dat*) near
εἰκών, εἰκόνος, ἡ	image, likeness [crafted or non-crafted]
ἐκκλίνω	avoid, turn away/aside (from)

▹ List 17 2×

ἐκκόπτω	cut off/down; do away with
ἐκλεκτός, -ή, -όν	chosen, elect
ἐλαία, -ας, ἡ	olive tree
ἐλεάω	have compassion (on), show mercy to [later byform of ἐλεέω]
ἐλεύθερος, -έρα, -ον	free
ἔνδειξις, ἐνδείξεως, ἡ	indication, demonstration
ἐνδύω	(*act*) dress/clothe (someone); (*mid*) put on, wear
ἕνεκα/ἕνεκεν	(+*gen*) because of, for the sake of
ἐξαπατάω	deceive, seduce
ἐξομολογέω	(*mid*) confess, admit; profess, acknowledge

▹ List 18 2×

ἐξουθενέω	look down on, treat with contempt; reject
ἔπαινος, ἐπαίνου, ὁ	praise, recognition, commendation
ἐπαισχύνομαι	be ashamed (of)
ἐπιθυμέω	long for, desire (+*gen/acc obj*)
ἐπιτυγχάνω	obtain, attain (+*gen/acc obj*)
ἔρις, -ιδος, ἡ	strife, contention
εὐδοκέω	be well pleased; determine, resolve
εὐλογητός, -ή, -όν	blessed, praised
εὐλογία, -ας, ἡ	praise; blessing; gift; flattery
εὐπρόσδεκτος, -ον	acceptable

▷ List 19 2×

ζῆλος, ζήλου/ζήλους, ὁ/τό	zeal; jealousy
ζωοποιέω/ζῳοποιέω	give life to, make alive
θῆλυς, θήλεια, θῆλυ	(*subst*) female, woman
θνητός, -ή, -όν	mortal
Ἰακώβ, ὁ (*indecl*)	Jacob
Ἰσαάκ, ὁ (*indecl*)	Isaac
Ἰσραηλίτης, -ου, ὁ	Israelite
καθάπερ	(just) as
καθίστημι/καθιστάνω	make, cause to be ▷
καινότης, -ητος, ἡ	newness

▷ List 20 2×

κάμπτω	(*trans*) bend; (*intrans*) bend
καρποφορέω	bear fruit
κατακαυχάομαι	boast against, exult over (+*gen obj*)
καταλλαγή, -ῆς, ἡ	reconciliation
καταλλάσσω	reconcile
κατέχω	hold back, restrain, suppress ▷
καύχησις, -ήσεως, ἡ	boasting
κοινωνέω	have a share, take part in; share
κοίτη, -ης, ἡ	bed; sexual intercourse
κρυπτός, -ή, -όν	hidden, secret

▷ List 21 2×

λατρεία, -ας, ἡ	cultic service, worship
λατρεύω	serve, worship [the carrying out of religious duties] (*+dat obj*)
λειτουργός, -οῦ, ὁ	minister, [cultic] servant
μακαρισμός, -οῦ, ὁ	blessedness
μακροθυμία, -ας, ἡ	patience; forbearance
μάχαιρα, -αίρης, ἡ	dagger, short sword
μενοῦνγε	on the contrary
μεστός, -ή, -όν	full
μεταδίδωμι	share, give a share of, impart
μεταλλάσσω	exchange

▷ List 22 2×

μέχρι	(*conj*) until; (*prep +gen*) until; as far as; to the point of
μοιχαλίς, -ίδος, ἡ	adulteress
μυστήριον, -ίου, τό	mystery, secret
οἰκοδομή, -ῆς, ἡ	building, structure; construction, building up
οἰκτίρω	have compassion on
ὁμολογέω	acknowledge; declare, confess
πάθημα, -ήματος, τό	suffering; emotion, passion
παραβάτης, -ου, ὁ	transgressor
παράκειμαι	be at hand, present
πληροφορέω	(*mid*) be fully assured/certain

▷ List 23 2×

πόσος, -η, -ον	[*interr* or *exclam*] how much?, how great?; how much?, how many?
πρᾶξις, πράξεως, ἡ	doing, activity; deed, action
προγινώσκω	know beforehand ▷
πρόθεσις, -έσεως, ἡ	setting forth, presentation; purpose
προορίζω	decide beforehand, predetermine
προσκαρτερέω	hold fast to, be devoted to [+*dat* of thing or person]
προσκόπτω	(*trans*) cause to strike against; hit (+*dat obj*); (*intrans*) stumble
προτίθημι	(*mid*) display publicly; set forth, intend, plan
Ῥώμη, -ης, ἡ	Rome
Σάρρα, -ας, ἡ	Sarah

▷ List 24 2×

Σιών, ἡ (*indecl*)	Zion
σκοτίζω	(*mid*) be(come) dark [literal or figurative]
σκότος, -ους, τό	darkness [literal or figurative]
Σπανία, -ας, ἡ	Spain
σπουδή, -ῆς, ἡ	haste; zeal, eagerness, diligence
στενοχωρία, -ας, ἡ	distress, difficulty
στηρίζω	set, establish; strengthen/make more firm [inwardly] ▷
συνίημι/συνίω	understand, comprehend ▷
τελέω	complete, finish; carry out (completely), accomplish; pay
τολμάω	dare, bring oneself (to), have the courage (to)

▷ List 25 — 2 to 1 ×

ἀββᾶ/ἀββά/αββα (*indecl*)	[Aram.] father
ἄβυσσος, ἀβύσσου, ἡ	abyss
ἀγαθωσύνη, -ῆς, ἡ	goodness
τύπος, -ου, ὁ	pattern, design, type
ὑψηλός, -ή, -όν	high, tall; exalted, proud, haughty
φρόνιμος, -ον	prudent, sensible, thoughtful, wise
φύραμα, -άματος, τό	something that is mixed or kneaded: mixture, batch (of dough), lump (of clay)
φυσικός, -ή, -όν	natural [in accordance with nature]
χρῆσις, χρήσεως, ἡ	use, function; relation, intimacy [often sexual intimacy]
χωρίζω	(*act*) divide, separate; (*mid*) separate oneself, leave, depart

▷ List 26 — 1 ×

ἁγιάζω	consecrate, make holy; regard as holy
ἁγιωσύνη, -ῆς, ἡ	holiness, sanctity
ἀδιάλειπτος, -ον	unceasing, constant
ἀδιαλείπτως	unceasingly, constantly
ἄδικος, -ον	unjust, unrighteous
ἀδόκιμος, -ον	unqualified, disqualified; worthless
ἀΐδιος, -ον	eternal
αἰνέω	praise
αἰχμαλωτίζω	put into captivity, make captive, capture
ἄκακος, -ον	innocent, guileless; simple, naïve

▷ List 27 1×

ἀκέραιος, -ον	unmixed, pure; innocent, pure
ἀκροατής, -οῦ, ὁ	hearer
Ἀκύλας, Ἀκύλα, ὁ	Aquila
ἀλαζών, -όνος, ὁ	boaster
ἀλάλητος, -ον	inexpressible
ἀληθής, -ές	true, trustworthy; real
ἀλλάσσω	change, alter; exchange
ἅμα	at the same time; together; (*prep +dat*) together with
ἁμάρτημα, -ήματος, τό	sin, sinful act
ἀμεταμέλητος, -ον	irrevocable

▷ List 28 1×

ἀμετανόητος, -ον	unrepentant
ἄμμος, -ου, ἡ	sand
Ἀμπλιᾶτος, -άτου, ὁ	Ampliatus
ἀναγγέλλω	report; disclose, announce
ἀνάγκη, -ης, ἡ	necessity, constraint, pressure; distress, anguish
ἀνάγω	lead/bring up
ἀναζάω	be alive again, return to life; come alive
ἀνάθεμα, -έματος, τό	accursed; curse
ἀνακαίνωσις, -ώσεως, ἡ	renewal
ἀνακεφαλαιόω	(*mid*) sum up

▷ List 29 — 1×

ἀναλογία, -ας, ἡ	proportion
Ἀνδρόνικος, -ίκου, ὁ	Andronicus
ἀνελεήμων, -ον	unmerciful
ἀνεξεραύνητος, -ον	unsearchable
ἀνεξιχνίαστος, -ον	beyond exploration, inscrutable
ἄνθραξ, -ακος, ὁ	charcoal
ἀνθρώπινος, -ίνη, -ον	human
ἀνόητος, -ον	unintelligent, senseless, foolish
ἀνταπόδομα, -όματος, τό	repayment [positive or negative]
ἀνταποκρίνομαι	reply; argue (with)

▷ List 30 — 1×

ἀντί	(+*gen*) instead of, in place of
ἀντιλέγω	argue (against), contradict; oppose
ἀντιμισθία, -ας, ἡ	recompense, exchange [positive or negative]
ἀντιστρατεύομαι	wage war against (+*dat obj*)
ἀντιτάσσω	(*mid +dat obj*) oppose, resist
ἀνυπόκριτος, -ον	without pretense, genuine, sincere
ἀξίως	worthily, in a manner worthy of
ἀόρατος, -ον	invisible
ἀπειθής, -ές	disobedient
Ἀπελλῆς, -οῦ, ὁ	Apelles

▷ List 31 1×

ἀπέναντι	(+*gen*) opposite; against, contrary to
ἀπιστέω	not believe; be unfaithful
ἁπλότης, -ητος, ἡ	sincerity
ἀποβολή, -ῆς, ἡ	throwing away; rejection; loss
ἀποκαραδοκία, -ας, ἡ	eager expectation
ἀπολαμβάνω	receive
ἀπολογέομαι	speak in one's defense, defend oneself
ἀποστολή, -ῆς, ἡ	sending off/forth; apostleship
ἀποστρέφω	turn (something) away (from something); put back, return
ἀποστυγέω	hate, abhor, loathe

▷ List 32 1×

ἀποτίθημι	(*mid*) put away, lay aside
ἀποτολμάω	be very bold, dare
ἀπώλεια, -είας, ἡ	destruction; waste
ἀρά, -ᾶς, ἡ	curse, imprecation
ἀριθμός, -οῦ, ὁ	number, total
Ἀριστόβουλος, -ούλου, ὁ	Aristobulus
ἄρχων, ἄρχοντος, ὁ	ruler; official
ἀσέλγεια, -είας, ἡ	licentiousness, excessive sensuality
ἀσθένημα, -ήματος, τό	weakness
ἀσθενής, -ές	weak; sick, ill

▷ List 33 — 1×

Ἀσία, -ας, ἡ	Asia
ἀσπίς, -ίδος, ἡ	asp
ἄστοργος, -ον	lacking affection, unfeeling
Ἀσύγκριτος, -ίτου, ὁ	Asyncritus
ἀσύνθετος, -ον	faithless; (*subst*) oath breaker, covenant breaker
ἀσχημοσύνη, -ης, ἡ	shameful behavior; shame
ἀφαιρέω	(*act*) remove, take away; (*mid*) take away, do away with ➤
ἀφθαρσία, -ας, ἡ	incorruptibility, immortality
ἄφθαρτος, -ον	incorruptible, immortal, undecaying
ἀφικνέομαι	come to, reach ➤

▷ List 34 — 1×

ἀφορίζω	separate; set apart
ἄφρων, -ον	senseless, foolish
Ἀχαΐα, -ας, ἡ	Achaia
ἀχρειόω	(*mid*) become worthless ➤
Βάαλ, ὁ (*indecl*)	[Heb.] Baal
βάπτισμα, -ίσματος, τό	baptism, (ceremonial) plunging/washing
βάρβαρος, -ον	foreign-speaking, foreign; (*subst*) foreigner, non-Hellene, non-Greek-speaking person
βδελύσσομαι	detest, abhor, consider utterly detestable
βέβαιος, -αία, -ον	steadfast, steady; firm, reliable, certain
βεβαιόω	confirm, establish; guarantee [legal term]

▹ List 35 1×

Βενιαμ(ε)ίν, ὁ (*indecl*)	Benjamin
βῆμα, βήματος, τό	step [as a measure of length]; platform; judicial bench, judgment seat
βούλημα, -ήματος, τό	purpose, intent, will
βρῶσις, βρώσεως, ὁ	food; eating, consumption
Γάϊος, -Γαΐου, ὁ	Gaius
γέ (*encl*)	indeed, even; yet, at least, though
γέμω	be full (of something) [+*gen* of thing]
γνωστός, -ή, -όν	known; capable of being known
Γόμορρα, -όρρας/όρρων, ἡ/τά	Gomorrah
γονεύς, -έως, ὁ	parent

▹ List 36 1×

γραπτός, -ή, -όν	written
γυμνότης, -ητος, ἡ	nakedness; without enough clothing
δέησις, δεήσεως, ἡ	entreaty; prayer, petition
δέομαι	ask, petition, pray [+*gen* of person(s) petitioned]
δεῦρο	come!, come here!, come on!; ἄχρι τοῦ δεῦρο until now
διαγγέλλω	proclaim, spread news far and wide
διακονέω	(+*dat obj*) serve; care for; wait on; administer
διάκρισις, -ίσεως, ἡ	differentiation, distinction; dispute
διαπορεύομαι	go/pass through
διαταγή, -ῆς, ἡ	ordinance, directive, command

1 CORINTHIANS

▷ List 1 — 16 to 9×

ἀνακρίνω	examine closely, inquire into; hear a case, put on trial, investigate	▸
ἄπιστος, -ον	unbelieving; unbelievable	
ἀσθενής, -ές	weak; sick, ill	
γαμέω	marry	▸
γνῶσις, γνώσεως, ἡ	knowledge [understanding/comprehension or that which is known]	
καταργέω	make useless; make ineffective, invalidate, nullify; set aside, eliminate	
μέλος, -ους, τό	member [of the human body], limb; member [of a group]	
πνευματικός, -ή, -όν	spiritual	
προφητεύω	prophesy [disclose divine will]; foretell; reveal	
σοφός, -ή, -όν	wise; skillful	

▷ List 2 — 9 to 6×

Ἀπολλῶς, Ἀπολλῶ, ὁ	Apollos	
ἄρτι	(just) now	
βρῶμα, βρώματος, τό	food	
ἐλεύθερος, -έρα, -ον	free	
νοῦς, νοός, ὁ	mind; understanding, intellect; thought	▸
ποτήριον, -ίου, τό	cup	
συνείδησις, -ήσεως, ἡ	consciousness, awareness; conscience	
συνέρχομαι	come together with, gather; go/come with, travel together with	▸
ὑποτάσσω	subject, subordinate	▸
χάρισμα, -ίσματος, τό	(gracious) gift	

▷ List 3 — 6 to 5×

διακρίνω	evaluate; make a distinction; judge, decide
εἰδωλόθυτος, -ον	(*subst*) meat sacrificed to an idol
ἐμαυτοῦ, -ῆς	myself, my (own) [when *gen*]
ἐπεί	since, because; for otherwise
ἔπειτα	then, next
εὐχαριστέω	thank, give thanks, be thankful
κοιμάω	(*mid*) sleep, fall asleep; die
νήπιος, -ία, -ον	(*subst*) infant; little child
παρθένος, -ου, ἡ	virgin; young woman [of marriageable age]
φυσιόω	(*trans act*) puff up, make proud; (*intrans mid*) be(come) proud/puffed up

▷ List 4 — 5×

ἐπουράνιος, -ον	heavenly
καταισχύνω	put to shame
καυχάομαι	boast (about) ▷
κερδαίνω	gain ▷
μεριμνάω	worry (about), be anxious; care for, be concerned about
μετέχω	(+*gen obj*) share, have a share in; partake of
μυστήριον, -ίου, τό	mystery, secret
μωρία, -ας, ἡ	foolishness
οἰκοδομή, -ῆς, ἡ	building, structure; construction, building up
ὀφείλω	owe, be indebted to; be obligated, ought; have to

▹ List 5 — 5 to 4×

ἄγαμος, -άμου, ὁ/ἡ	unmarried man/woman
ἁγιάζω	consecrate, make holy; regard as holy
ἀγνοέω	not know, be uninformed/ignorant; ignore, disregard
ἄνομος, -ον	lawless; without law
ἀρέσκω	please (+*dat obj*) ▸
ἀφθαρσία, -ας, ἡ	incorruptibility, immortality
πορνεία, -ας, ἡ	sexual immorality, fornication
ποτίζω	give to drink
προφητεία, -ας, ἡ	prophetic activity; prophecy [the gift]; prophecy [an utterance]
ὥσπερ	(just) as

▹ List 6 — 4×

διατάσσω	(*act/mid*) instruct, direct ▸
διερμηνεύω	interpret, explain; translate
εἰδωλολάτρης, -ου, ὁ	image worshiper, idolater
εἴδωλον, -ώλου, τό	idol, cultic image
ἐκτός	outside; ἐκτὸς εἰ μή unless, except; (*prep +gen*) outside; except
Ἕλλην, -ηνος, ὁ	Greek (person); a person of Hellenic culture, gentile
ἐνδύω	(*act*) dress/clothe (someone); (*mid*) put on, wear
ἔξεστιν	(*impers*) it is right/permitted [*3sg* of ἔξειμι]
ἐπαινέω	praise
ἐπειδή	when, after; since, because

▷ List 7 4×

ἐποικοδομέω	build (up)on
ζηλόω	be zealous for, strive after; be jealous
ζύμη, -ης, ἡ	fermented dough, leaven
ἰσχυρός, -ά, -όν	strong, mighty; (*comp*) ἰσχυρότερος, -έρα, -ον more powerful, stronger
κενός, -ή, -όν	empty [of content]; empty, fruitless; in vain, for nothing
Κηφᾶς, Κηφᾶ, ὁ	Cephas
κληρονομέω	(*intrans*) be an heir; (*trans*) acquire, obtain
μισθός, -οῦ, ὁ	pay, wages; recompense, reward
μωρός, -ά, -όν	foolish, stupid
πάντως	undoubtedly, certainly, by all means, at all, (+*neg*) by no means, not at all

▷ List 8 4 to 3×

ἀγοράζω	buy
Ἀδάμ, ὁ (*indecl*)	Adam
ἀνάγκη, -ης, ἡ	necessity, constraint, pressure; distress, anguish
πόρνος, -ου, ὁ	sexually immoral person, fornicator
τρέχω	run
φυτεύω	plant
χοϊκός, -ή, -όν	made of earth, earthy
χράομαι	use (+*dat/acc obj*)
χωρίζω	(*act*) divide, separate; (*mid*) separate oneself, leave, depart
ψυχικός, -ή, -όν	[that which pertains to ψυχή] natural, worldly

▶

▷ List 9 3×

ἀνθρώπινος, -ίνη, -ον	human	
ἀπαρχή, -ῆς, ἡ	firstfruits	
ἀποκαλύπτω	reveal, disclose	▸
ἀποκάλυψις, -ύψεως, ἡ	revelation, disclosure	
ἀποστερέω	steal, defraud; deprive	
ἅρπαξ	ravenous, rapacious; (*subst*) robber, swindler	▸
ἀστήρ, -έρος, ὁ	(luminous) celestial body, star	
βασιλεύω	reign, rule, be king	
γέ (*encl*)	indeed, even; yet, at least, though	
γένος, -ους, τό	people group, family; offspring, descendant; kind, class	

▷ List 10 3×

γνώμη, -ης, ἡ	judgment, opinion; purpose, intent, will	
διαίρεσις, -έσεως, ἡ	distinction, difference; distribution, apportionment	
δοκιμάζω	examine, evaluate; determine, put to the test; approve	
εἰκών, εἰκόνος, ἡ	image, likeness [crafted or non-crafted]	
εἶτα	then, next; furthermore	
ἐκλέγομαι	choose; select	
ἐλάχιστος, -ίστη, -ον	least, smallest [in status, value, or size]	
ἐλπίζω	hope (for); expect	▸
ἐξουθενέω	look down on, treat with contempt; reject	
ἐξουσιάζω	exercise authority (over) (+*gen obj*)	

▷ List 11 3×

ζωοποιέω/ζῳοποιέω	give life to, make alive
θεμέλιος, -ίου, ὁ	foundation
θυσιαστήριον, -ίου, τό	altar
θύω	sacrifice; slaughter, kill
ἴαμα, ἰάματος, τό	healing
ἰδιώτης, -ου, ὁ	layperson, uninstructed person; outsider, one not in the know
καλῶς	well, appropriately, effectively; correctly
καταγγέλλω	announce, proclaim, declare
κατακαλύπτω	(*mid*) cover oneself [with a veil]
κατέχω	hold fast/to; possess ▹

▷ List 12 3×

καύχημα, -ήματος, τό	boast [expression of pride or basis for pride]
κήρυγμα, -ύγματος, τό	proclamation
κλητός, -ή, -όν	called, invited
κοινωνία, -ας, ἡ	(close) fellowship; participation, sharing; generosity
κοπιάω	be weary/tired; labor, toil
κρείττων, κρεῖττον / κρείσσων, κρεῖσσον	better, superior [rank or value]; [*neut acc sg* as *adv*] better
κρίμα, -ατος, τό	judgment [process of evaluation]; judgment [end result], judicial verdict; lawsuit
μανθάνω	learn ▹
μερίζω	(*trans act*) divide; distribute, allot; (*intrans mid-pass*) be divided [with regard to oneself]
νῖκος, νίκους, τό	victory

▷ List 13 3×

νυνί	now, at this time
οἰκέω	(*intrans*) dwell, live; (*trans*) inhabit
ὅλως	completely, wholly, altogether; actually
ὁμοίως	likewise, in the same way
πεινάω	hunger, be hungry [physically or metaphorically]
πειράζω	test; tempt
περισσεύω	(*intrans*) abound (in), overflow, be left over ▶
περισσός, -ή, -όν	extraordinary, remarkable; abundant, superfluous; (*comp*) περισσότερος, -έρα, -ον greater, better, excessive
πλεονέκτης, -ου, ὁ	greedy person
πορνεύω	fornicate, commit sexual immorality

▷ List 14 3×

σαρκικός, -ή, -όν	material, physical, fleshly; worldly, (merely) human
σιγάω	be/keep silent
Στεφανᾶς, Στεφανᾶ, ὁ	Stephanas
συμφέρω	(*impers*) it is beneficial/of advantage; it is better; (*subst ptc*) benefit, profit ▶
σχίσμα, -ατος, τό	division, dissension; tear, crack
τέλειος, -εία, -ον	complete, perfect, mature [of character or behavior]
τυγχάνω	happen upon, εἰ τύχοι it may be; τυχόν perhaps ▶
ὑστερέω	(*intrans mid*) be in need; come short (of); be lacking
φανερός, -ά, -όν	visible, plain, evident, known; (*subst*) the open
φθαρτός, -ή, -όν	perishable

▷ List 15 — 3 to 2×

ἀδελφή, -ῆς, ἡ	sister
ἀδικέω	(*intrans*) do wrong, be in the wrong; (*trans*) wrong; injure
ἄδικος, -ον	unjust, unrighteous
ἄζυμος, -ον	unleavened, (*subst*) unleavened bread
ἀήρ, ἀέρος, ὁ	air
ἀθανασία, -ας, ἡ	immortality
αἰσχρός, -ά, -όν	shameful, disgraceful
ἀκατακάλυπτος, -ον	uncovered
ἀκοή, -ῆς, ἡ	hearing, listening; ear; news, rumor, report, message
φθείρω	corrupt, ruin, destroy

▷ List 16 — 2×

ἀκροβυστία, -ας, ἡ	foreskin; uncircumcision; one who is uncircumcised
ἀλλάσσω	change, alter; exchange ▸
ἀλοάω	thresh
ἀνά	ἀνὰ μέσον in the midst of, between (+*gen*); ἀνὰ μέρος in turn
ἀνάθεμα, -έματος, τό	accursed; curse
ἀνάμνησις, -ήσεως, ἡ	reminder, remembrance
ἀναπληρόω	fill (up); supply; fulfill
ἀροτριάω	plow
ἄρχων, ἄρχοντος, ὁ	ruler; official
ἀσθένεια, -είας, ἡ	sickness, disease; weakness

▹ List 17 2×

ἀσθενέω	be sick; be weak
ἀσχημονέω	behave disgracefully/dishonorably
ἀτιμία, -ας, ἡ	dishonor, disgrace
ἄτιμος, -ον	dishonored, without honor; (*comp*) ἀτιμότερος, -έρα, -ον less honored/esteemed
αὐξάνω/αὔξω	(*trans*) make grow/increase; (*intrans*) grow, increase
ἄφθαρτος, -ον	incorruptible, immortal, undecaying
ἄφωνος, -ον	silent; mute; incapable of conveying meaning
βάρβαρος, -ον	foreign-speaking, foreign; (*subst*) foreigner, non-Hellene, non-Greek-speaking person
βεβαιόω	confirm, establish; guarantee [legal term]
βιωτικός, -ή, -όν	of/belonging to (daily) life, ordinary, everyday

▹ List 18 2×

βοῦς, βοός, ὁ	ox
γάλα, -ακτος, τό	milk
γαμίζω	give (a woman) in marriage; marry, take as spouse [disputed sense]
γνωρίζω	make known, inform; know
γογγύζω	grumble, complain; whisper, murmur
δεῖπνον, δείπνου, τό	dinner; feast, banquet
δηλόω	make clear, disclose, reveal, explain
διακονία, -ας, ἡ	service, serving; (ministerial) service, ministry
διδακτός, -ή, -όν	taught, instructed; taught, imparted
διδαχή, -ῆς, ἡ	teaching [activity or content]

▷ List 19 2×

δικαιόω	justify, consider right/righteous, make righteous; vindicate, put in the right
διόπερ	therefore, for this very reason
δουλόω	enslave
ἐγκρατεύομαι	control oneself, exercise self-control
ἑδραῖος, -αία, -ον	firm, steadfast
εἴπερ	if indeed; since
ἐκδέχομαι	wait (for), expect
ἐνεργέω	(*intrans*) be at work/active; (*trans*) work, produce
ἐνέργημα, -ήματος, τό	activity, action, performance
ἐνίστημι	(*pf*) be present/here ▷

▷ List 20 2×

ἐντροπή, -ῆς, ἡ	shame, humiliation
ἐπίγειος, -ον	earthly
ἐπιμένω	remain, stay; persist, continue
ἐπιστολή, -ῆς, ἡ	letter
ἐπιταγή, -ῆς, ἡ	command
ἐπιτρέπω	permit, give permission, allow (+*dat obj*)
ἔρις, -ιδος, ἡ	strife, contention
ἑρμηνεία, -ας, ἡ	interpretation, explanation; translation
εὐδοκέω	be well pleased; determine, resolve
εὐσχήμων, -ον	noble, dignified, respectable, presentable ▷

▷ List 21 2×

Ἔφεσος, -έσου, ἡ	Ephesus
ἐχθρός, -ά, -όν	hated; hostile; (*subst*) enemy
θνητός, -ή, -όν	mortal
ἱκανός, -ή, -όν	sufficient; able, qualified, worthy
καθάπερ	(just) as
κακία, -ας, ἡ	wickedness; malice; trouble, misfortune
καταντάω	come (to), arrive (at), [extended sense] attain (to)
καταχράομαι	use to the full, make full use of
κείρω	shear (wool), cut (hair)
κενόω	(*trans act*) make empty; render void, make (something) nothing; (*intrans mid*) be(come) empty; be(come) void

▷ List 22 2×

κέντρον, -ου, τό	goad; point, sting [of an animal]
κλάω	break
κλῆσις, κλήσεως, ἡ	call, calling, invitation; state, condition, position
κοιλία, -ας, ἡ	stomach; womb; heart [figurative, representing one's inner desires and feelings]
κοινωνός, -οῦ, ὁ/ἡ	companion, partner, sharer
κολλάω	(*intrans mid*) cling (to), join (with), join oneself (to)
κομάω	have long hair, let one's hair grow long
κόπος, -ου, ὁ	trouble, hardship; labor, toil
κριτήριον, -ίου, τό	law court; lawsuit
κρυπτός, -ή, -όν	hidden, secret

▷ List 23 2×

λογεία, -ας, ἡ	collection (of money)
λοίδορος, -όρου, ὁ	reviler, verbally abusive person
Μακεδονία, -ας, ἡ	Macedonia
μαρτύριον, -ίου, τό	testimony, witness, proof
μάταιος, -αία, -ον	empty, idle, vain, useless
μέθυσος, -ύσου, ὁ	drunkard
μέλει	(*impers*) it is a concern to/of interest to [*3sg* of μέλω]
μήτι	not ➢
μιμητής, -οῦ, ὁ	imitator
μυρίος, -α, -ον	innumerable, countless; (*pl*) ten thousand

▷ List 24 2×

νεφέλη, -ης, ἡ	cloud
νομίζω	think, suppose, believe
ξυράω	(*mid*) have oneself shaved
οἰκονόμος, -ου, ὁ	household manager/steward; administrator, manager
οἷος, οἵα, οἷον	such as, of what sort; οἷος . . . τοιοῦτος (such) as . . . so also
ὁσάκις	as often as
οὔπω	not yet
οὖς, ὠτός, τό	ear; hearing, understanding
παλαιός, -ά, -όν	old
παραγγέλλω	command, instruct, give orders

▹ List 25 2×

πάρειμι	be present/here, have come
παρουσία, -ας, ἡ	presence; arrival, coming
πειρασμός, -οῦ, ὁ	test, trial; temptation
περιτέμνω	circumcise
πέτρα, -ας, ἡ	rock [formation or piece]
πλανάω	(*act*) lead astray, deceive; (*mid*) wander, go astray, be misled
ποίμνη, -ης, ἡ	flock [of sheep]
πόρνη, -ης, ἡ	sex worker
προπέμπω	send (someone) on their way [with assistance]
πώς (*encl*)	somehow, perhaps, in any way, at all

▹ List 26 2×

σάλπιγξ, σάλπιγγος, ἡ	trumpet; trumpet call
σατανᾶς, σατανᾶ, ὁ	[Heb.] Satan
σκανδαλίζω	cause (someone) to sin; shock, offend
σός, σή, σόν	your, yours
σταυρός, -οῦ, ὁ	cross
στέγω	endure, bear
συγχαίρω	rejoice (with)
σύμφορος, -ον	beneficial, advantageous, profitable
συναναμίγνυμι	(*mid +dat obj*) associate with
συνευδοκέω	approve (of), agree (with); consent (to)

▷ List 27 2×

συνήθεια, -είας, ἡ	custom, habit
Τιμόθεος, -έου, ὁ	Timothy
τράπεζα, -έζης, ἡ	table, [extended sense] meal
ὑμέτερος, -έρα, -ον	your, yours; in/about you
φεύγω	flee; escape; avoid ➢
φθορά, -ᾶς, ἡ	corruption, decay, ruin, destruction
φορέω	bear constantly/regularly
φρήν, φρενός, ἡ	mind; thinking, understanding
φρόνιμος, -ον	prudent, sensible, thoughtful, wise
φύραμα, -άματος, τό	something that is mixed or kneaded: mixture, batch (of dough), lump (of clay)

▷ List 28 2 to 1×

α′	1 [in the book title ΠΡΟΣ ΚΟΡΙΝΘΙΟΥΣ Α "1 Corinthians"]
ἀγενής, -ές	low, base
ἁγιασμός, -οῦ, ὁ	holiness, consecration
ἀγνωσία, -ας, ἡ	ignorance
ἀγωνίζομαι	exert effort, strive; struggle, fight
ἀδάπανος, -ον	free of charge, costing nothing
ἄδηλος, -ον	unclear, indistinct
ἀδήλως	uncertainly
ψάλλω	sing, make music
ὠφελέω	help, benefit, be of use to (+*dat/acc obj*); accomplish

▷ List 29 — 1×

ἀδικία, -ας, ἡ	injustice, unrighteousness; wrongdoing, misdeed
ἀδόκιμος, -ον	unqualified, disqualified
ἀθετέω	nullify, invalidate; reject
αἴνιγμα, -ίγματος, τό	riddle; indirect image; ἐν αἰνίγματι indirectly
αἵρεσις, -έσεως, ἡ	faction, sect
ἀκάθαρτος, -ον	impure, unclean [cultic or moral]
ἄκαρπος, -ον	unfruitful; useless
ἀκαταστασία, -ας, ἡ	instability, disorder; turmoil, disturbance
ἀκρασία, -ας, ἡ	lack of self-control
Ἀκύλας, Ἀκύλα, ὁ	Aquila

▷ List 30 — 1×

ἄκων, ἄκουσα, ἆκον	unwilling(ly)
ἀλαλάζω	shout aloud, wail loudly, sound loudly
ἁμάρτημα, -ήματος, τό	sin, sinful act
ἀμέριμνος, -ον	free from concern, without worry
ἀμετακίνητος, -ον	immovable
ἀμπελών, -ῶνος, ὁ	vineyard
ἀναγκαῖος, -αία, -ον	necessary, important
ἀναμιμνῄσκω	remind
ἀνάξιος, -ον	unworthy
ἀναξίως	in an unworthy/dishonoring manner

▶

▷ List 31 1×

ἀναπαύω	give rest, refresh
ἀνδρίζομαι	act like a man, show courage
ἀνέγκλητος, -ον	irreproachable, blameless
ἀνέχω	(*mid +gen/acc obj*) bear with, tolerate, put up with
ἀντί	(+*gen*) instead of, in place of; ἀνθ' ὧν because
ἀντίκειμαι	oppose (+*dat obj*)
ἀντίλημψις, -ήμψεως, ἡ	help, aid, helpful deed
ἀπάγω	lead off, take away, [extended sense] lead astray
ἄπειμι	be absent/away
ἀπεκδέχομαι	await

▷ List 32 1×

ἀπελεύθερος, -έρου, ὁ	freedperson, emancipated slave
ἀπερισπάστως	without distraction
ἀποδείκνυμι	point out; display; prove
ἀπόδειξις, -είξεως, ἡ	demonstration, proof
ἀποκρύπτω	hide, conceal, keep hidden ▷
ἀπολογία, -ας, ἡ	defense [a speech or the act of making a defense]
ἀπολούω	(*mid*) wash away from oneself, wash oneself, have oneself washed
ἀπολύτρωσις, -ώσεως, ἡ	release, liberation, deliverance, redemption
ἀποστολή, -ῆς, ἡ	sending off/forth; apostleship
ἀποφέρω	take/carry away, transport, carry ▷

▷ List 33 1×

ἀπρόσκοπος, -ον	without offense, blameless; inoffensive
ἅπτω	(*mid +gen obj*) touch, hold, cling to; have sexual relations with
ἀργύριον, -ίου, τό	silver [metal]; money <TH only>
ἄργυρος, -ύρου, ὁ	silver [metal]; money <NA/UBS, SBL only>
ἄρρωστος, -ον	ill, sick
ἀρσενοκοίτης, -ου, ὁ	men who have sex with males
ἀρχιτέκτων, -ονος, ὁ	master builder
Ἀσία, -ας, ἡ	Asia
ἀσπασμός, -οῦ, ὁ	greeting
ἀστατέω	be homeless

▷ List 34 1×

ἀσχήμων, -ον	unpresentable, unseemly
ἄτομος, -ον	indivisible, ἐν ἀτόμῳ in a moment, split second
αὐλέω	play the flute
αὐλός, -οῦ, ὁ	flute
αὔριον	next day, tomorrow; soon, shortly
ἀφόβως	without fear
ἄφρων, -ον	senseless, foolish
Ἀχαΐα, -ας, ἡ	Achaia
Ἀχαϊκός, -οῦ, ὁ	Achaicus
ἄψυχος, -ον	lifeless, inanimate

▷ List 35 1×

βάθος, -ους, τό	depth
Βαρναβᾶς, Βαρναβᾶ, ὁ	Barnabas
βλασφημέω	slander, speak disrespectfully about, revile
βουλή, -ῆς, ἡ	intention, motive; decision, plan, purpose
βούλομαι	want, desire; intend, plan
βραβεῖον, -είου, τό	prize, award
βρόχος, -ου, ὁ	noose, [figurative] restriction
βρῶσις, βρώσεως, ὁ	food; eating, consumption
Γάϊος, Γαΐου, ὁ	Gaius
Γαλατία, -ας, ἡ	Galatia

▷ List 36 1×

γεώργιον, -ίου, τό	cultivated land, field, orchard
γρηγορέω	be (fully) awake/alert; be watchful/on the alert
γυμνιτεύω	be poorly clothed
γυμνός, -ή, -όν	naked, bare, [figurative] uncovered; inadequately dressed; lightly dressed
δείκνυμι	show, make known; explain ▷
δειπνέω	eat a meal, dine
δέρω	violently mistreat, beat
δή (*postp*)	now, then, so [difficult to translate well and concisely] ▷
δῆλος, δήλη, δῆλον	evident, clear
διαθήκη, -ης, ἡ	will, testament; covenant

2 CORINTHIANS

▷ List 1 — 20 to 7×

ἀσθενέω	be sick; be weak
διακονία, -ας, ἡ	service, serving; (ministerial) service, ministry
ἐπιστολή, -ῆς, ἡ	letter
καυχάομαι	boast (about)
κίνδυνος, -ύνου, ὁ	danger
λυπέω	(*act*) cause grief/sorrow; (*mid*) grieve, be sad/distressed
παράκλησις, -ήσεως, ἡ	encouragement, exhortation; comfort, consolation
περισσεύω	(*intrans*) abound (in), overflow, be left over; ▸ (*trans*) cause (something) to abound, increase
Τίτος, -ου, ὁ	Titus
συνίστημι/συνιστάνω/ συνιστάω	(*trans pres/aor*) recommend, commend; establish, prove

▷ List 2 — 7 to 5×

ἀνέχω	(*mid +gen/acc obj*) bear with, tolerate, ▸ put up with
ἀσθένεια, -είας, ἡ	sickness, disease; weakness
ἄφρων, -ον	senseless, foolish
γνῶσις, γνώσεως, ἡ	knowledge [understanding/comprehension or that which is known]
κατεργάζομαι	do; produce, bring about; prepare ▸
καύχησις, -ήσεως, ἡ	boasting; reason for boasting
λύπη, -ης, ἡ	grief, sadness; pain
Μακεδονία, -ας, ἡ	Macedonia
ναί	yes
περισσοτέρως	(*comp*) (even) more; (*superl*) especially

▷ List 3 5×

διάκονος, -όνου, ὁ/ἡ	servant, helper; ministerial attendant ["deacon(ess)"]
ἐλπίζω	hope (for); expect ▸
ζῆλος, ζήλου/ζήλους, ὁ/τό	zeal; jealousy
θαρρέω	have courage, be confident/bold [the Attic spelling of θαρσέω]
νόημα, νοήματος, τό	thought, intention, purpose; understanding, mind
πάρειμι	be present/here, have come
πολλάκις	often, many times
πώς (*encl*)	somehow, perhaps, in any way, at all
σπουδή, -ῆς, ἡ	haste; zeal, eagerness, diligence
ὑπερβολή, -ῆς, ἡ	excess, surpassing quality/character, εἰς/καθ' ὑπερβολήν to an extraordinary degree, beyond measure

▷ List 4 5 to 4×

ἄπειμι	be absent/away
ἁπλότης, -ητος, ἡ	sincerity
δοκιμή, -ῆς, ἡ	testing; (proven) character; proof
ἐμαυτοῦ, -ῆς	myself, my (own) [when *gen*]
ἐπιτελέω	finish; complete, accomplish, fulfill (a duty)
εὐλογία, -ας, ἡ	praise; blessing; gift
καθάπερ	(just) as
κάλυμμα, -ύμματος, τό	head covering, veil
καταργέω	make useless; make ineffective, invalidate, nullify; set aside, eliminate
χαρίζομαι	give graciously/freely; forgive

▹ List 5 — 4 to 3×

ἀγνοέω	not know, be uninformed/ignorant; not understand; ignore, disregard
ἀδικέω	(*intrans*) do wrong, be in the wrong; (*trans*) wrong; injure
κοινωνία, -ας, ἡ	(close) fellowship; participation, sharing; generosity
κόπος, -ου, ὁ	trouble, hardship; labor, toil
οἰκοδομή, -ῆς, ἡ	building, structure; construction, building up
πεποίθησις, -ήσεως, ἡ	trust, confidence
πλεονεκτέω	exploit, take advantage of
προθυμία, -ας, ἡ	willingness, eagerness, readiness
τολμάω	dare, bring oneself (to), have the courage (to)
ὑστέρημα, -ήματος, τό	need, deficiency; lack, shortcoming

▹ List 6 — 3×

ἀδόκιμος, -ον	unqualified, disqualified; worthless
ἀναγινώσκω	read (aloud) ➤
ἀνάγκη, -ης, ἡ	necessity, constraint, pressure; distress, anguish
ἄνεσις, -έσεως, ἡ	relief, rest
ἄπιστος, -ον	unbelieving; unbelievable
ἀφορμή, -ῆς, ἡ	opportunity
ἀφροσύνη, -ης, ἡ	lack of sense, thoughtlessness, foolishness
Ἀχαΐα, -ας, ἡ	Achaia
γράμμα, -ατος, τό	letter [of the alphabet]; document, writing, letter
δέομαι	ask, petition, pray [+*gen* of person(s) petitioned]

▷ List 7 3×

διακονέω	(+*dat obj*) serve; care for; wait on; administer
δοκιμάζω	examine, evaluate; determine, put to the test; approve
δυνατός, -ή, -όν	able, capable, strong, powerful; possible
ἐκδημέω	be away from home, be away (from)
ἐνδημέω	be at home, stay/remain in a place
ἕνεκα/ἕνεκεν	(+*gen*) because of, for the sake of
ἕτοιμος, -οίμη, -ον	ready, (*subst*) what has already been done
εὐχαριστία, -ας, ἡ	thankfulness, gratitude; thanksgiving
ἡδέως	gladly; (*superl*) ἥδιστα most/very gladly
θλίβω	compress, make narrow; press upon; oppress, afflict ▹

▷ List 8 3×

ἱκανός, -ή, -όν	sufficient; able, qualified
καθαίρεσις, -έσεως, ἡ	tearing down, destruction, demolition
κανών, κανόνος, ὁ	standard, rule; limit, boundary; area, sphere
καταλλάσσω	reconcile
καταναρκάω	burden, be a burden to (+*gen obj*)
καύχημα, -ήματος, τό	boast [expression of pride or basis for pride]
μετασχηματίζω	(*mid*) change one's form, disguise oneself
μήτι	not ▹
οἷος, οἵα, οἷον	such as, of what sort; οἷος . . . τοιοῦτος (such) as . . . so also
ὀσμή, -ῆς, ἡ	smell, odor, fragrance

▷ List 9 3×

πάθημα, -ήματος, τό	suffering; emotion, passion
παρουσία, -ας, ἡ	presence; arrival, coming
προλέγω	tell beforehand/in advance
ῥύομαι	save, rescue, deliver
σατανᾶς, σατανᾶ, ὁ	[Heb.] Satan
σπουδαῖος, -αία, -ον	eager, earnest, diligent; (*comp*) σπουδαιότερος, -έρα, -ον very earnest
στενοχωρέω	(*mid-pass*) be distressed/in difficulty; be restricted/confined
συνείδησις, -ήσεως, ἡ	consciousness, awareness; conscience
τρίς	three times
ὑπακοή, -ῆς, ἡ	obedience

▷ List 10 3 to 2×

ἁγνός, -ή, -όν	pure
ἁγνότης, -ητος, ἡ	purity [moral]
ἀγρυπνία, -ας, ἡ	sleeplessness
ἀεί	always, constantly
ἀκαταστασία, -ας, ἡ	instability, disorder; turmoil, disturbance
ἀλλότριος, -ία, -ον	another's; foreign
ὑπομονή, -ῆς, ἡ	endurance, perseverance, steadfastness
ὑστερέω	(*trans act +gen/acc obj*) lack; (*intrans act*) lack, fail; be inferior; (*intrans mid*) be in need
φείδομαι	spare (+*gen obj*); refrain (from)
χράομαι	use (+*dat/acc obj*); act, function

▷ List 11 — 2×

ἄμετρος, -ον	immeasurable, εἰς τὰ ἄμετρα excessively
ἀνακαλύπτω	uncover, unveil ▶
ἀποκάλυψις, -ύψεως, ἡ	revelation, disclosure
ἁρπάζω	seize; take away, snatch
ἀρραβών, -ῶνος, ὁ	down payment, deposit, pledge
ἀτενίζω	look intently (at), stare (at) [+*dat* or εἰς]
ἀτιμία, -ας, ἡ	dishonor, disgrace
αὐθαίρετος, -ον	of one's own accord, voluntarily
αὐξάνω/αὔξω	(*trans*) make grow/increase; (*intrans*) grow, increase
βαρέω	weigh down, burden

▷ List 12 — 2×

βουλεύω	(*mid*) deliberate; decide
βούλομαι	want, desire; intend, plan
γέ (*encl*)	indeed, even; yet, at least, though
γονεύς, -έως, ὁ	parent
δέησις, δεήσεως, ἡ	entreaty; prayer, petition
διαθήκη, -ης, ἡ	will, testament; covenant
δόκιμος, -ον	approved
δυνατέω	be able (to); be effective/powerful
ἐγγράφω	engrave, inscribe, write down (on) ▶
ἐγκακέω	lose heart, be discouraged

▷ List 13 2×

εἰκών, εἰκόνος, ἡ	image, likeness [crafted or non-crafted]
εἰλικρίνεια, -είας, ἡ	sincerity, purity of motive
ἐνεργέω	(*intrans*) be at work/active; (*trans*) work, produce
ἐξαπορέω	(*mid*) despair, be in great despair
ἐπαίρω	(*act*) lift up; (*mid*) lift oneself up, swell up, be arrogant
ἐπεί	since, because; for otherwise
ἐπενδύομαι	(*mid*) put on (clothing) [over an existing garment]; be fully clothed
ἐπιποθέω	long for, strongly desire
ἐπιπόθησις, -ήσεως, ἡ	longing, yearning
εὐδοκέω	be well pleased; determine, resolve

▷ List 14 2×

εὐλογητός, -ή, -όν	blessed, praised
εὐπρόσδεκτος, -ον	acceptable
εὔχομαι	pray (for); wish (for)
ἐφικνέομαι	reach, extend (to) ▸
ἡνίκα	when, at the time when, ἡνίκα ἄν (+*subj*) whenever
θερίζω	reap, harvest
θνητός, -ή, -όν	mortal
ἰσότης, -ητος, τό	equality, [extended sense] fairness
καθό	how; insofar as, to the degree that
καλύπτω	cover; hide, conceal ▸

▹ List 15 2×

καταισχύνω	put to shame
κατάκρισις, -ίσεως, ἡ	condemnation
καταλλαγή, -ῆς, ἡ	reconciliation
καταπίνω	swallow (up), gulp (down), [extended sense] devour ➢
κατέναντι	(+*gen*) ahead/in front of, opposite; in the sight of, before
κοινωνός, -οῦ, ὁ/ἡ	companion, partner, sharer
Κορίνθιος, -ίου, ὁ	Corinthian
Κόρινθος, -ίνθου, ἡ	Corinth
λάμπω	give light, shine
Μακεδών, Μακεδόνος, ὁ	Macedonian

▹ List 16 2×

μάρτυς, μάρτυρος, ὁ	witness
μεταμέλομαι	regret; change one's mind
μετάνοια, -οίας, ἡ	change of mind and heart, repentance
μέτρον, -ου, τό	measure [instrument or result of measuring]
μωμάομαι	find fault, blame
νηστεία, -ας, ἡ	hunger, fasting
νυνί	now, at this time
ὅπλον, -ου, τό	tool, weapon
ὀφείλω	owe, be indebted to; be obligated, ought; have to
πανουργία, -ας, ἡ	trickery, craftiness

▷ List 17 2×

παρασκευάζω	(*trans act*) prepare; (*intrans mid*) get ready, prepare oneself
παρρησία, -ας, ἡ	plainness; openness; boldness
περισσεία, -ας, ἡ	surplus, abundance
περίσσευμα, -εύματος, τό	that which is left over, excess, surplus
περισσός, -ή, -όν	extraordinary; abundant, superfluous; (*comp*) περισσότερος, -έρα, -ον greater, better, excessive
πέρυσι	last year, a year ago
πλάξ, πλακός, ἡ	tablet
πλατύνω	widen
πλεονάζω	(*intrans*) increase, abound; have too much; (*trans*) (cause to) increase
πληγή, -ῆς, ἡ	blow, striking, beating; wound

▷ List 18 2×

πλουτίζω	make rich, enrich
πράσσω	do, accomplish, perform
προαμαρτάνω	sin previously ▸
προενάρχομαι	begin beforehand
προσαναπληρόω	supply/fill up in addition
πτωχεία, -ας, ἡ	poverty
σαρκικός, -ή, -όν	material, physical, fleshly; worldly, (merely) human
σκῆνος, σκήνους, τό	tent, [figurative] (human) body
σκότος, -ους, τό	darkness [literal or figurative]
σπλάγχνον, -ου, τό	[always *pl*] entrails; seat of emotion [similar to English's "heart"]; compassion, affection

▷ List 19 — 2×

σπόρος, -ου, ὁ	seed
στενάζω	sigh, groan
στενοχωρία, -ας, ἡ	distress, difficulty
συγκρίνω	combine; compare
συμπέμπω	send along with, send at the same time
συμφέρω	(*impers*) it is beneficial/of advantage; (*subst ptc*) benefit, profit ▷
συνεργός, -όν	helpful, contributing; [only *subst* in NT] fellow worker
ταπεινός, -ή, -όν	humble; lowly; abject, submissive
ταπεινόω	bring low; humble [positive], humiliate [negative]
Τιμόθεος, -έου, ὁ	Timothy

▷ List 20 — 2 to 1×

ἀβαρής, -ές	without weight, [figurative] not burdensome
ἀγανάκτησις, -ήσεως, ἡ	indignation
ἁγιότης, -ητος, ἡ	holiness <TH, SBL only>
ὑπεραίρω	(*trans act*) lift up over; (*intrans mid*) exalt oneself; become arrogant
ὑπερβάλλω	surpass, exceed
ὑπερλίαν	exceedingly, beyond measure, in super capacity <ὑπὲρ λίαν in TH>
ὑπόστασις, -άσεως, ἡ	substantial nature, essence; undertaking; confidence; plan
φειδομένως	sparingly
φθείρω	corrupt, ruin, destroy ▷
φωτισμός, -οῦ, ὁ	illumination

▷ List 21 1×

ἁγιωσύνη, -ῆς, ἡ	holiness, sanctity
ἀδικία, -ας, ἡ	injustice, unrighteousness; wrongdoing, misdeed
ἁδρότης, -ητος, ἡ	abundance
αἰσχύνη, -ης, ἡ	shame, dishonor; [sense/experience of] shame; shameful deed
αἰσχύνω	(*mid*) be ashamed
αἰχμαλωτίζω	put into captivity, make captive, capture
ἀκαθαρσία, -ας, ἡ	uncleanness, filth; immorality
ἀκάθαρτος, -ον	impure, unclean [cultic or moral]
ἀληθής, -ές	true, trustworthy; real
ἀμεταμέλητος, -ον	not to be regretted

▷ List 22 1×

ἀναγγέλλω	report; disclose, announce
ἀναγκάζω	compel, force; urge
ἀναγκαῖος, -αία, -ον	necessary, important
ἀνάγνωσις, -ώσεως, ἡ	reading
ἀνακαινόω	renew
ἀναμιμνῄσκω	(*trans act*) remind; (*intrans mid*) remember
ἀναπαύω	(*trans act*) give rest, refresh; (*intrans mid*) rest
ἀναστρέφω	(*act*) return, go back; (*mid*) conduct oneself, live
ἀνεκδιήγητος, -ον	indescribable, ineffable
ἀνομία, -ας, ἡ	lawlessness [condition or action]

▸

▹ List 23 1×

ἀντιμισθία, -ας, ἡ	recompense, exchange [positive or negative]
ἀνυπόκριτος, -ον	without pretense, genuine, sincere
ἅπαξ	once; once and for all
ἀπαρασκεύαστος, -ον	not ready, unprepared
ἀπεῖπον	(*mid*) refuse, repudiate, renounce [*aor* of defunct present ἀπολέγω]
ἀπόκριμα, -ίματος, τό	judicial decision/sentence
ἀπολογέομαι	speak in one's defense, defend oneself
ἀπολογία, -ας, ἡ	defense [a speech or the act of making a defense]
ἀπορέω	be perplexed/at a loss
ἀποτάσσω	(*mid*) say goodbye (to)

▹ List 24 1×

ἀποτόμως	severely, sharply
ἅπτω	(*mid +gen obj*) touch, hold, cling to
Ἁρέτας, -α, ὁ	Aretas
ἀριστερός, -ά, -όν	left; (*subst*) left hand
ἀρκέω	(*act*) be enough/sufficient; (*mid*) be content/satisfied
ἁρμόζω	(*mid*) betroth
ἄρρητος, -ον	not to be spoken/divulged
ἀρχαῖος, -αία, -ον	old, ancient
ἀσέλγεια, -είας, ἡ	licentiousness, excessive sensuality
ἀσθενής, -ές	weak; sick, ill

▷ List 25 1×

Ἀσία, -ας, ἡ	Asia
αὐγάζω	see
αὐτάρκεια, -είας, ἡ	sufficiency; contentment
ἀφίστημι	(*trans*) draw away, incite; (*intrans*) withdraw, depart; keep away ▸
ἀφορίζω	(*intrans mid*) be separate
ἀχειροποίητος, -ον	not made/done by hand
β′	2 [in the book title ΠΡΟΣ ΚΟΡΙΝΘΙΟΥΣ Β "2 Corinthians"]
βάθος, -ους, τό	depth
βάρος, -ους, τό	weight; burden
βαρύς, -εῖα, -ύ	heavy; burdensome; weighty, serious

▷ List 26 1×

βέβαιος, -αία, -ον	steadfast, steady; firm, reliable, certain
βεβαιόω	confirm, establish; guarantee [legal term]
βελιάρ, ὁ (*indecl*)	Beliar
βῆμα, βήματος, τό	step [as a measure of length]; platform; judicial bench, judgment seat
βοηθέω	help, come to the aid of (+*dat obj*)
βρῶσις, βρώσεως, ὁ	food; eating, consumption
βυθός, -οῦ, ὁ	the deep, deep water
γένημα, -ήματος, τό	fruit, (*pl*) produce
γένος, -ους, τό	people group, family; offspring, descendant; kind, class
γνήσιος, -ία, -ον	legitimate, true [validity of family membership]; genuine

▷ List 27 1×

γνώμη, -ης, ἡ	judgment, opinion; purpose, intent, will
γνωρίζω	make known, inform; know
γυμνός, -ή, -όν	naked, bare, [figurative] uncovered; inadequately dressed; lightly dressed
γυμνότης, -ητος, ἡ	nakedness; without enough clothing
δάκρυον, -ύου, τό	tear(drop)
Δαμασκηνός, -ή, -όν	of Damascus, (*subst*) Damascene
Δαμασκός, -οῦ, ἡ	Damascus
δαπανάω	spend (money)
δεκατέσσαρες, -α	fourteen
δεκτός, -ή, -όν	acceptable, pleasing; accepted, welcome; favorable

▷ List 28 1×

δέρω	violently mistreat, beat
διαφθείρω	destroy; corrupt
δίψος, -ους, τό	thirst
διωγμός, -οῦ, ὁ	persecution
δόλιος, -ία, -ον	deceitful
δόλος, -ου, ὁ	deceit, cunning, craftiness
δολόω	falsify, distort
δότης, -ου, ὁ	giver
δυσφημία, -ας, ἡ	slander, defamation
δωρεά, -ᾶς, ἡ	gift

▷ List 29 — 1×

δωρεάν	freely; without cause
Ἑβραῖος, -ίου, ὁ	Hebrew [ethnicity]
ἐγκαταλείπω	leave behind; forsake, abandon
ἐγκρίνω	reckon among, classify
ἐθνάρχης, -ου, ὁ	leader of an ethnic community, ethnarch
εἶδος, εἴδους, τό	form, appearance; sight
εἴδωλον, -ώλου, τό	idol, cultic image
εἵνεκεν	because, on account of
εἰρηνεύω	be at peace, keep the peace
εἰσδέχομαι	welcome, receive

▷ List 30 — 1×

ἐκδαπανάω	expend completely, exhaust
ἐκδικέω	grant justice; carry out justice, avenge, punish
ἐκδίκησις, -ήσεως, ἡ	carrying out of justice; vengeance; punishment
ἐκδύω	(*trans act*) take/strip clothes off; (*intrans mid*) be stripped
ἐκκόπτω	cut off/down; do away with ▷
ἐκτός	outside; ἐκτὸς εἰ μή unless, except; (*prep +gen*) outside; except <NA/UBS, SBL only>
ἐκφεύγω	escape; flee ▷
ἐκφοβέω	terrify
ἐλαττονέω	receive/have less
ἐλαφρία, -ας, ἡ	levity

▹ List 31 1×

ἐλαφρός, -ή, -όν	light, easy to bear
ἐλεέω	have compassion (on), show mercy to
ἐλευθερία, -ας, ἡ	freedom, liberty
ἐμπεριπατέω	walk among
ἐναντίον	(+*gen*) in front of, before; (*adv*) τοὐναντίον instead, on the contrary
ἐνδείκνυμι	(*mid*) show, demonstrate, exhibit
ἔνδειξις, ἐνδείξεως, ἡ	indication, demonstration
ἐνδύνω	slip in
ἐνοικέω	live/dwell in
ἐντυπόω	carve in/on

▹ List 32 1×

ἐξαπατάω	deceive, seduce
ἔξεστιν	(*impers*) it is right/permitted [*3sg* of ἔξειμι] ▹
ἐξίστημι/ἐξιστάνω	(*intrans*) be amazed; be out of one's mind ▹
ἐξουθενέω	look down on, treat with contempt; reject
ἔξωθεν	(from) outside; (*prep* +*gen*) outside
ἔπαινος, ἐπαίνου, ὁ	praise, recognition, commendation
ἐπακούω	listen closely to, hear (+*gen obj*)
ἐπιβαρέω	burden, be a burden to
ἐπίγειος, -ον	earthly
ἐπιείκεια, -είας, ἡ	graciousness, clemency

▷ List 33 1×

ἐπικαλέω	(*mid*) call upon, invoke, appeal
ἐπισκηνόω	take up residence, dwell
ἐπίστασις, -άσεως, ἡ	attention, care
ἐπιστρέφω	(*intrans act/mid*) return; turn (around); change (one's thinking or behavior)
ἐπιταγή, -ῆς, ἡ	command
ἐπιτιμία, -ας, ἡ	punishment
ἐπιχορηγέω	provide, supply, furnish
ἐργάτης, -ου, ὁ	worker, laborer; doer
ἐρεθίζω	provoke [negative], excite, stir up [positive]
ἐρημία, -ας, ἡ	desolate place, desert, wilderness; desolation

▷ List 34 1×

ἐριθεία, -ᾶς, ἡ	selfish ambition
ἔρις, -ιδος, ἡ	strife, contention
ἑσσόομαι	be inferior to, worse off than
ἔσω	inside, within
ἔσωθεν	(from) within, (from) inside; inside, within
ἑτεροζυγέω	be mismatched (with)
ἑτοίμως	readily
Εὕα, -ας, ἡ	Eve
εὐάρεστος, -ον	pleasing
εὐφημία, -ας, ἡ	good repute; word of praise

▷ List 35 1×

εὐφραίνω	make glad
εὐχαριστέω	thank, give thanks, be thankful
εὐωδία, -ας, ἡ	sweet aroma, fragrance
ζηλόω	be zealous for, strive after
ζημιόω	(*mid*) lose, suffer loss
ζωοποιέω/ζῳοποιέω	give life to, make alive
ἡγέομαι	consider, regard
ἥσσων, ἧσσον	lesser, inferior, worse; [*neut* as *adv*] less
θανατόω	put to death
θαῦμα, θαύματος, τό	wonder, marvel

▷ List 36 1×

θησαυρίζω	store (up), save
θησαυρός, -οῦ, ὁ	repository, container, chest; treasure
θριαμβεύω	triumph (over); lead in triumph
θυγάτηρ, θυγατρός, ἡ	daughter
θυμός, -οῦ, ὁ	desire, passion; anger, wrath
θύρα, -ας, ἡ	door; entrance
θυρίς, θυρίδος, ἡ	window
ἰδιώτης, -ου, ὁ	layperson, uninstructed person; outsider, one not in the know
ἱκανότης, -ητος, τό	sufficiency, fitness, competence
ἱκανόω	make adequate/qualified/fit

GALATIANS

▷ List 1	8 to 4×
βαστάζω	pick up; carry, bear
δικαιόω	justify, consider right/righteous, make righteous; vindicate, put in the right
δουλεύω	be a slave; slave (for), serve (+*dat obj*)
ἐλευθερία, -ας, ἡ	freedom, liberty
ἐλεύθερος, -έρα, -ον	free
ἐνεργέω	(*intrans*) be at work/active; (*trans*) work, produce
θερίζω	reap, harvest
παιδίσκη, -ης, ἡ	female slave
περιτέμνω	circumcise ▸
περιτομή, -ῆς, ἡ	circumcision; one who is circumcised

▷ List 2	4 to 3×
ἀκροβυστία, -ας, ἡ	foreskin; uncircumcision; one who is uncircumcised
ἀναγκάζω	compel, force; urge
ἄρτι	(just) now
Βαρναβᾶς, Βαρναβᾶ, ὁ	Barnabas
διαθήκη, -ης, ἡ	will, testament; covenant
εἰκῇ	without cause; in vain
ἔνειμι	be in(side) ▸
ἔπειτα	then, next
Κηφᾶς, Κηφᾶ, ὁ	Cephas
ποτέ (*encl*)	when, at some time; formerly, once; (+*rel pron*) whatever

▷ List 3 — 3 to 2×

Ἁγάρ, ἡ (*indecl*)	Hagar
ἀθετέω	nullify, invalidate; reject
ἀκοή, -ῆς, ἡ	hearing, listening; ear; news, rumor, report, message
ζηλόω	be zealous for, strive after
κατάρα, -ας, ἡ	curse
καταργέω	make useless; make ineffective, invalidate, nullify; set aside, eliminate; [+ἀπό] separate, set free
κληρονόμος, -ου, ὁ	heir; beneficiary, heir
προλέγω	tell beforehand/in advance
σταυρός, -οῦ, ὁ	cross
τρέχω	run ▶

▷ List 4 — 2×

ἀνάθεμα, -έματος, τό	accursed; curse
ἀνέρχομαι	go/come up ▶
ἀνόητος, -ον	unintelligent, senseless, foolish
ἀποκαλύπτω	reveal, disclose ▶
ἀποκάλυψις, -ύψεως, ἡ	revelation, disclosure
Ἀραβία, -ας, ἡ	Arabia
ἀρέσκω	please (+*dat obj*) ▶
ἀφορίζω	separate; set apart
Γαλάτης, -ου, ὁ	Galatian
διαφέρω	be unlike, differ; differ in worth, surpass, be worth more (than) ▶

▷ List 5	2×
δουλεία, -ας, ἡ	slavery
Ἕλλην, -ηνος, ὁ	Greek (person); a person of Hellenic culture, gentile
ἐξαγοράζω	(*act*) buy up/off, redeem; (*mid*) take advantage of
ἐξαποστέλλω	send out/off, dispatch
ἐπιθυμία, -ας, ἡ	desire, longing; lust, craving
ἐπικατάρατος, -ον	cursed
Ἰουδαϊσμός, -οῦ, ὁ	Judeanism/Judaism
καλῶς	well, appropriately, effectively; correctly
κατηχέω	report, inform; teach, instruct
καυχάομαι	boast (about)

▷ List 6	2×
κληρονομέω	(*intrans*) be an heir; (*trans*) acquire, obtain
μεσίτης, -ου, ὁ	mediator, arbitrator
νήπιος, -ία, -ον	(*subst*) infant; little child
παιδαγωγός, -οῦ, ὁ	guardian, guide
πάρειμι	be present/here, have come
πορθέω	destroy utterly, annihilate
πραΰτης, -ητος, τό	humility, gentleness
προσανατίθημι	(*mid*) contribute; consult with (+*dat obj*)
πτωχός, -ή, -όν	poor; deficient, inferior
πώς (*encl*)	somehow, perhaps, in any way, at all

▷ List 7 — 2 to 1×

ἀββᾶ/ἀββά/αββα (*indecl*)	[Aram.] father
ἀγαθωσύνη, -ῆς, ἡ	goodness
Σ(ε)ινᾶ (*indecl*)	Sinai
στοιχεῖον, -είου, τό	(basic) element, (fundamental) part, elemental force/spirit
στοιχέω	be in line (with), conform (to), agree (with)
συγκλείω	enclose, catch; confine ▷
ταράσσω	agitate, disturb [physically, mentally, or spiritually] ▷
Τίτος, -ου, ὁ	Titus
φύσις, -εως, τό	nature [inherent/basic qualities, features, or character]
ὠδίνω	suffer labor/birth pains

▷ List 8 — 1×

ἀγνοέω	not know, be uninformed/ignorant
ἀδικέω	(*trans*) wrong; injure
αἵρεσις, -έσεως, ἡ	faction, sect
ἀκαθαρσία, -ας, ἡ	uncleanness, filth; immorality
ἀκυρόω	nullify, make void
ἀληθεύω	tell/speak the truth
ἀλλάσσω	change, alter; exchange
ἀλληγορέω	express figuratively
ἀναλόω	consume, destroy
ἀναπληρόω	fill (up); supply; fulfill

▷ List 9 1×

ἀναστατόω	unsettle, trouble, disturb
ἀναστροφή, -ῆς, ἡ	conduct, way of life
ἀνατίθημι	(*mid*) set before (for consideration), present
ἀνθίστημι	resist, oppose, withstand (+*dat obj*) ▸
ἀντίκειμαι	oppose (+*dat obj*)
Ἀντιόχεια, -είας, ἡ	Antioch
ἄνω	above; up(ward)
ἄνωθεν	from above; πάλιν ἄνωθεν all over again
ἀπεκδέχομαι	await
ἀποκόπτω	(*act*) cut off/away; (*mid*) castrate oneself

▷ List 10 1×

ἀπολαμβάνω	receive ▸
ἀπορέω	be perplexed/at a loss
ἀποστολή, -ῆς, ἡ	sending off/forth; apostleship
ἆρα	[interrogative particle that may imply suspense, anxiety, or impatience]
ἄρσην, -εν	male ▸
ἀσέλγεια, -είας, ἡ	licentiousness, excessive sensuality
ἀσθένεια, -είας, ἡ	sickness, disease; weakness
ἀσθενής, -ές	weak; sick, ill
ἀφορμή, -ῆς, ἡ	opportunity
βάρος, -ους, τό	weight; burden

▷ List 11 1×

βασκαίνω	bewitch ➢
βιβλίον, -ου, τό	scroll; document
βοάω	call/cry out, shout
Γαλατία, -ας, ἡ	Galatia
γέ (*encl*)	indeed, even; yet, at least, though
γένος, -ους, τό	people group, family; offspring, descendant; kind, class
γνωρίζω	make known, inform; know
γράμμα, -ατος, τό	letter [of the alphabet]; document, writing, letter
δάκνω	bite
Δαμασκός, -οῦ, ἡ	Damascus

▷ List 12 1×

δεκαπέντε (*indecl*)	fifteen
δεκατέσσαρες, -α	fourteen
δέομαι	ask, petition, pray [+*gen* of person(s) petitioned]
δῆλος, δήλη, δῆλον	evident, clear
διάκονος, -όνου, ὁ/ἡ	servant, helper; ministerial attendant ["deacon(ess)"]
διαμένω	remain, persist
διατάσσω	(*act/mid*) instruct, direct ➢
διχοστασία, -ας, ἡ	dissension
δοκιμάζω	examine, evaluate; determine, put to the test; approve
δουλόω	enslave

▷ **List 13**	1×
δυνατός, -ή, -όν	able, capable, strong, powerful; possible
δωρεάν	freely; without cause; in vain
ἐγκακέω	lose heart, be discouraged
ἐγκόπτω	hinder
ἐγκράτεια, -είας, ἡ	self-control
ἐθνικῶς	like a gentile
εἰδωλολατρία, -ας, ἡ	image worship, idolatry
εἴκω	yield
ἐκκλείω	shut out, exclude
ἐκλύω	(*mid-pass*) become weary/weak, give out/up

▷ **List 14**	1×
ἐκπίπτω	fall off; fall from, be deprived of (+*gen obj*) ▸
ἐκπτύω	spit out, [extended sense] disdain
ἔλεος, ἐλέους, τό	compassion, mercy
ἐλευθερόω	set free
ἐμαυτοῦ, -ῆς	myself, my (own) [when *gen*]
ἐμμένω	remain/stay in, [extended sense] persist/persevere in, stand fast
ἐναντίον	(+*gen*) in front of, before; (*adv*) τοὐναντίον instead, on the contrary
ἐνάρχομαι	begin
ἐνδύω	(*act*) dress/clothe (someone); (*mid*) put on, wear
ἐνευλογέω	bless

▷ List 15 1×

ἐνέχω	(*act*) bear a grudge, be hostile; (*mid*) be subject to
ἐνιαυτός, -οῦ, ὁ	year
ἐνίστημι	(*pf*) be present/here ➢
ἐξαιρέω	(*act*) take out; (*mid*) rescue, deliver, set free ➢
ἐξορύσσω	dig/tear out
ἐξουθενέω	look down on, treat with contempt; reject
ἐπαγγέλλομαι	promise
ἐπιδιατάσσομαι	supplement/add to (a will) [legal terminology]
ἐπιθυμέω	long for, desire (+*gen/acc obj*)
ἐπιμένω	remain, stay; persist, continue

▷ List 16 1×

ἐπιστρέφω	(*intrans act/mid*) return, go/come back; turn (around); change (one's thinking or behavior); (*trans act*) turn, redirect ➢
ἐπιτελέω	finish; complete, accomplish, fulfill (a duty)
ἐπίτροπος, -όπου, ὁ	manager; guardian
ἐπιχορηγέω	provide, supply, furnish
ἐριθεία, -ᾶς, ἡ	selfish ambition
ἔρις, -ιδος, ἡ	strife, contention
εὐδοκέω	be well pleased; determine, resolve
εὐθέως	immediately
εὐλογία, -ας, ἡ	praise; blessing; gift
εὐπροσωπέω	make a good show

▷ List 17 — 1×

εὐφραίνω	(*trans act*) make glad; (*intrans mid*) be glad, enjoy oneself, rejoice
ἔχθρα, -ας, ἡ	enmity, hatred
ἐχθρός, -ά, -όν	hated; hostile; (*subst*) enemy
ζῆλος, ζήλου/ζήλους, ὁ/τό	zeal; jealousy
ζηλωτής, -οῦ, ὁ	enthusiast, loyalist; zealot
ζυγός, -οῦ, ὁ	yoke
ζύμη, -ης, ἡ	fermented dough, leaven
ζυμόω	leaven, ferment, make (dough) rise
ζωοποιέω/ζῳοποιέω	give life to, make alive
θῆλυς, θήλεια, θῆλυ	(*subst*) female, woman

▷ List 18 — 1×

θυμός, -οῦ, ὁ	desire, passion; anger, wrath
ἴδε	[attention-getter] look!, pay attention!
ἰουδαΐζω	live in a Judean/Jewish manner
Ἰουδαϊκῶς	in a Judean/Jewish manner
Ἰσαάκ, ὁ (*indecl*)	Isaac
ἱστορέω	visit [to obtain information]
ἰσχύω	be strong/powerful/able; prevail; be in force [legal term]
κανών, κανόνος, ὁ	standard, rule
καταγινώσκω	condemn (+*gen obj*)
καταδουλόω	enslave

▸

▷ List 19 1×

καταλύω	(*trans*) tear down, destroy; abolish, bring to an end
καταρτίζω	restore, put in order; prepare, make ready
κατασκοπέω	spy on
κατεσθίω	devour, consume
καύχημα, -ήματος, τό	boast [expression of pride or basis for pride]
κενόδοξος, -ον	vainglorious, conceited
κενός, -ή, -όν	empty [of content]; empty, fruitless; in vain, for nothing
Κιλικία, -ας, ἡ	Cilicia
κληρονομία, -ας, ἡ	inheritance; property, possession
κλίμα, -ατος, τό	region

▷ List 20 1×

κοιλία, -ας, ἡ	stomach; womb; heart [figurative, representing one's inner desires and feelings]
κοινωνέω	have a share, take part in; share
κοινωνία, -ας, ἡ	(close) fellowship; participation, sharing; generosity
κοπιάω	be weary/tired; labor, toil
κόπος, -ου, ὁ	trouble, hardship; labor, toil
κρεμάννυμι	(*trans act*) make (something) hang; (*intrans mid*) hang ➢
κρίμα, -ατος, τό	judgment [process of evaluation]; judgment [end result], judicial verdict
κτίσις, -εως, τό	creation [act or product]
κυρόω	confirm, ratify
κῶμος, κώμου, ὁ	unseemly/excessive partying, carousal

▹ **List 21**	**1×**
μακαρισμός, -οῦ, ὁ	blessedness
μακροθυμία, -ας, ἡ	patience; forbearance
μάλιστα	most of all, especially
μανθάνω	learn
μαρτύρομαι	testify
μέθη, -ης, ἡ	drunkenness
μεταστρέφω	change, alter; distort, twist
μετατίθημι	(*trans act*) transfer, move to a new place; change, alter; (*intrans mid*) change one's mind, turn away
μέχρι	(*conj*) until; (*prep +gen*) until; as far as; to the point of
μήν, μηνός, ὁ	month

▹ **List 22**	**1×**
μνημονεύω	remember (*+gen/acc obj*)
μορφόω	form, shape
μυκτηρίζω	turn up one's nose at, treat with contempt, mock
ξύλον, -ου, τό	wood; object made of wood [e.g., club, stocks, cross]; tree
οἰκεῖος, -εία, -ον	in/of the house, (*subst pl*) household members
οἰκονόμος, -ου, ὁ	household manager/steward; administrator, manager
ὅμως	nevertheless; likewise
ὄντως	really, truly, actually
ὁποῖος, -οία, -ον	of what sort, what kind of; as
ὀρθοποδέω	walk straight, [extended sense] act rightly

▹ List 23 1×

ὀφειλέτης, -ου, ὁ	debtor
ὄφελον	O that, would that, wish
πάθημα, -ήματος, τό	suffering; emotion, passion
παράβασις, -άσεως, ἡ	transgression, violation
παραβάτης, -ου, ὁ	transgressor
παράδοσις, -όσεως, ἡ	tradition
παράπτωμα, -ώματος, τό	transgression
παρατηρέω	watch closely, keep an eye on; carefully observe (a custom or tradition)
παρείσακτος, -ον	secretly brought in
παρεισέρχομαι	come in (beside), [extended sense] slip in

▸

▹ List 24 1×

παρέχω	bring about, make happen; present, provide
πατρικός, -ή, -όν	ancestral
πειράζω	test; tempt
πειρασμός, -οῦ, ὁ	test, trial; temptation
πεισμονή, -ῆς, ἡ	persuasion
περισσοτέρως	(*comp*) (even) more; (*superl*) especially
πηλίκος, -η, -ον	[*interr* or *exclam*] how large?; how great?
πλανάω	(*act*) lead astray, deceive; (*mid*) wander, go astray, be misled
πλήρωμα, -ώματος, τό	that which fills; that which completes; fullness
πλησίον	(+*gen*) near; (*subst*) neighbor

▷ List 25 1×

πνευματικός, -ή, -όν	spiritual
πορνεία, -ας, ἡ	sexual immorality, fornication
πράσσω	do, accomplish, perform
προγράφω	write beforehand/in advance; set forth/display publicly
προευαγγελίζομαι	proclaim good news in advance
προθεσμία, -ας, ἡ	appointed day/time
προκαλέω	call out, provoke, challenge
προκόπτω	advance, progress
προκυρόω	ratify/confirm in advance
προλαμβάνω	take/receive beforehand; catch, overtake, detect ▸

▷ List 26 1×

προοράω	foresee; see previously ▸
προστίθημι	add on/to; continue (to), do again [indicates the repetition of another verb's action]
πρότερος, -έρα, -ον	former, earlier; [*neut sg* as *adv*] before, formerly
ῥήσσω/ῥήγνυμι	(*trans*) break apart, tear, rend; (*intrans*) burst forth, break out
σκάνδαλον, -άλου, τό	trap; cause of sin ["stumbling block"]; offense
σκοπέω	pay attention to, examine; look to, consider
σπουδάζω	strive, make every effort (to), be eager (to)
στεῖρα, στείρας, ἡ	barren woman
στήκω	stand
στίγμα, -ατος, τό	mark (on the body), brand

▷ List 27 1×

στῦλος, στύλου, ὁ	pillar, column [metaphorically, a thing/person that provides support]
συμπαραλαμβάνω	take along with ▷
συναπάγω	lead away with/together
συνεσθίω	eat with
συνηλικιώτης, -ου, ὁ	contemporary
συνίστημι/συνιστάνω/ συνιστάω	(*trans pres/aor*) recommend, commend; establish, prove
συνυποκρίνομαι	join in pretense ▷
Συρία, -ας, ἡ	Syria
συσταυρόω	crucify with ▷
συστοιχέω	correspond (to)

▷ List 28 1×

ταχέως	quickly, without delay; soon
τεκνίον, -ου, τό	little child <TH only>
τελέω	complete, finish; carry out (completely), accomplish; pay
τετρακόσιοι, -αι, -α	four hundred
τίκτω	give birth to, bear, [inanimate] produce
τοσοῦτος, -αύτη, -οῦτο(ν)	so many; so much/great; such
τριάκοντα (*indecl*)	thirty
υἱοθεσία, -ας, ἡ	adoption
ὑμέτερος, -έρα, -ον	your, yours
ὑπερβολή, -ῆς, ἡ	excess, surpassing quality/character, καθ' ὑπερβολήν to an extraordinary degree, beyond measure

▷ List 29 — 1×

ὑπόκρισις, -ίσεως, ἡ	pretense, hypocrisy
ὑποστέλλω	withdraw
ὑποστρέφω	return, turn back
ὑποταγή, -ῆς, ἡ	submission
φανερός, -ά, -όν	visible, plain, evident, known; (*subst*) the open
φαρμακεία, -ας, ἡ	sorcery, witchcraft
φθονέω	envy, be jealous of (+*dat obj*)
φθόνος, -ου, ὁ	envy
φθορά, -ᾶς, ἡ	corruption, decay, ruin, destruction
φόνος, -ου, ὁ	killing <TH only>

▷ List 30 — 1×

φορτίον, -ου, τό	load; burden
φρεναπατάω	deceive
φρονέω	think
φρουρέω	keep watch; guard, protect; detain, confine
φυλάσσω	observe, follow
φύραμα, -άματος, τό	something that is mixed or kneaded: mixture, batch (of dough), lump (of clay)
χαρίζομαι	give graciously/freely; forgive
χάριν	(+*gen* preceding or following) because of, for the sake of
χρηστότης, -ητος, ἡ	kindness, goodness
ψευδάδελφος, -έλφου, ὁ	false brother/member

▷ List 31 1×

ψεύδομαι	lie, speak falsely
ὦ	(*interj*) O [address]; oh!
ὥσπερ	(just) as
ὠφελέω	help, benefit, be of use to (+*dat/acc obj*); accomplish

EPHESIANS

▷ List 1 — 6 to 3 ×

ἀμφότεροι, -αι, -α	both
γνωρίζω	make known, inform; know
ἐνεργέω	(*intrans*) be at work/active; (*trans*) work, produce
ἐπουράνιος, -ον	heavenly
κτίζω	create
μυστήριον, -ίου, τό	mystery, secret
οἰκοδομή, -ῆς, ἡ	building, structure; construction, building up
πλήρωμα, -ώματος, τό	that which fills, content; that which completes, complement; fullness
πλοῦτος, πλούτου, ὁ/τό	wealth, riches; abundance
ποτέ (*encl*)	when, at some time; formerly, once

▷ List 2 — 3 ×

ἀπολύτρωσις, -ώσεως, ἡ	release, liberation, deliverance, redemption
ἐνδύω	(*act*) dress/clothe (someone); (*mid*) put on, wear
ἐνέργεια, -είας, ἡ	working, action, activity
ἔπαινος, ἐπαίνου, ὁ	praise, recognition, commendation
κληρονομία, -ας, ἡ	inheritance; property, possession
κλῆσις, κλήσεως, ἡ	call, calling, invitation
μέτρον, -ου, τό	measure [instrument or result of measuring]
μηκέτι	no longer
οἰκονομία, -ας, ἡ	management, administration; arrangement, plan
ὀνομάζω	name, call; utter, mention

▷ List 3 — 3 to 2×

ἀκαθαρσία, -ας, ἡ	uncleanness, filth; immorality
ἄμωμος, -ον	unblemished; blameless
ἀναλαμβάνω	lift up; take up/along ▷
ἀπαλλοτριόω	alienate, estrange, separate
ὀργή, -ῆς, ἡ	anger; wrath
παράπτωμα, -ώματος, τό	transgression
πνευματικός, -ή, -όν	spiritual
σκότος, -ους, τό	darkness [literal or figurative]
ὑπερβάλλω	surpass, exceed
ὑποτάσσω	subject, subordinate

▷ List 4 — 2×

ἀπείθεια, -είας, ἡ	disobedience
ἀποκάλυψις, -ύψεως, ἡ	revelation, disclosure
ἀποτίθημι	(*mid*) put away, lay aside
αὐξάνω/αὔξω	(*trans*) make grow/increase; (*intrans*) grow, increase
γέ (*encl*)	indeed, even; yet, at least, though
δέησις, δεήσεως, ἡ	entreaty; prayer, petition
δέσμιος, -ίου, ὁ	prisoner
διάβολος, -ον	slanderous; (*subst*) adversary; devil
διάκονος, -όνου, ὁ/ἡ	servant, helper; ministerial attendant ["deacon(ess)"]
διάνοια, -οίας, ἡ	mind, understanding; thought, disposition

▷ List 5	2×
δωρεά, -ᾶς, ἡ	gift
ἐγγύς	near [spatial or temporal]
ἐκτρέφω	nourish; rear/bring up (from childhood)
ἐλέγχω	expose; reprove; convict, accuse
ἑνότης, -ητος, ἡ	unity
ἐπίγνωσις, -ώσεως, ἡ	knowledge
ἐπιθυμία, -ας, ἡ	desire, longing; lust, craving
εὐδοκία, -ας, ἡ	goodwill; favor
εὐχαριστέω	thank, give thanks, be thankful
ἔχθρα, -ας, ἡ	enmity, hatred

▷ List 6	2×
ἰσχύς, -ύος, ἡ	strength
κλέπτω	steal
κράτος, -ους, τό	strength, might, power; rule, sovereignty
μακράν	far off/away [spatial or temporal]
μεθοδεία, -ας, ἡ	craftiness, scheming
μέλος, -ους, τό	member [of the human body], limb; member [of a group]
νοέω	understand; consider, think about
νοῦς, νοός, ὁ	mind; understanding, intellect; thought
ξένος, -η, -ον	strange, foreign; (*subst*) stranger, foreigner
πανοπλία, -ας, ἡ	suit of armor, full armor

▷ List 7 2×

παρρησία, -ας, ἡ	plainness; openness; boldness
πλεονεξία, -ας, ἡ	greed; greedy act, extortion
πρόθεσις, -έσεως, ἡ	setting forth, presentation; purpose
προορίζω	decide beforehand, predetermine
προσαγωγή, -ῆς, ἡ	access
προσευχή, -ῆς, ἡ	prayer
συμμέτοχος, -ον	(*subst*) sharer, partner
συναρμολογέω	fit/join together
σφραγίζω	seal; seal up; mark with a seal; certify
ὑπακούω	obey

▷ List 8 2 to 1×

ἀγαθωσύνη, -ῆς, ἡ	goodness
ἁγιάζω	consecrate, make holy; regard as holy
ἄγνοια, -οίας, ἡ	ignorance
ἀγρυπνέω	stay alert, be watchful
ᾄδω	sing
ὑπεράνω	(+*gen*) (high) above
ὕψος, -ους, τό	height [dimension or position]
φωτίζω	(*intrans*) shine; (*trans*) illuminate, light up; enlighten, give light to
χαρίζομαι	give graciously/freely; forgive
χάριν	(+*gen* preceding or following) because of, for the sake of

▷ List 9 1×

ἀήρ, ἀέρος, ὁ	air
ἄθεος, -ον	without god
αἰσχρός, -ά, -όν	shameful, disgraceful
αἰσχρότης, -ητος, ἡ	shamefulness, shameful conduct
αἰχμαλωσία, -ας, ἡ	captivity
αἰχμαλωτεύω	take captive, capture
ἀκάθαρτος, -ον	impure, unclean [cultic or moral]
ἄκαρπος, -ον	unfruitful; useless
ἀκριβῶς	diligently, carefully, well
ἀκροβυστία, -ας, ἡ	foreskin; uncircumcision; one who is uncircumcised

▷ List 10 1×

ἀκρογωνιαῖος, -αία, -ον	at the extreme angle/corner, (*subst*) foundation, cornerstone	
ἀληθεύω	tell/speak the truth	
ἅλυσις, ἁλύσεως, ἡ	chain, [extended sense] imprisonment	
ἀναγινώσκω	read (aloud)	▸
ἀνακεφαλαιόω	(*mid*) sum up	
ἀνανεόομαι	renew	
ἀναστρέφω	(*act*) return, go back; (*mid*) conduct oneself, live	▸
ἀναστροφή, -ῆς, ἡ	conduct, way of life	
ἄνεμος, ἀνέμου, ὁ	wind	
ἀνεξιχνίαστος, -ον	beyond exploration, inscrutable	

▷ List 11 1×

ἀνέχω	(*mid +gen/acc obj*) bear with, tolerate, put up with	
ἀνήκω	be proper/fitting	
ἀνθίστημι	resist, oppose, withstand (+*dat obj*)	▷
ἀνθρωπάρεσκος, -ον	(*subst*) people pleaser	
ἀνίημι	let go, loose	▷
ἄνοιξις, ἀνοίξεως, ἡ	opening [activity]	
ἀντί	(+*gen*) instead of, in place of	
ἀξίως	worthily, in a manner worthy of	
ἀπαλγέω	put away sorrow, become callous; be disheartened/despondent	
ἅπας, ἅπασα, ἅπαν	whole, all; (*subst*) everyone, all, everything	

▷ List 12 1×

ἀπατάω	deceive, mislead	
ἀπάτη, -ης, ἡ	deception, deceit	
ἀπειλή, -ῆς, ἡ	threat	
ἁπλότης, -ητος, ἡ	sincerity	
ἀποκαλύπτω	reveal, disclose	▷
ἀποκαταλλάσσω	reconcile	
ἀποκρύπτω	hide, conceal, keep hidden	▷
ἀρραβών, -ῶνος, ὁ	down payment, deposit, pledge	
ἄρχων, ἄρχοντος, ὁ	ruler; official	
ἀσέλγεια, -είας, ἡ	licentiousness, excessive sensuality	

▷ List 13 1×

ἄσοφος, -ον	unwise, foolish
ἀσωτία, -ας, ἡ	recklessness, dissipation, debauchery
αὔξησις, -ήσεως, ἡ	growth, increase
ἄφεσις, ἀφέσεως, ἡ	release; forgiveness (of)
ἁφή, -ῆς, ἡ	joint, ligament
ἀφθαρσία, -ας, ἡ	incorruptibility, immortality
ἄφρων, -ον	senseless, foolish
βάθος, -ους, τό	depth
βάπτισμα, -ίσματος, τό	baptism, (ceremonial) plunging/washing
βέλος, -ους, τό	arrow

▷ List 14 1×

βλασφημία, -ας, ἡ	slander, defamation, reviling
βουλή, -ῆς, ἡ	intention, motive; decision, plan, purpose
γνῶσις, γνώσεως, ἡ	knowledge [understanding/comprehension or that which is known]
γονεύς, -έως, ὁ	parent
γόνυ, γόνατος, τό	knee
διαθήκη, -ης, ἡ	will, testament; covenant
διακονία, -ας, ἡ	service, serving; (ministerial) service, ministry
διδασκαλία, -ας, ἡ	teaching, instruction [activity or content]
δόγμα, -ατος, τό	decree, ordinance
δοκιμάζω	examine, evaluate; determine, put to the test

▷ List 15 1×

δόμα, -ατος, τό	gift
δουλεύω	be a slave; slave (for), serve (+*dat obj*)
δῶρον, δώρου, τό	gift [general or votive]
ἐγκακέω	lose heart, be discouraged
εἰδωλολάτρης, -ου, ὁ	image worshiper, idolater
ἐκλέγομαι	choose; select
ἐκπορεύομαι	go/come out
ἐλάχιστος, -ίστη, -ον	least, smallest [in status, value, or size]
ἔλεος, ἐλέους, τό	compassion, mercy
ἐλεύθερος, -έρα, -ον	free

▷ List 16 1×

ἐνδείκνυμι	(*mid*) show, demonstrate, exhibit	▷
ἔνδοξος, -ον	distinguished, highly esteemed, notable	
ἐνδυναμόω	(*trans act*) strengthen; (*intrans mid*) become strong	
ἐξαγοράζω	(*act*) buy up/off, redeem; (*mid*) take advantage of	
ἐξισχύω	be able/strong enough/in a position to	
ἐπέρχομαι	come (up)on, approach	
ἐπιδύω	(*intrans*) set (up)on	
ἐπιφαύσκω	shine out	▷
ἐπιχορηγία, -ας, ἡ	assistance, help	
ἐποικοδομέω	build (up)on	

▷ List 17 1×

ἐργασία, -ας, ἡ	work, labor, activity, [extended sense] business, trade; profit
ἔσω	inside, within
ἑτοιμασία, -ας, ἡ	readiness, preparation
εὖ	well
εὐαγγελιστής, -οῦ, ὁ	proclaimer of good news, evangelist
εὐάρεστος, -ον	pleasing
εὐλογητός, -ή, -όν	blessed, praised
εὐλογία, -ας, ἡ	praise; blessing; gift
εὔνοια, -οίας, ἡ	good attitude, willingness
εὔσπλαγχνος, -ον	tenderhearted, compassionate

▷ List 18 1×

εὐτραπελία, -ας, ἡ	coarse jesting, obscene speech
εὐχαριστία, -ας, ἡ	thankfulness, gratitude; thanksgiving
εὐωδία, -ας, ἡ	sweet aroma, fragrance
Ἐφέσιος, -ία, -ον	Ephesian
Ἔφεσος, -έσου, ἡ	Ephesus
ἡλικία, -ας, ἡ	maturity; stature [physical]
ἥλιος, -ίου, ὁ	sun
θάλπω	comfort, care for
θεμέλιος, -ίου, ὁ	foundation
θεμελιόω	lay a foundation, found, establish

▷ List 19	1×
θυμός, -οῦ, ὁ	desire, passion; anger, wrath
θυρεός, -οῦ, ὁ	shield
θυσία, -ας, ἡ	sacrifice, offering
θώραξ, -ακος, ὁ	breastplate; chest
καθαρίζω	cleanse, make clean
καθεύδω	be sleeping/asleep
κακία, -ας, ἡ	wickedness; malice; trouble, misfortune
κάμπτω	(*trans*) bend; (*intrans*) bend
καταβολή, -ῆς, ἡ	foundation
καταλαμβάνω	grasp, attain; understand, realize ▷

▷ List 20	1×
καταλείπω	leave (behind); cause to be left over
καταντάω	come (to), arrive (at), [extended sense] attain (to)
καταργέω	make useless; make ineffective, invalidate, nullify; set aside, eliminate
καταρτισμός, -οῦ, ὁ	equipping, training
κατενώπιον	(+*gen*) before, opposite, in front of
κατεργάζομαι	do; produce, bring about
κατοικητήριον, -ίου, τό	dwelling, abode
κατώτερος, -έρα, -ον	lower [*comp* of κάτω]
καυχάομαι	boast (about)
κενός, -ή, -όν	empty [of content]; empty, fruitless; in vain, for nothing

▷ List 21 1×

κληρόω	(*act*) appoint by lot; (*mid*) obtain by lot
κλυδωνίζομαι	(*pass*) be tossed about by waves
κομίζω	(*act*) bring; (*mid*) receive
κοπιάω	be weary/tired; labor, toil
κοσμοκράτωρ, -ορος, ὁ	world ruler
κραταιόω	(*mid*) become strong
κραυγή, -ῆς, ἡ	shout(ing), cry(ing) out
κρυφῇ	in secret, secretly
κυβεία, -ας, ἡ	trickery
κυριότης, -ητος, ἡ	lordship, dominion, ruling power

▷ List 22 1×

λουτρόν, -οῦ, τό	bath, washing
λυπέω	(*act*) cause grief/sorrow; (*mid*) grieve, be sad/distressed
μακροθυμία, -ας, ἡ	patience; forbearance
μακροχρόνιος, -ον	long-lasting, long-lived
μανθάνω	learn
μαρτύρομαι	testify; insist, implore
ματαιότης, -ητος, ἡ	futility, purposelessness
μάχαιρα, -αίρης, ἡ	dagger, short sword
μέγεθος, -έθους, τό	greatness
μεθύσκω	(*mid*) get drunk

➤

▷ List 23 1×

μεσότοιχον, -οίχου, τό	dividing wall
μεταδίδωμι	share, give a share of, impart
μέχρι	(*conj*) until; (*prep +gen*) until; as far as; to the point of
μῆκος, μήκους, τό	length
μιμητής, -οῦ, ὁ	imitator
μνεία, -ας, ἡ	remembrance, memory; mention
μνημονεύω	remember (*+gen/acc obj*)
μωρολογία, -ας, ἡ	foolish talk
νήπιος, -ία, -ον	(*subst*) infant; little child
νουθεσία, -ας, ἡ	instruction, warning, admonition

▷ List 24 1×

νυνί	now, at this time
οἰκεῖος, -εία, -ον	in/of the house, (*subst pl*) household members
οἶνος, οἴνου, ὁ	wine
ὀργίζω	(*mid*) be(come) angry
ὁσιότης, -ητος, ἡ	piety, devoutness
ὀσμή, -ῆς, ἡ	smell, odor, fragrance
ὀσφῦς, -ύος, ἡ	waist, loins
ὀφείλω	owe, be indebted to; be obligated, ought; have to
ὀφθαλμοδουλία, -ας, ἡ	eye-service [service done to impress others]
παιδεία, -ας, ἡ	instruction, discipline, training

▹ List 25 1×

παλαιός, -ά, -όν	old
πάλη, -ης, ἡ	wrestling, struggle
πανουργία, -ας, ἡ	trickery, craftiness
πάροικος, -οίκου, ὁ	foreign, alien; (*subst*) stranger; (resident) foreigner
παροργίζω	make angry
παροργισμός, -οῦ, ὁ	anger
παρρησιάζομαι	speak freely/boldly
πατριά, -ᾶς, ἡ	family, clan
παύω	(*trans act*) make stop/cease; (*intrans mid*) stop, cease
πεποίθησις, -ήσεως, ἡ	trust, confidence

▹ List 26 1×

περιζώννυμι/ περιζωννύω	(*act*) gird about; (*mid*) gird oneself
περικεφαλαία, -ας, ἡ	helmet
περιποίησις, -ήσεως, ἡ	keeping safe, preservation; possessing, possession
περισσεύω	(*intrans*) abound (in), overflow, be left over; (*trans*) cause (something) to abound, increase
περιτομή, -ῆς, ἡ	circumcision; one who is circumcised
περιφέρω	carry about/around
πικρία, -ας, ἡ	bitterness
πλάνη, -ης, ἡ	error, deceit
πλάτος, -ους, τό	breadth, width
πλεονέκτης, -ου, ὁ	greedy person

▷ List 27 1×

πλήν	nevertheless, but, only; (*prep* +*gen*) except ▸
πλησίον	(+*gen*) near; (*subst*) neighbor
πλούσιος, -ία, -ον	rich, wealthy; rich (in), abounding (in)
ποίημα, -ήματος, τό	[anything made or done] work, workmanship, creation
ποιμήν, ποιμένος, ὁ	shepherd
πολιτεία, -ας, ἡ	citizenship; behavior/way of life [of a respectable citizen]
πολυποίκιλος, -ον	much variegated/diversified, manifold
πονηρία, -ας, ἡ	wickedness, maliciousness
πορνεία, -ας, ἡ	sexual immorality, fornication
πόρνος, -ου, ὁ	sexually immoral person, fornicator

▷ List 28 1×

πράσσω	do, accomplish, perform
πραΰτης, -ητος, τό	humility, gentleness
πρέπω	(*impers*) it is fitting/appropriate/right
πρεσβεύω	be/serve as an ambassador
προγράφω	write beforehand/in advance
προελπίζω	hope beforehand/first ▸
προετοιμάζω	prepare beforehand
προσκαρτέρησις, -ήσεως, ἡ	perseverance, persistence
προσκολλάω	(*mid*) stick/cleave to, join with
προσφορά, -ᾶς, ἡ	sacrificing, offering [activity]; sacrifice, offering [item brought]

▷ List 29 1×

προσωπολημψία, -ας, ἡ	partiality
πρότερος, -έρα, -ον	former, earlier
προτίθημι	(*mid*) display publicly; set forth, intend, plan
πυρόω	burn (up), set on fire [literal or metaphorical]
πώρωσις, -ώσεως, ἡ	obtuseness, hardness
ῥιζόω	(*mid*) take root; (*pass*) be planted ▷
ῥυτίς, -ίδος, ἡ	wrinkle
σαπρός, -ά, -όν	bad, rotten
σβέννυμι	extinguish, put out ▷
σκοτόω	(*mid*) be(come) darkened [literal or figurative]

▷ List 30 1×

σοφός, -ή, -όν	wise; skillful
σπίλος, -ου, ὁ	spot, blemish
σπουδάζω	strive, make every effort (to), be eager (to)
σταυρός, -οῦ, ὁ	cross
συγκαθίζω	(*trans*) cause to sit down with; (*intrans*) sit down together ▷
συγκληρονόμος, -ον	(*subst*) co-heir
συγκοινωνέω	participate (in), take part (in), share (with)
συζωοποιέω	make alive together with ▷
συμβιβάζω	bring/fit together, unite
συμπολίτης, -ητος, ἡ	fellow citizen

▷ List 31 1×

σύνδεσμος, -έσμου, ὁ	[that which binds together] binding, bond
συνεγείρω	raise (someone/something) (up) with
σύνεσις, -έσεως, ἡ	understanding, comprehension [mental faculty]; insight [content of what is understood]
συνίημι/συνίω	understand, comprehend
συνοικοδομέω	build together
σύσσωμος, -ον	belonging to the same body
σωτήρ, -ῆρος, ὁ	savior, deliverer
σωτήριον, -ίου, τό	salvation, deliverance
ταπεινοφροσύνη, -ῆς, ἡ	humility
τέλειος, -εία, -ον	complete, perfect, mature [of character or behavior]

▷ List 32 1×

τιμάω	honor; set a price
τρόμος, -ου, ὁ	trembling
Τυχικός, -οῦ, ὁ	Tychicus
υἱοθεσία, -ας, ἡ	adoption
ὕμνος, -ου, ὁ	hymn, song of praise
ὑπερεκπερισσοῦ	beyond the highest degree/extent, infinitely beyond, beyond all measure
ὑποδέω	(*mid*) put on [+*acc* of footwear], put footwear on [+*acc* of body part]
φθείρω	corrupt, ruin, destroy
φραγμός, -οῦ, ὁ	fence, hedge, [extended sense] partition/division
φρόνησις, -ήσεως, ἡ	understanding, discernment, insight

▷ **List 33**	1 ×
φύσις, -εως, τό	nature [inherent/basic qualities, features, or character]
χαριτόω	show grace (to), bestow favor (on)
χειροποίητος, -ον	made by hand
χρηστός, -ή, -όν	serviceable; good; kind
χρηστότης, -ητος, ἡ	kindness, goodness
ψάλλω	sing, make music
ψαλμός, -οῦ, ὁ	psalm, song of praise [in general or specifically in reference to OT psalms]
ψεῦδος, ψεύδους, τό	lie, falsehood
ᾠδή, -ῆς, ἡ	song

PHILIPPIANS

▷ List 1	10 to 2×
ἄμεμπτος, -ον	blameless, faultless
δέησις, δεήσεως, ἡ	entreaty; prayer, petition
δεσμός, -οῦ, ὁ	(*sg*) binding, impediment; (*pl*) bonds, chains, [extended sense] imprisonment
ἡγέομαι	consider, regard
καταλαμβάνω	grasp, attain; seize, secure ▷
κοινωνία, -ας, ἡ	(close) fellowship; participation, sharing; generosity
περισσεύω	(*intrans*) abound (in), overflow, be left over; (*trans*) cause (something) to abound, increase
πλήν	nevertheless, but, only; (*prep +gen*) except ▷
ὑπερέχω	surpass, be superior to, excel, (+*gen*) be better/more important than
φρονέω	think

▷ List 2	2×
ἀναγκαῖος, -αία, -ον	necessary, important
ἀπολογία, -ας, ἡ	defense [a speech or the act of making a defense]
ἀπώλεια, -είας, ἡ	destruction; waste
ἀσθενέω	be sick; be weak
γνωρίζω	make known, inform; know
Ἑβραῖος, -ίου, ὁ	Hebrew [ethnicity]
ἐλπίζω	hope (for); expect
ἐνεργέω	(*intrans*) be at work/active; (*trans*) work, produce
ἔπαινος, ἐπαίνου, ὁ	praise, recognition, commendation
Ἐπαφρόδιτος, -ίτου, ὁ	Epaphroditus

▷ List 3 2×

ἐπίγειος, -ον	earthly
ἐπιζητέω	seek after, search for; seek, want
ἐπιποθέω	long for, strongly desire
ἐριθεία, -ᾶς, ἡ	selfish ambition
εὐδοκία, -ας, ἡ	goodwill; favor
ζημία, -ας, ἡ	loss
θυσία, -ας, ἡ	sacrifice, offering
καταγγέλλω	announce, proclaim, declare
καύχημα, -ήματος, τό	boast [expression of pride or basis for pride]
κενός, -ή, -όν	empty [of content]; empty, fruitless; in vain, for nothing

▷ List 4 2×

κέρδος, -ους, τό	gain, profit
λειτουργία, -ας, ἡ	service [cultic or generic]
λύπη, -ης, ἡ	grief, sadness; pain
μανθάνω	learn
μεριμνάω	worry (about), be anxious; care for, be concerned about
μέχρι	(*conj*) until; (*prep +gen*) until; as far as; to the point of
μορφή, -ῆς, ἡ	(outward) form, appearance
παρουσία, -ας, ἡ	presence; arrival, coming
περιτομή, -ῆς, ἡ	circumcision; one who is circumcised
προκοπή, -ῆς, ἡ	progress, advancement

▶

▹ List 5 2×

σκοπέω	pay attention to, examine; look to, consider
σπλάγχνον, -ου, τό	[always *pl*] entrails; seat of emotion [similar to English's "heart"]; compassion, affection
σταυρός, -οῦ, ὁ	cross
στήκω	stand; stand firm
συγχαίρω	rejoice (with)
συναθλέω	struggle/contend together, struggle/contend with (+*dat obj*)
συνεργός, -όν	helpful, contributing; [only *subst* in NT] fellow worker
ταπεινόω	bring low; humble [positive], humiliate [negative]
ταχέως	quickly, without delay; soon
Τιμόθεος, -έου, ὁ	Timothy

▹ List 6 2 to 1×

ἁγνός, -ή, -όν	pure
ἁγνῶς	purely, sincerely
ἀγών, -ῶνος, ὁ	(athletic) contest; struggle
ἀδημονέω	be troubled/distressed
αἱρέω	(*mid*) choose; prefer
αἴσθησις, -ήσεως, ἡ	perception, insight, discernment
αἰσχύνη, -ης, ἡ	shame, dishonor; [sense/experience of] shame; shameful deed
αἰσχύνω	(*mid*) be ashamed
Φιλιππήσιος, -ίου, ὁ	Philippian
χαρίζομαι	give graciously/freely; forgive

▷ **List 7** 1×

αἴτημα, -ήματος, τό	request
ἀκαιρέομαι	have no opportunity
ἀκέραιος, -ον	unmixed, pure; innocent, pure
ἀληθής, -ές	true, trustworthy; real
ἄλυπος, -ον	free from anxiety
ἄμωμος, -ον	unblemished; blameless
ἀναθάλλω	make flourish again, revive
ἀναλύω	(*trans*) undo, untie; (*intrans*) depart; return
ἀναπληρόω	fill (up); supply; fulfill
ἀντίκειμαι	oppose (+*dat obj*)

▷ **List 8** 1×

ἄνω	above; up(ward)
ἀξίως	worthily, in a manner worthy of
ἅπαξ	once; once and for all
ἄπειμι	be absent/away
ἀπεκδέχομαι	await
ἀπέχω	(*trans act*) receive in full
ἀποβαίνω	move off, disembark; turn out, lead to, result in ▸
ἀποκαλύπτω	reveal, disclose
ἀποκαραδοκία, -ας, ἡ	eager expectation
ἀπουσία, -ας, ἡ	absence

▹ List 9 1×

ἀπρόσκοπος, -ον	without offense, blameless; inoffensive
ἀρετή, -ῆς, ἡ	excellence [often referring to character or civic performance], virtue
ἁρπαγμός, -οῦ, ὁ	something used for one's own advantage ▸
ἀσφαλής, -ές	certain, sure, dependable, safe
αὐτάρκης, -ες	self-sufficient, content
ἀφόβως	without fear
ἀφοράω	fix one's eyes (on); determine, see ▸
βεβαίωσις, -ώσεως, ἡ	confirmation, guarantee
Βενιαμ(ε)ίν, ὁ (*indecl*)	Benjamin
βίβλος, -ου, ἡ	written account, book

▹ List 10 1×

βούλομαι	want, desire; intend, plan
βραβεῖον, -είου, τό	prize, award
γένος, -ους, τό	people group, family; offspring, descendant; kind, class
γνήσιος, -ία, -ον	legitimate, true [validity of family membership]; genuine
γνησίως	genuinely, sincerely
γνῶσις, γνώσεως, ἡ	knowledge [understanding/comprehension or that which is known]
γογγυσμός, -οῦ, ὁ	discreet talk; murmuring, grumbling
γόνυ, γόνατος, τό	knee
δεκτός, -ή, -όν	acceptable, pleasing; accepted, welcome; favorable
διάκονος, -όνου, ὁ/ἡ	servant, helper; ministerial attendant ["deacon(ess)"]

▷ List 11 — 1×

διαλογισμός, -οῦ, ὁ	reasoning, thought; dispute
διαστρέφω	turn aside, mislead; make crooked, distort ➤
διαφέρω	be unlike, differ; differ in worth, surpass, be worth more (than)
διότι	because, since; for; because of this
δίς	twice
δοκιμάζω	examine, evaluate; determine, put to the test; approve
δοκιμή, -ῆς, ἡ	testing; (proven) character; proof
δόμα, -ατος, τό	gift
δόσις, -εως, ἡ	giving; gift
δουλεύω	be a slave; slave (for), serve (+*dat obj*)

▷ List 12 — 1×

ἐγγύς	near [spatial or temporal]
εἰλικρινής, -ές	pure, sincere
ἐλεέω	have compassion (on), show mercy to
ἐμαυτοῦ, -ῆς	myself, my (own) [when *gen*]
ἐνάρχομαι	begin
ἔνδειξις, ἐνδείξεως, ἡ	indication, demonstration
ἐνδυναμόω	(*trans act*) strengthen; (*intrans mid*) become strong
ἐνέργεια, -είας, ἡ	working, action, activity
ἔντιμος, -ον	honored, distinguished; valuable, precious
ἐξανάστασις, -άσεως, ἡ	resurrection

▷ List 13 1×

ἐξαυτῆς	immediately, at once
ἐξομολογέω	(*mid*) confess, admit; profess, acknowledge
ἐπειδή	when, after; since, because
ἐπεκτείνομαι	stretch out for, reach out toward
ἐπέχω	hold on to; observe, pay attention to (+*dat obj*)
ἐπίγνωσις, -ώσεως, ἡ	knowledge
ἐπιεικής, -ές	reasonable, fair, yielding
ἐπιθυμία, -ας, ἡ	desire, longing; lust, craving
ἐπιλανθάνομαι	(+*gen/acc obj*) forget; neglect, ignore
ἐπιμένω	remain, stay; persist, continue

▷ List 14 1×

ἐπιπόθητος, -ον	longed for, desired
ἐπίσκοπος, -όπου, ὁ	overseer, guardian
ἐπιτελέω	finish; complete, accomplish, fulfill (a duty)
ἐπιχορηγία, -ας, ἡ	assistance, help
ἐπουράνιος, -ον	heavenly
ἐργάτης, -ου, ὁ	worker, laborer; doer
ἔρις, -ιδος, ἡ	strife, contention
ἑτέρως	otherwise, differently
εὐάρεστος, -ον	pleasing
Εὐοδία, -ας, ἡ	Euodia

▷ List 15 1×

εὔφημος, -ον	praiseworthy, commendable
εὐχαριστέω	thank, give thanks, be thankful
εὐχαριστία, -ας, ἡ	thankfulness, gratitude; thanksgiving
εὐψυχέω	be heartened/glad
εὐωδία, -ας, ἡ	sweet aroma, fragrance
ἐχθρός, -ά, -όν	hated; hostile; (*subst*) enemy
ζῆλος, ζήλου/ζήλους, ὁ/τό	zeal; jealousy
ζημιόω	(*mid*) lose, suffer loss
Θεσσαλονίκη, -ης, ἡ	Thessalonica
ἴσος, -η, -ον	equal, same

▷ List 16 1×

ἰσόψυχος, -ον	of like soul/mind
ἰσχύω	be strong/powerful/able; prevail
καίπερ	although
Καῖσαρ, Καίσαρος, ὁ	Caesar
καλῶς	well, appropriately, effectively; correctly
κάμπτω	(*trans*) bend; (*intrans*) bend
καταντάω	come (to), arrive (at), [extended sense] attain (to)
κατατομή, -ῆς, ἡ	mutilation
καταχθόνιος, -ον	under the earth
κατεργάζομαι	do; produce, bring about

▷ List 17 1×

καυχάομαι	boast (about)
κεῖμαι	be lying/reclining/resting; exist for, be set for
κενοδοξία, -ας, ἡ	vanity, conceit
κενόω	(*trans act*) make empty; render void, make (something) nothing
κερδαίνω	gain ▷
Κλήμης, Κλήμεντος, ὁ	Clement
κλῆσις, κλήσεως, ἡ	call, calling, invitation
κοιλία, -ας, ἡ	stomach; womb; heart [figurative, representing one's inner desires and feelings]
κοινωνέω	have a share, take part in; share
κοπιάω	be weary/tired; labor, toil

▷ List 18 1×

κρείττων, κρεῖττον / κρείσσων, κρεῖσσον	better, superior [rank or value]
κύων, κυνός, ὁ	dog [also, of persons, used as an invective]
λατρεύω	serve, worship [the carrying out of religious duties] (+*dat obj*)
λειτουργός, -οῦ, ὁ	minister, [cultic] servant
λῆμψις, λήμψεως, ἡ	receiving
Μακεδονία, -ας, ἡ	Macedonia
μάλιστα	most of all, especially
μάρτυς, μάρτυρος, ὁ	witness
μεγαλύνω	make large/great; magnify, exalt, glorify
μεγάλως	greatly

▷ List 19 1×

μενοῦνγε	on the contrary; ἀλλὰ μενοῦνγε but more than that
μετασχηματίζω	(*act*) change the form (of something/someone); (*mid*) change one's form, disguise oneself
μνεία, -ας, ἡ	remembrance, memory; mention
μυέω	initiate (into the mysteries)
ναί	yes
νόημα, νοήματος, τό	thought, intention, purpose; understanding, mind
νοῦς, νοός, ὁ	mind; understanding, intellect; thought
οἰκτιρμός, -οῦ, ὁ	compassion, mercy
οἴομαι	think, suppose, expect
οἷος, οἵα, οἷον	such as, of what sort

▷ List 20 1×

ὀκνηρός, -ά, -όν	idle, sluggish; bothersome
ὀκταήμερος, -ον	on the eighth day
ὁμοίωμα, -ώματος, τό	likeness
ὀπίσω	behind, back; (*prep +gen*) behind; after [temporal or spatial]
ὀσμή, -ῆς, ἡ	smell, odor, fragrance
πάθημα, -ήματος, τό	suffering; emotion, passion
παραβολεύομαι	risk, expose to danger (+*dat obj*)
παράκλησις, -ήσεως, ἡ	encouragement, exhortation; comfort, consolation
παραμένω	stay; continue, persevere [in a state or condition]
παραμύθιον, -ίου, τό	comfort, consolation

▷ List 21 1×

παραπλήσιος, -ία, -ον	[*neut* as *adv*] close to, coming near to
παρρησία, -ας, ἡ	plainness; openness; boldness
πεινάω	hunger, be hungry [physically or metaphorically]
πεποίθησις, -ήσεως, ἡ	trust, confidence
περισσοτέρως	(*comp*) (even) more; (*superl*) especially
πλεονάζω	(*intrans*) increase, abound; (*trans*) (cause to) increase
πλοῦτος, πλούτου, ὁ/τό	wealth, riches; abundance
πολίτευμα, -εύματος, τό	citizenship; state; government
πολιτεύω	(*mid*) live as a citizen, [extended sense] conduct oneself, live one's life
πολλάκις	often, many times

▷ List 22 1×

ποτέ (*encl*)	when, at some time; formerly, once; [+ἤδη] at last
πραιτώριον, -ίου, τό	the praetorium
πράσσω	do, accomplish, perform
προσδέχομαι	receive, welcome; wait for, await, expect
προσευχή, -ῆς, ἡ	prayer
προσφιλής, -ές	pleasing, lovely
πρόφασις, -άσεως, ἡ	pretext, excuse
πτύρω	(*pass*) be frightened/terrified (by)
πώς (*encl*)	somehow, perhaps, in any way, at all
σεμνός, -ή, -όν	worthy of reverence/respect

▷ List 23	1×
σκολιός, -ά, -όν	crooked, bent, [extended sense] perverse, unjust
σκοπός, -οῦ, ὁ	goal, aim
σκύβαλον, -άλου, τό	dung, [extended sense] refuse
σπένδω	pour (something) out as a drink offering
σπουδαίως	with haste; eagerly; (*comp*) σπουδαιοτέρως all the more eager
στέφανος, -άνου, ὁ	wreath, crown
στοιχέω	be in line (with), conform (to), agree (with)
συγκοινωνέω	participate (in), take part (in), share (with)
συγκοινωνός, -οῦ, ὁ	partner, participant
σύζυγος, -ον	yoked together, (*subst*) comrade, companion

▷ List 24	1×
συλλαμβάνω	(*act*) capture, seize; (*mid +dat obj*) assist, help
συμμιμητής, -οῦ, ὁ	fellow imitator
συμμορφίζομαι	(*pass*) be conformed (to)
σύμμορφος, -ον	of the same form as, resembling
σύμψυχος, -ον	of one mind, united
συνέχω	enclose, surround; hold, confine; constrain, affect
Συντύχη, -ης, ἡ	Syntyche
συστρατιώτης, -ου, ὁ	fellow soldier
σχῆμα, σχήματος, τό	appearance, form, shape
σωτήρ, -ῆρος, ὁ	savior, deliverer

▷ List 25 1×

ταπεινοφροσύνη, -ῆς, ἡ	humility
ταπείνωσις, -ώσεως, ἡ	humiliation; low status, humble station
τέλειος, -εία, -ον	complete, perfect, mature [of character or behavior]
τελειόω	complete, finish; bring (something) to its goal/conclusion; perfect
τολμάω	dare, bring oneself (to), have the courage (to)
τρέχω	run
τρόμος, -ου, ὁ	trembling
τρόπος, -ου, ὁ	manner, way
τύπος, -ου, ὁ	pattern, design
ὑπακούω	obey

▷ List 26 1×

ὑπερυψόω	highly exalt
ὑπήκοος, -ον	obedient
ὑποτάσσω	subject, subordinate
ὑστερέω	(*intrans mid*) be in need; come/fall short (of); be lacking
ὑστέρημα, -ήματος, τό	need, deficiency; lack, shortcoming
ὑστέρησις, -ήσεως, ἡ	need, lack, poverty
φαίνω	(*act*) shine; (*mid*) appear
φανερός, -ά, -όν	visible, plain, evident, known; (*subst*) the open
φθάνω	precede; arrive, reach, overtake; attain
φθόνος, -ου, ὁ	envy

▷ List 27	1×
Φίλιπποι, -ίππων, οἱ	Philippi
φρουρέω	keep watch; guard, protect; detain, confine
φυλή, -ῆς, ἡ	tribe; people group
φωστήρ, -ῆρος, τό	that which gives light; (luminous) celestial body, star; radiance, splendor
χορτάζω	(*intrans mid*) eat one's fill; be satisfied

COLOSSIANS

▷ List 1 — 4 to 3×

ἀναγινώσκω	read (aloud)
αὐξάνω/αὔξω	(*trans*) make grow/increase; (*intrans*) grow, increase
γνωρίζω	make known, inform; know
διάκονος, -όνου, ὁ/ἡ	servant, helper; ministerial attendant ["deacon(ess)"]
ἐπίγνωσις, -ώσεως, ἡ	knowledge
εὐχαριστέω	thank, give thanks, be thankful
κτίζω	create
Λαοδίκεια, -είας, ἡ	Laodicea
μυστήριον, -ίου, τό	mystery, secret
περιτομή, -ῆς, ἡ	circumcision; one who is circumcised

▷ List 2 — 3 to 2×

ἀγωνίζομαι	exert effort, strive; struggle, fight
ἀδικέω	(*intrans*) do wrong, be in the wrong; (*trans*) wrong; injure
ἀκροβυστία, -ας, ἡ	foreskin; uncircumcision; one who is uncircumcised
ἄνω	above; up(ward)
ἀόρατος, -ον	invisible
ἀπεκδύομαι	strip/take off of oneself
ἀποκαταλλάσσω	reconcile
εἰκών, εἰκόνος, ἡ	image, likeness [crafted or non-crafted]
ταπεινοφροσύνη, -ῆς, ἡ	humility
χαρίζομαι	give graciously/freely; forgive

▷ List 3 2×

ἐνδύω	(*act*) dress/clothe (someone); (*mid*) put on, wear
ἐνέργεια, -είας, ἡ	working, action, activity
Ἐπαφρᾶς, Ἐπαφρᾶ, ὁ	Epaphras
εὐχαριστία, -ας, ἡ	thankfulness, gratitude; thanksgiving
καρποφορέω	bear fruit
κτίσις, -εως, τό	creation [act or product]
μακροθυμία, -ας, ἡ	patience; forbearance
νουθετέω	warn, instruct, admonish
νυνί	now, at this time
ὀργή, -ῆς, ἡ	anger; wrath

▷ List 4 2×

παράπτωμα, -ώματος, τό	transgression
πλήρωμα, -ώματος, τό	that which fills, content; that which completes, complement; fullness
πλοῦτος, πλούτου, ὁ/τό	wealth, riches; abundance
πνευματικός, -ή, -όν	spiritual
ποτέ (*encl*)	when, at some time; formerly, once
προσευχή, -ῆς, ἡ	prayer
πρωτότοκος, -ον	firstborn [literal or figurative]
σταυρός, -οῦ, ὁ	cross
στοιχεῖον, -είου, τό	(basic) element, (fundamental) part, elemental force/spirit
συμβιβάζω	bring/fit together, unite

▷ List 5 — 2 to 1×

ἀγών, -ῶνος, ὁ	(athletic) contest; struggle
ᾄδω	sing
ἀθυμέω	become dispirited, lose heart
αἰσχρολογία, -ας, ἡ	obscene speech, foul language
σύνδεσμος, -έσμου, ὁ	[that which binds together] binding, bond
σύνδουλος, -ούλου, ὁ	fellow slave
συνεγείρω	raise (someone/something) (up) with
σύνεσις, -έσεως, ἡ	understanding, comprehension [mental faculty]; insight [content of what is understood]
τέλειος, -εία, -ον	complete, perfect, mature [of character or behavior]
ὑπακούω	obey

▷ List 6 — 1×

ἀκαθαρσία, -ας, ἡ	uncleanness, filth; immorality
ἅλας, -ατος, τό	salt
ἅμα	at the same time; together; (*prep +dat*) together with
ἄμωμος, -ον	unblemished; blameless
ἀνακαινόω	renew
ἀνέγκλητος, -ον	irreproachable, blameless
ἀνέχω	(*mid +gen/acc obj*) bear with, tolerate, put up with
ἀνεψιός, -οῦ, ὁ	cousin
ἀνήκω	(*impers*) it is proper/fitting
ἀνθρωπάρεσκος, -ον	(*subst*) people pleaser

▷ **List 7**	**1×**
ἀνταναπληρόω	fill up, supplement
ἀνταπόδοσις, -όσεως, ἡ	repayment, reward
ἀξίως	worthily, in a manner worthy of
ἀπαλλοτριόω	alienate, estrange, separate
ἀπάτη, -ης, ἡ	deception, deceit
ἀπείθεια, -είας, ἡ	disobedience
ἄπειμι	be absent/away
ἀπέκδυσις, -ύσεως, ἡ	removal, putting/stripping off
ἁπλότης, -ητος, ἡ	sincerity
ἀπόκειμαι	lay/put away [for safekeeping], reserve

▷ **List 8**	**1×**
ἀποκρύπτω	hide, conceal, keep hidden ➤
ἀπόκρυφος, -ον	hidden
ἀπολαμβάνω	receive ➤
ἀπολύτρωσις, -ώσεως, ἡ	release, liberation, deliverance, redemption
ἀποτίθημι	(*mid*) put away, lay aside
ἀπόχρησις, -ήσεως, ἡ	consuming, consumption, using up
ἅπτω	(*mid +gen obj*) touch, hold, cling to
ἀρεσκεία, -ας, ἡ	desire to please
Ἀρίσταρχος, -άρχου, ὁ	Aristarchus
ἀρτύω	prepare, make ready, [of food] season

▷ List 9 1×

Ἄρχιππος, -ίππου, ὁ	Archippus
ἀσπασμός, -οῦ, ὁ	greeting
αὔξησις, -ήσεως, ἡ	growth, increase
ἀφειδία, -ας, ἡ	unsparing/severe treatment
ἄφεσις, ἀφέσεως, ἡ	release; forgiveness (of)
ἁφή, -ῆς, ἡ	joint, ligament
ἀχειροποίητος, -ον	not made/done by hand
βάπτισμα, -ίσματος, τό	baptism, (ceremonial) plunging/washing <TH only>
βαπτισμός, -οῦ, ὁ	baptism, (ceremonial) plunging/washing <NA/UBS, SBL only>
βάρβαρος, -ον	foreign-speaking, foreign; (*subst*) foreigner, non-Hellene, non-Greek-speaking person

▷ List 10 1×

Βαρναβᾶς, Βαρναβᾶ, ὁ	Barnabas
βεβαιόω	confirm, establish; guarantee [legal term]
βλασφημία, -ας, ἡ	slander, defamation, reviling
βραβεύω	direct, control, rule
βρῶσις, βρώσεως, ὁ	food; eating, consumption
γέ (*encl*)	indeed, even; yet, at least, though
γεύομαι	taste, partake (+*gen/acc obj*)
γνῶσις, γνώσεως, ἡ	knowledge [understanding/comprehension or that which is known]
γονεύς, -έως, ὁ	parent
γρηγορέω	be (fully) awake/alert; be watchful/on the alert

▷ List 11 1×

δειγματίζω	make an example of, disgrace
δεσμός, -οῦ, ὁ	(*sg*) binding, impediment; (*pl*) bonds, chains, [extended sense] imprisonment
δηλόω	make clear, disclose, reveal, explain
Δημᾶς, Δημᾶ, ὁ	Demas
διακονία, -ας, ἡ	service, serving; (ministerial) service, ministry
διάνοια, -οίας, ἡ	mind, understanding; thought, disposition
διδασκαλία, -ας, ἡ	teaching, instruction [activity or content]
δόγμα, -ατος, τό	decree, ordinance
δογματίζω	(*mid*) submit to rules/ordinances
δουλεύω	be a slave; slave (for), serve (+*dat obj*)

▷ List 12 1×

δυναμόω	strengthen, enable
ἑδραῖος, -αία, -ον	firm, steadfast
ἐθελοθρησκ(ε)ία, -ας, ἡ	self-imposed worship, religion thought up by oneself
εἰδωλολατρία, -ας, ἡ	image worship, idolatry
εἰκῇ	without cause; in vain
εἰρηνοποιέω	make peace
ἐκλεκτός, -ή, -όν	chosen, elect
ἐλεύθερος, -έρα, -ον	free
Ἕλλην, -ηνος, ὁ	Greek (person); a person of Hellenic culture, gentile
ἐμβατεύω	enter into; go into detail about

▷ List 13 1×

ἔνειμι	be in(side) ▶
ἐνεργέω	(*intrans*) be at work/active; (*trans*) work, produce
ἐνοικέω	live/dwell in
ἔνταλμα, -άλματος, τό	commandment
ἐξαγοράζω	(*act*) buy up/off, redeem; (*mid*) take advantage of
ἐξαλείφω	wipe away/out; destroy
ἑορτή, -ῆς, ἡ	festival; feast
ἐπιθυμία, -ας, ἡ	desire, longing; lust, craving
ἐπιμένω	remain, stay; persist, continue
ἐπιστολή, -ῆς, ἡ	letter

▷ List 14 1×

ἐπιχορηγέω	provide, supply, furnish
ἐποικοδομέω	build (up)on
ἐρεθίζω	provoke [negative], excite, stir up [positive]
εὐάρεστος, -ον	pleasing
εὐδοκέω	be well pleased; determine, resolve
εὐχάριστος, -ον	thankful, grateful
ἐχθρός, -ά, -όν	hated; hostile; (*subst*) enemy
ἡλίκος, -η, -ον	such, what size [context indicates whether it is "how great" or "how small"]
θεμελιόω	lay a foundation, found, establish
θεότης, -ητος, τό	divinity, divine nature

▷ List 15 1×

θησαυρός, -οῦ, ὁ	repository, container, chest; treasure
θιγγάνω	touch (*+gen obj*) ➤
θρησκεία, -ας, ἡ	religion, religious service
θριαμβεύω	triumph (over); lead in triumph
θυμός, -οῦ, ὁ	desire, passion; anger, wrath
θύρα, -ας, ἡ	door; entrance
ἰατρός, -οῦ, ὁ	physician
Ἱεράπολις, -όλεως, ἡ	Hierapolis
ἱκανόω	make adequate/qualified/fit
Ἰοῦστος, Ἰούστου, ὁ	Justus

▷ List 16 1×

ἰσότης, -ητος, τό	equality, [extended sense] fairness
κακία, -ας, ἡ	wickedness; malice; trouble, misfortune
καταβραβεύω	pass judgment against, condemn
καταγγέλλω	announce, proclaim, declare
κατενώπιον	(+*gen*) before, opposite, in front of
κενός, -ή, -όν	empty [of content]; empty, fruitless; in vain, for nothing
κληρονομία, -ας, ἡ	inheritance; property, possession
κλῆρος, κλήρου, ὁ	lot; allotment, share
Κολοσσαεύς, -έως, ὁ	Colossian
Κολοσσαί, -ῶν, αἱ	Colossae

▷ List 17 1×

κομίζω	(*act*) bring; (*mid*) receive
κοπιάω	be weary/tired; labor, toil
κράτος, -ους, τό	strength, might, power; rule, sovereignty
κρύπτω	(*trans*) hide (something); (*intrans mid*) hide (oneself), be hidden
κυριότης, -ητος, ἡ	lordship, dominion, ruling power
Λαοδικεύς, -έως, ὁ	Laodicean
Λουκᾶς, Λουκᾶ, ὁ	Luke
μανθάνω	learn ▷
Μᾶρκος, Μάρκου, ὁ	Mark
μεθίστημι/μεθιστάνω	move, transfer, [extended sense] remove

▷ List 18 1×

μέλος, -ους, τό	member [of the human body], limb; member [of a group]
μερίς, -ίδος, ἡ	part, portion, share
μετακινέω	(*mid*) move (oneself), shift (from)
μνημονεύω	remember (*+gen/acc obj*)
μομφή, -ῆς, ἡ	blame, cause for complaint
νεκρόω	put to death
νεομηνία/νουμηνία, -ας, ἡ	new moon, first of the month
νέος, -α, -ον	new; young
νοῦς, νοός, ὁ	mind; understanding, intellect; thought
Νύμφα, -ας, ἡ	Nympha

▹ List 19 1×

οἰκονομία, -ας, ἡ	management, administration; arrangement, plan
οἰκτιρμός, -οῦ, ὁ	compassion, mercy
Ὀνήσιμος, -ίμου, ὁ	Onesimus
ὁρατός, -ή, -όν	visible
οὗ	(to) where
ὀφθαλμοδουλία, -ας, ἡ	eye-service [service done to impress others]
πάθημα, -ήματος, τό	suffering; emotion, passion
πάθος, -ους, τό	passion
παλαιός, -ά, -όν	old
παράδοσις, -όσεως, ἡ	tradition

▹ List 20 1×

παραλογίζομαι	deceive
πάρειμι	be present/here, have come
παρέχω	(*mid*) grant [something from one's own means]
παρηγορία, -ας, ἡ	comfort
παρρησία, -ας, ἡ	plainness; openness; boldness
παύω	(*trans act*) make stop/cease; (*intrans mid*) stop, cease
περισσεύω	(*intrans*) abound (in), overflow, be left over
περιτέμνω	circumcise
πιθανολογία, -ας, ἡ	persuasive speech, plausible arguments
πικραίνω	(*intrans mid*) become bitter, [extended sense] become embittered

▹

▷ List 21 1×

πλεονεξία, -ας, ἡ	greed; greedy act, extortion
πληροφορέω	(*mid*) be fully assured/certain
πληροφορία, -ας, ἡ	assurance, certainty
πλησμονή, -ῆς, ἡ	satiety, satisfaction
πλουσίως	richly, abundantly
πόνος, -ου, ὁ	hard work, toil; pain, affliction, distress
πορνεία, -ας, ἡ	sexual immorality, fornication
πόσις, -εως, ἡ	drinking; drink
πρᾶξις, πράξεως, ἡ	doing, activity; deed, action
πραΰτης, -ητος, τό	humility, gentleness

▷ List 22 1×

προακούω	hear before(hand)
προσηλόω	nail (to), fasten (to)
προσκαρτερέω	hold fast to, be devoted to [+*dat* of thing or person]
προσωπολημψία, -ας, ἡ	partiality
πρωτεύω	be first, have first place
ῥιζόω	(*mid*) take root; (*pass*) be planted
ῥύομαι	save, rescue, deliver
σκιά, -ᾶς, ἡ	shadow, [extended sense] outline, (mere) representation; shade
σκότος, -ους, τό	darkness [literal or figurative]
Σκύθης, -ου, ὁ	Scythian

▶

▷ List 23 1×

σπλάγχνον, -ου, τό	[always *pl*] entrails; seat of emotion [similar to English's "heart"]; compassion, affection
στερέωμα, -ώματος, τό	foundation, firmness, steadfastness
συζωοποιέω	make alive together with ▷
συλαγωγέω	take captive [literally or figuratively]
συναιχμάλωτος, -ώτου, ὁ	fellow prisoner
συνεργός, -όν	helpful, contributing; [only *subst* in NT] fellow worker
συνθάπτω	bury together (with) ▷
συνίστημι/συνιστάνω/ συνιστάω	(*trans pres/aor*) recommend, commend; establish, prove; (*intrans pf*) stand with/by; exist
σωματικῶς	bodily
τάξις, -εως, ἡ	order [sequence]; order, arrangement; orderliness

▷ List 24 1×

τελειότης, -ητος, ἡ	completeness, perfection
Τιμόθεος, -έου, ὁ	Timothy
Τυχικός, -οῦ, ὁ	Tychicus
ὕμνος, -ου, ὁ	hymn, song of praise
ὑπεναντίος, -α, -ον	opposed, against
ὑπομονή, -ῆς, ἡ	endurance, perseverance, steadfastness
ὑποτάσσω	subject, subordinate
ὑστέρημα, -ήματος, τό	need, deficiency; lack, shortcoming
φθορά, -ᾶς, ἡ	corruption, decay, ruin, destruction
φιλοσοφία, -ας, ἡ	philosophy

▹ List 25	1×
φρονέω	think
φυσιόω	(*trans act*) puff up, make proud; (*intrans mid*) be(come) proud/puffed up
χειρόγραφον, -άφου, τό	handwritten document, record of debts
χρηστότης, -ητος, ἡ	kindness, goodness
ψαλμός, -οῦ, ὁ	psalm, song of praise [in general or specifically in reference to OT psalms]
ψεύδομαι	lie, speak falsely
ᾠδή, -ῆς, ἡ	song

1 THESSALONIANS

▷ LIST 1	4 TO 3×
ἁγιασμός, -οῦ, ὁ	holiness, consecration
ἀδιαλείπτως	unceasingly, constantly
ἀρέσκω	please (+*dat obj*) ▸
διότι	because, since; for; because of this
δοκιμάζω	examine, evaluate; determine, put to the test; approve
εὐχαριστέω	thank, give thanks, be thankful
καθάπερ	(just) as
καθεύδω	be sleeping/asleep
κοιμάω	(*mid*) sleep, fall asleep; die
παρουσία, -ας, ἡ	presence; arrival, coming

▷ LIST 2	3 TO 2×
ἀθετέω	nullify, invalidate; reject
ἀκαθαρσία, -ας, ἡ	uncleanness, filth; immorality
ἅμα	at the same time; together; (*prep* +*dat*) together with
ἀμέμπτως	blamelessly
ἀπέχω	(*intrans act*) be far away, distant; (*intrans mid*) abstain from, keep away from
κόπος, -ου, ὁ	trouble, hardship; labor, toil
Μακεδονία, -ας, ἡ	Macedonia
ὀργή, -ῆς, ἡ	anger; wrath
περισσεύω	(*intrans*) abound (in), overflow, be left over; (*trans*) cause (something) to abound, increase ▸
Τιμόθεος, -έου, ὁ	Timothy

▷ List 3 — 2×

Ἀχαΐα, -ας, ἡ	Achaia
γρηγορέω	be (fully) awake/alert; be watchful/on the alert
εἴσοδος, -όδου, ἡ	entrance [location or activity]; reception, welcome
ἐπιθυμία, -ας, ἡ	desire, longing; lust, craving
εὐδοκέω	be well pleased; determine, resolve
Θεσσαλονικεύς, -έως, ὁ	Thessalonian
κενός, -ή, -όν	empty [of content]; empty, fruitless; in vain, for nothing
κλέπτης, -ου, ὁ	thief
μάρτυς, μάρτυρος, ὁ	witness
μηκέτι	no longer

▷ List 4 — 2×

μιμητής, -οῦ, ὁ	imitator
μνεία, -ας, ἡ	remembrance, memory; mention
μνημονεύω	remember (+*gen/acc obj*)
νήφω	be sober/temperate
νουθετέω	warn, instruct, admonish
παραμυθέομαι	console, comfort
πειράζω	test; tempt
περιλείπομαι	remain, be left
προλέγω	tell beforehand/in advance
σκότος, -ους, τό	darkness [literal or figurative]

▷ List 5 2 to 1×

α′	1 [in the book title ΠΡΟΣ ΘΕΣΣΑΛΟΝΙΚΕΙΣ Α "1 Thessalonians"]
ἁγιάζω	consecrate, make holy; regard as holy
ἁγιωσύνη, -ῆς, ἡ	holiness, sanctity
ἀγνοέω	not know, be uninformed/ignorant; not understand; ignore, disregard
ἀγών, -ῶνος, ὁ	(athletic) contest; struggle
ἀήρ, ἀέρος, ὁ	air
στέγω	endure, bear
στηρίζω	set, establish; strengthen/make more firm [inwardly] ▸
ὑπερεκπερισσοῦ	beyond the highest degree/extent, infinitely beyond, beyond all measure
φθάνω	precede; arrive, reach, overtake; attain

▷ List 6 1×

Ἀθῆναι, -ῶν, αἱ	Athens
αἰφνίδιος, -ον	sudden
ἀκοή, -ῆς, ἡ	hearing, listening; ear; news, rumor, report, message
ἀκριβῶς	diligently, carefully, well
ἀληθινός, -ή, -όν	true, trustworthy; real
ἀληθῶς	truly, actually
ἄμεμπτος, -ον	blameless, faultless
ἀναγινώσκω	read (aloud)
ἀνάγκη, -ης, ἡ	necessity, constraint, pressure; distress, anguish
ἀναμένω	wait for

▷ List 7 1×

ἀναπληρόω	fill (up); supply; fulfill
ἀνταποδίδωμι	give/pay back [favorable or unfavorable actions]
ἀντέχω	(*mid +gen obj*) cling/be devoted to
ἀντί	(+*gen*) instead of, in place of
ἀξίως	worthily, in a manner worthy of
ἀπάντησις, -ήσεως, ἡ	meeting
ἅπαξ	once; once and for all
ἀπορφανίζω	make an orphan of someone, bereave
ἁρπάζω	seize; take away, snatch
ἄρτι	(just) now

▷ List 8 1×

ἀρχάγγελος, -έλου, ὁ	archangel
ἀσθενής, -ές	weak; sick, ill
ἀσφάλεια, -είας, ἡ	security; certainty
ἄτακτος, -ον	undisciplined, disorderly
βάρος, -ους, τό	weight; burden; influence, authority
γαστήρ, γαστρός, ἡ	belly; womb
δέομαι	ask, petition, pray [+*gen* of person(s) petitioned]
διάκονος, -όνου, ὁ/ἡ	servant, helper; ministerial attendant ["deacon(ess)"] <TH only>
διαμαρτύρομαι	[generally more emphatic than similar words] bear witness, attest; warn, exhort (+*dat obj*)
δικαίως	[juridical] justly, fairly; [of character] uprightly, justly

▷ List 9 1×

δίς	twice
δόλος, -ου, ὁ	deceit, cunning, craftiness
δουλεύω	be a slave; slave (for), serve (+*dat obj*)
ἐγκόπτω	hinder
εἶδος, εἴδους, τό	form, appearance
εἴδωλον, -ώλου, τό	idol, cultic image
εἰρηνεύω	be at peace, keep the peace
ἔκδικος, -ον	(*subst*) avenger
ἐκδιώκω	drive/chase out
ἐκλογή, -ῆς, ἡ	choice, election

▷ List 10 1×

ἐκφεύγω	escape; flee ▶
ἐναντίος, -α, -ον	opposite, facing; opposed, contrary
ἐνδύω	(*act*) dress/clothe (someone); (*mid*) put on, wear
ἐνεργέω	(*intrans*) be at work/active; (*trans*) work, produce
ἐνορκίζω	put under oath, make someone swear
ἐξηχέω	(*intrans mid*) resound, ring out/forth ▶
ἐξουθενέω	look down on, treat with contempt; reject
ἔπειτα	then, next
ἐπιβαρέω	burden, be a burden to
ἐπιποθέω	long for, strongly desire

▷ List 11 1×

ἐπίσταμαι	understand; know <TH only>
ἐπιστολή, -ῆς, ἡ	letter
ἐπιστρέφω	(*intrans act/mid*) return, go/come back; turn (around); change (one's thinking or behavior)
εὐσχημόνως	appropriately, decently; properly
εὐχαριστία, -ας, ἡ	thankfulness, gratitude; thanksgiving
ἐφίστημι	stand by/near; [with reference to events] come/spring upon <NA/UBS, SBL only> ▷
ἡγέομαι	consider, regard
ἤπιος, -ία, -ον	gentle, kind <TH only>
ἡσυχάζω	rest
θάλπω	comfort, care for

▷ List 12 1×

θεοδίδακτος, -ον	taught by God
θλίβω	compress, make narrow; press upon; oppress, afflict ▷
θώραξ, -ακος, ὁ	breastplate; chest
καταλαμβάνω	grasp, attain; seize; overtake ▷
καταλείπω	leave (behind); cause to be left over
καταρτίζω	restore, put in order; prepare, make ready
κατευθύνω	guide, direct
κατέχω	hold fast/to ▷
καύχησις, -ήσεως, ἡ	boasting
κεῖμαι	be lying/reclining/resting; exist for, be set for

▷ List 13 1×

κέλευσμα, κελεύσματος, τό	commanding shout
κολακεία, -ας, ἡ	flattery
κοπιάω	be weary/tired; labor, toil
κτάομαι	procure for oneself, get, acquire
κωλύω	hinder, prevent
λυπέω	(*act*) cause grief/sorrow; (*mid*) grieve, be sad/distressed
μακροθυμέω	be patient
μαρτύρομαι	testify
μεθύσκω	(*mid*) get drunk
μεθύω	be drunk

▷ List 14 1×

μεταδίδωμι	share, give a share of, impart
μόχθος, -ου, ὁ	toil, hardship
νεφέλη, -ης, ἡ	cloud
νήπιος, -ία, -ον	(*subst*) infant; little child <NA/UBS, SBL only>
οἷος, οἵα, οἷον	such as, of what sort
ὄλεθρος, ὀλέθρου, ὁ	destruction
ὀλιγόψυχος, -ον	discouraged
ὁλόκληρος, -ον	complete, whole
ὁλοτελής, -ές	entirely complete, perfect in every way
ὁμείρομαι	long for (+*gen obj*)

▷ List 15 1×

ὁποῖος, -οία, -ον	of what sort, what kind of; as
ὁσίως	devoutly
πάθος, -ους, τό	passion
παραγγελία, -ας, ἡ	command, order, instruction
παραγγέλλω	command, instruct, give orders
παράκλησις, -ήσεως, ἡ	encouragement, exhortation; comfort, consolation
παρρησιάζομαι	speak freely/boldly; be bold, have the courage
περικεφαλαία, -ας, ἡ	helmet
περιποίησις, -ήσεως, ἡ	keeping safe, preservation; possessing, possession; gaining, acquisition
περισσοτέρως	(*comp*) (even) more; (*superl*) especially

▷ List 16 1×

πλάνη, -ης, ἡ	error, deceit
πλεονάζω	(*intrans*) increase, abound; (*trans*) (cause to) increase
πλεονεκτέω	exploit, take advantage of
πλεονεξία, -ας, ἡ	greed; greedy act, extortion
πληροφορία, -ας, ἡ	assurance, certainty
πορνεία, -ας, ἡ	sexual immorality, fornication
ποτέ (*encl*)	when, at some time; formerly, once; (+*neg*) never
πρᾶγμα, πράγματος, τό	deed, act, matter, thing, occurrence
πράσσω	do, accomplish, perform
προΐστημι	lead, manage, be at the head of (+*gen obj*)

▷ List 17 1×

προπάσχω	suffer previously/before	▶
προσευχή, -ῆς, ἡ	prayer	
πρόφασις, -άσεως, ἡ	pretext, excuse	
προφητεία, -ας, ἡ	prophetic activity; prophecy [the gift]; prophecy [an utterance]	
πώς (*encl*)	somehow, perhaps, in any way, at all	
ῥύομαι	save, rescue, deliver	▶
σαίνω	fawn upon, beguile [so as to deceive]; agitate, disturb, shake	
σάλπιγξ, σάλπιγγος, ἡ	trumpet; trumpet call	
σατανᾶς, σατανᾶ, ὁ	[Heb.] Satan	
σβέννυμι	extinguish, put out, [extended sense] quench, suppress	▶

▷ List 18 1×

Σιλουανός, -οῦ, ὁ	Silvanus
σκεῦος, σκεύους, τό	object, thing; vessel, container
σπουδάζω	strive, make every effort (to), be eager (to)
στέφανος, -άνου, ὁ	wreath, crown
στήκω	stand; stand firm
συμφυλέτης, -ου, ὁ	fellow countryman
συνεργός, -όν	helpful, contributing; [only *subst* in NT] fellow worker <NA/UBS, SBL only>
τοιγαροῦν	for that very reason, therefore
τροφός, -οῦ, ἡ	[one who tends to the nourishment of a child] nurse, nursing mother
τύπος, -ου, ὁ	mark; pattern, design, example

▷ List 19 1×

ὑβρίζω	mistreat spitefully, insult
ὑπερβαίνω	go beyond, step over; transgress/sin against
ὑπομονή, -ῆς, ἡ	endurance, perseverance, steadfastness
ὑστέρημα, -ήματος, τό	need, deficiency; lack, shortcoming
φιλαδελφία, -ας, ἡ	brotherly/sisterly love
φίλημα, -ήματος, τό	kiss
Φίλιπποι, -ίππων, οἱ	Philippi
φιλοτιμέομαι	have as an ambition (to do something), strive eagerly, aspire
ὠδίν, -ῖνος, ἡ	birth pains
ὥσπερ	(just) as

2 THESSALONIANS

▷ List 1	4 to 2×
ἀδικία, -ας, ἡ	injustice, unrighteousness; wrongdoing, misdeed
ἀνομία, -ας, ἡ	lawlessness [condition or action]
ἀποκαλύπτω	reveal, disclose ▹
ἀτάκτως	disorderly
ἐνδοξάζομαι	(*pass*) be glorified/honored
ἐνέργεια, -είας, ἡ	working, action, activity
ἐπιστολή, -ῆς, ἡ	letter
μήτε	[continuing a previous *neg*] and not, neither, nor
παραγγέλλω	command, instruct, give orders
παρουσία, -ας, ἡ	presence; arrival, coming

▷ List 2	2×
εὐχαριστέω	thank, give thanks, be thankful
Θεσσαλονικεύς, -έως, ὁ	Thessalonian
θλίβω	compress, make narrow; press upon; oppress, afflict ▹
κατέχω	hold fast/to; hold back, restrain, suppress ▹
μιμέομαι	imitate
ὀφείλω	owe, be indebted to; be obligated, ought; have to
παράδοσις, -όσεως, ἡ	tradition
στηρίζω	set, establish; strengthen/make more firm [inwardly] ▹
τρόπος, -ου, ὁ	manner, way; conduct, way of life
ὑπακούω	obey

▷ LIST 3 2 TO 1×

ἀγαθωσύνη, -ῆς, ἡ	goodness
ἁγιασμός, -οῦ, ὁ	holiness, consecration
αἱρέω	(*mid*) choose; prefer ➢
ἀναιρέω	do away with, destroy, kill ➢
ἄνεσις, -έσεως, ἡ	relief, rest
ἀνέχω	(*mid*) bear with, tolerate, put up with (+*gen/acc obj*); endure ➢
ἄνομος, -ον	lawless
ἀνταποδίδωμι	give/pay back [favorable or unfavorable actions]
ὑπομονή, -ῆς, ἡ	endurance, perseverance, steadfastness
ψεῦδος, ψεύδους, τό	lie, falsehood

▷ LIST 4 1×

ἀντί	(+*gen*) instead of, in place of; ἀνθ᾽ ὧν because
ἀντίκειμαι	oppose (+*dat obj*)
ἀξιόω	consider worthy
ἀπαρχή, -ῆς, ἡ	firstfruits <NA/UBS, SBL only>
ἅπας, ἅπασα, ἅπαν	whole, all; (*subst*) everyone, all, everything <TH only>
ἀπάτη, -ης, ἡ	deception, deceit
ἀποδείκνυμι	point out; display; prove
ἀποκάλυψις, -ύψεως, ἡ	revelation, disclosure
ἀποστασία, -ας, ἡ	rebellion, defection; apostasy
ἀπώλεια, -είας, ἡ	destruction; waste

▷ List 5 1×

ἄρτι	(just) now
ἀσπασμός, -οῦ, ὁ	greeting
ἀτακτέω	live a disorderly life, behave inappropriately
ἄτοπος, -ον	out of place, wrong, wicked
β′	2 [in the book title ΠΡΟΣ ΘΕΣΣΑΛΟΝΙΚΕΙΣ Β "2 Thessalonians"]
δίκη, -ης, ἡ	punishment, justice
διωγμός, -οῦ, ὁ	persecution
δωρεάν	freely; without cause
ἐγκακέω	lose heart, be discouraged
ἐγκαυχάομαι	boast (in/about)

▷ List 6 1×

εἴπερ	if indeed; since
ἐκδίκησις, -ήσεως, ἡ	carrying out of justice; vengeance; punishment
ἔνδειγμα, ἐνδείγματος, τό	evidence
ἐνεργέω	(*intrans*) be at work/active; (*trans*) work, produce
ἐνίστημι	(*pf*) be present/here ▸
ἐντρέπω	(*mid*) be ashamed ▸
ἐξαπατάω	deceive, seduce
ἐπιβαρέω	burden, be a burden to
ἐπισυναγωγή, -ῆς, ἡ	gathering, assembling; meeting
ἐπιφάνεια, -είας, ἡ	appearing, appearance

▷ List 7 1×

εὐδοκέω	be well pleased; determine, resolve
εὐδοκία, -ας, ἡ	goodwill; favor
ἐχθρός, -ά, -όν	hated; hostile; (*subst*) enemy
ἡγέομαι	consider, regard
ἡσυχία, -ας, ἡ	quietness, peace and quiet; silence
θροέω	(*mid*) be alarmed/disturbed
ἰσχύς, -ύος, ἡ	strength
καλοποιέω	do good/what is right
καταξιόω	consider worthy
καταργέω	make ineffective, nullify; set aside, eliminate

▷ List 8 1×

κατευθύνω	guide, direct
κλῆσις, κλήσεως, ἡ	call, calling, invitation
κόπος, -ου, ὁ	trouble, hardship; labor, toil
μαρτύριον, -ίου, τό	testimony, witness, proof
μνημονεύω	remember (+*gen/acc obj*)
μόχθος, -ου, ὁ	toil, hardship
μυστήριον, -ίου, τό	mystery, secret
νουθετέω	warn, instruct, admonish
νοῦς, νοός, ὁ	mind; understanding, intellect; thought ➤
ὄλεθρος, ὀλέθρου, ὁ	destruction

▷ List 9 — 1×

παράκλησις, -ήσεως, ἡ	encouragement, exhortation; comfort, consolation
περιεργάζομαι	meddle, be a busybody
περιποίησις, -ήσεως, ἡ	keeping safe, preservation; possessing, possession; gaining, acquisition
πλάνη, -ης, ἡ	error, deceit
πλεονάζω	(*intrans*) increase, abound; (*trans*) (cause to) increase
ῥύομαι	save, rescue, deliver ▷
σαλεύω	shake; disturb, upset
σατανᾶς, σατανᾶ, ὁ	[Heb.] Satan
σέβασμα, -άσματος, τό	object of worship/awe
σημειόω	(*mid*) note down, mark; take note of

▷ List 10 — 1×

Σιλουανός, -οῦ, ὁ	Silvanus
στέλλω	(*mid*) keep away; avoid
στήκω	stand; stand firm
συναναμίγνυμι	(*mid +dat obj*) associate with
ταχέως	quickly, without delay; soon
τέρας, -ατος, τό	wonder, marvel, portent
Τιμόθεος, -έου, ὁ	Timothy
τίνω	pay a penalty
τρέχω	run; progress quickly ▷
τύπος, -ου, ὁ	pattern, model, example

▷ List 11 — 1×

ὑπεραίρω	(*trans act*) lift up over; (*intrans mid*) exalt oneself; become arrogant
ὑπεραυξάνω	increase abundantly
φλόξ, φλογός, ἡ	flame
φυλάσσω	guard, protect

1 TIMOTHY

▷ **List 1** — **8 to 4×**

διδασκαλία, -ας, ἡ	teaching, instruction [activity or content]
ἐλπίζω	hope (for); expect ▸
εὐσέβεια, -είας, ἡ	devoutness, piety
καλῶς	well, appropriately, effectively; correctly
νέος, -α, -ον	new; young ▸
ὄντως	really, truly, actually
παραγγέλλω	command, instruct, give orders
προΐστημι	lead, manage, be at the head of (+*gen obj*)
προσέχω	look after, pay attention/attend to (+*dat obj*)
χήρα, -ας, ἡ	widow

▷ **List 2** — **4 to 3×**

ἀνεπίλημπτος, -ον	blameless, irreproachable
βέβηλος, -ον	profane, worldly, impure
βούλομαι	want, desire; intend, plan
γαμέω	marry
διάβολος, -ον	slanderous; (*subst*) adversary; devil
διάκονος, -όνου, ὁ/ἡ	servant, helper; ministerial attendant ["deacon(ess)"]
ἐκτρέπω	(*mid*) turn away/aside from ▸
συνείδησις, -ήσεως, ἡ	consciousness, awareness; conscience
Τιμόθεος, -έου, ὁ	Timothy
ὡσαύτως	in the same way, likewise

▷ List 3 — 3 to 2×

ἁγνεία, -ας, ἡ	moral purity; chastity
ἀγωνίζομαι	exert effort, strive; struggle, fight
Ἀδάμ, ὁ (*indecl*)	Adam
ἀντίκειμαι	oppose (+*dat obj*)
ἐμπίπτω	fall in(to) ▸
ἐπαρκέω	help, aid (+*dat obj*)
εὐχαριστία, -ας, ἡ	thankfulness, gratitude; thanksgiving
μάλιστα	most of all, especially
μανθάνω	learn ▸
σωτήρ, -ῆρος, ὁ	savior, deliverer

▷ List 4 — 2×

ἀπόδεκτος, -ον	pleasing; ἀποδεκτός acceptable, approved
ἀποδοχή, -ῆς, ἡ	acceptance
ἀργός, -ή, -όν	idle, having nothing to do; lazy; useless
ἀστοχέω	miss the mark; fail, stray/deviate (from)
βλασφημέω	slander, speak disrespectfully about, revile
δέησις, δεήσεως, ἡ	entreaty; prayer, petition
δεσπότης, -ου, ὁ	master, lord
διακονέω	(+*dat obj*) serve; care for; wait on; administer
εἶτα	then, next; furthermore
ἐλεέω	have compassion (on), show mercy to

▷ List 5 2×

ἔντευξις, ἐντεύξεως, ἡ	petition; prayer, intercession
ἐπαγγέλλομαι	promise; profess
ἐπακολουθέω	(+*dat obj*) follow close upon/after; devote oneself to
ἐπιλαμβάνομαι	take/lay hold of (+*gen obj*)
ἑτεροδιδασκαλέω	give divergent instruction/false teaching
ἡγέομαι	consider, regard
ἡσυχία, -ας, ἡ	quietness, peace and quiet; silence
καθαρός, -ά, -όν	clean; pure; innocent
καταφρονέω	despise, look down on, disregard (+*gen obj*)
κοπιάω	be weary/tired; labor, toil

▷ List 6 2×

κόσμιος, -ία, -ον	well-ordered, respectable, appropriate
κρίμα, -ατος, τό	judgment [process of evaluation]; judgment [end result], judicial verdict
μάρτυς, μάρτυρος, ὁ	witness
μήτε	[continuing a previous *neg*] and not, neither, nor
μῦθος, μύθου, ὁ	story, tale, myth
μυστήριον, -ίου, τό	mystery, secret
νηφάλιος, -ία, -ον	temperate, self-controlled
οἶνος, οἴνου, ὁ	wine
ὁμολογία, -ας, ἡ	profession, confession
ὀρέγω	(*mid* +*gen obj*) aspire to, long for

▷ List 7 2×

παγίς, -ίδος, ἡ	snare, trap
παραγγελία, -ας, ἡ	command, order, instruction
παραιτέομαι	request; excuse oneself; reject, refuse
παρέχω	bring about, make happen; provide
πλουτέω	be rich
πορισμός, -οῦ, ὁ	means of gain
προάγω	(*intrans*) go before, precede [spatially or temporally]
πρόδηλος, -ον	clear, evident, obvious
προσευχή, -ῆς, ἡ	prayer
προσμένω	remain, stay

▷ List 8 2×

προφητεία, -ας, ἡ	prophetic activity; prophecy [the gift]; prophecy [an utterance]
σατανᾶς, σατανᾶ, ὁ	[Heb.] Satan
σεμνός, -ή, -όν	worthy of reverence/respect
σεμνότης, -ητος, ἡ	dignity, solemnity
σωφροσύνη, -ης, ἡ	reasonableness, good judgment
τυφόω	(*mid*) be conceited/arrogant
ὑγιαίνω	be well; (*attr ptc*) correct, sound [describing Christian instruction or teaching]
ὑποταγή, -ῆς, ἡ	submission
φυλάσσω	observe, follow; guard, protect
χράομαι	use (+*dat/acc obj*)

▷ List 9 — 2 to 1 ×

α′	1 [in the book title ΠΡΟΣ ΤΙΜΟΘΕΟΝ Α "1 Timothy"]
ἀγαθοεργέω	do good, benefit (someone)
ἁγιάζω	consecrate, make holy; regard as holy
ἁγιασμός, -οῦ, ὁ	holiness, consecration
ἀγνοέω	be uninformed/ignorant; not understand
ἁγνός, -ή, -όν	pure
ἀγών, -ῶνος, ὁ	(athletic) contest; struggle
ἀδελφή, -ῆς, ἡ	sister
ὦ	(*interj*) O [address]; oh!
ὠφέλιμος, -ον	useful, helpful, beneficial

▷ List 10 — 1 ×

ἀδηλότης, -ητος, ἡ	uncertainty
ἀθανασία, -ας, ἡ	immortality
ἀθετέω	nullify, invalidate; reject
αἰδώς, -οῦς, ἡ	sense of honor, respect (for oneself or others)
αἰσχροκερδής, -ές	shamelessly greedy
Ἀλέξανδρος, -άνδρου, ὁ	Alexander
ἀλλότριος, -ία, -ον	another's
ἄλλως	otherwise
ἀλοάω	thresh
ἅμα	at the same time

▹ List 11 1×

ἄμαχος, -ον	noncombative, peaceable
ἀμελέω	not care (for), disregard (+*gen obj*)
ἀμοιβή, -ῆς, ἡ	requital, repayment
ἀνάγνωσις, -ώσεως, ἡ	reading
ἀναλαμβάνω	lift up ➤
ἀναστρέφω	(*mid*) conduct oneself, live
ἀναστροφή, -ῆς, ἡ	conduct, way of life
ἀνδραποδιστής, -οῦ, ὁ	kidnapper, slave dealer
ἀνδροφόνος, -ου, ὁ	murderer
ἀνέγκλητος, -ον	irreproachable, blameless

▹ List 12 1×

ἀνόητος, -ον	unintelligent, senseless, foolish
ἄνομος, -ον	lawless
ἀνόσιος, -ον	unholy, profane
ἀντίθεσις, -έσεως, ἡ	contradiction
ἀντιλαμβάνω	(*mid +gen obj*) help, aid; be devoted to
ἀντίλυτρον, -ύτρου, τό	ransom
ἀνυπόκριτος, -ον	without pretense, genuine, sincere
ἀνυπότακτος, -ον	not made subject, [of people] rebellious
ἀξιόω	consider worthy
ἀόρατος, -ον	invisible

▷ List 13 1×

ἅπας, ἅπασα, ἅπαν	whole, all; (*subst*) everyone, all, everything
ἀπατάω	deceive, mislead
ἀπέραντος, -ον	endless, countless
ἀπέχω	(*intrans mid*) abstain from, keep away from
ἀπιστία, -ας, ἡ	unbelief; unfaithfulness
ἄπιστος, -ον	unbelieving; unbelievable
ἀπόβλητος, -ον	rejected
ἀποθησαυρίζω	store up
ἀπόλαυσις, -αύσεως, ἡ	enjoyment
ἀποπλανάω	(*act*) mislead; (*mid*) go astray

▷ List 14 1×

ἀποστερέω	steal, defraud
ἀπρόσιτος, -ον	unapproachable
ἀπωθέω	(*mid*) push back; reject
ἀπώλεια, -είας, ἡ	destruction; waste
ἀρκέω	(*mid*) be content/satisfied
ἀρνέομαι	deny; refuse; disown
ἀρσενοκοίτης, -ου, ὁ	men who have sex with males
ἀσεβής, -ές	ungodly
ἀσθένεια, -είας, ἡ	sickness, disease; weakness
ἄσπιλος, -ον	spotless; without fault

▷ List 15 1×

αὐθεντέω	domineer (+*gen obj*)
αὐτάρκεια, -είας, ἡ	sufficiency; contentment
ἄφθαρτος, -ον	incorruptible, immortal, undecaying
ἀφιλάργυρος, -ον	not loving money
ἀφίστημι	withdraw, depart; keep away
ἀφορμή, -ῆς, ἡ	opportunity
βαθμός, -οῦ, ὁ	step (of a stair); standing, rank
βαρέω	weigh down, burden
βασιλεύω	reign, rule, be king
βίος, -ου, ὁ	life, manner of living; livelihood, means of living

▷ List 16 1×

βλαβερός, -ά, -όν	harmful
βλασφημία, -ας, ἡ	slander, defamation, reviling
βλάσφημος, -ον	slanderous, defaming, reviling
βοῦς, βοός, ὁ	ox
βραδύνω	delay, be slow
βρῶμα, βρώματος, τό	food
βυθίζω	(*trans act*) (cause) to sink, plunge
γενεαλογία, -ας, ἡ	genealogy
γνήσιος, -ία, -ον	legitimate, true [validity of family membership]; genuine
γνῶσις, γνώσεως, ἡ	knowledge [understanding/comprehension or that which is known]

▹ List 17 1×

γραώδης, -ες	characteristic of an elderly woman
γυμνάζω	train, practice, discipline
γυμνασία, -ας, ἡ	training, exercise
δείκνυμι	show, make known; explain ▸
διαβεβαιόομαι	speak confidently, insist, maintain strongly
διάγω	spend one's life, live
διακονία, -ας, ἡ	service, serving; (ministerial) service, ministry
διαλογισμός, -οῦ, ὁ	reasoning, thought; dispute
διαμαρτύρομαι	[generally more emphatic than similar words] bear witness, attest; warn, exhort (+*dat obj*)
διαπαρατριβή, -ῆς, ἡ	constant arguing

▹ List 18 1×

διατροφή, -ῆς, ἡ	sustenance, food
διαφθείρω	destroy; corrupt ▸
διδακτικός, -ή, -ον	skillful in teaching
δικαιόω	justify, consider right/righteous, make righteous; vindicate, put in the right
δίλογος, -ον	insincere
διπλοῦς, διπλῆ, διπλοῦν	double
διώκτης, -ου, ὁ	persecutor
δοκιμάζω	examine, evaluate; determine, put to the test; approve
δουλεύω	be a slave; slave (for), serve (+*dat obj*)
δυνάστης, -ου, ὁ	ruler, sovereign; court official

▷ List 19 1×

ἑδραίωμα, -ώματος, τό	support [that which provides a firm base]
εἰσφέρω	lead/bring in ➢
ἔκγονος, -ον	born of; (*subst*) descendant; grandchild
ἐκζήτησις, -ήσεως, ἡ	speculation
ἐκλεκτός, -ή, -όν	chosen, elect
ἐκτός	outside; ἐκτὸς εἰ μή unless, except
ἐκφέρω	carry/bring out; produce ➢
ἐλάσσων, ἔλασσον	less; inferior; younger
ἐλέγχω	expose; reprove; convict, accuse
ἔλεος, ἐλέους, τό	compassion, mercy

▷ List 20 1×

ἐνδείκνυμι	(*mid*) show, demonstrate, exhibit ➢
ἐνδυναμόω	strengthen
ἐντρέφω	nurture, bring up
ἐξαπατάω	deceive, seduce
ἑξήκοντα (*indecl*)	sixty
ἔξωθεν	(from) outside
ἐπαίρω	lift up ➢
ἐπέχω	hold on to; observe, pay attention to (+*dat obj*)
ἐπίγνωσις, -ώσεως, ἡ	knowledge
ἐπιεικής, -ές	reasonable, fair, yielding

▷ List 21	1×
ἐπίθεσις, -έσεως, ἡ	laying on
ἐπιθυμέω	long for, desire (+*gen/acc obj*)
ἐπιθυμία, -ας, ἡ	desire, longing; lust, craving
ἐπιμελέομαι	take care of, care for (+*gen obj*)
ἐπιμένω	remain, stay; persist, continue
ἐπίορκος, -ον	perjured, (*subst*) perjurer
ἐπιπλήσσω	chastise, rebuke
ἐπισκοπή, -ῆς, ἡ	visitation; oversight
ἐπίσκοπος, -όπου, ὁ	overseer, guardian
ἐπίσταμαι	understand; know

▷ List 22	1×
ἐπιταγή, -ῆς, ἡ	command
ἐπιτίθημι	lay/put upon
ἐπιτρέπω	permit, give permission, allow (+*dat obj*)
ἐπιφάνεια, -είας, ἡ	appearing, appearance
ἐργάτης, -ου, ὁ	worker, laborer; doer
ἔρις, -ιδος, ἡ	strife, contention
Εὕα, -ας, ἡ	Eve
εὐεργεσία, -ας, ἡ	doing of good, beneficence; good deed
εὐμετάδοτος, -ον	generous
εὐσεβέω	show profound respect for, venerate

▷ List 23 1×

Ἔφεσος, -έσου, ἡ	Ephesus
ζήτησις, -ήσεως, ἡ	investigation; discussion; controversy
ζυγός, -οῦ, ὁ	yoke
ζωογονέω/ζῳογονέω	keep/preserve alive
ἤρεμος, -ον	quiet, tranquil
ἡσύχιος, -ον	quiet, well-ordered, at rest
θεμέλιος, -ίου, ὁ	foundation
θεοσέβεια, -είας, ἡ	reverence to God, godliness
θλίβω	compress; press upon; oppress, afflict ▷
θνῄσκω	die ▷

▷ List 24 1×

ἱματισμός, -οῦ, ὁ	clothing, apparel
καταλέγω	(*pass*) be enrolled
καταστολή, -ῆς, ἡ	attire
καταστρηνιάω	have strong desires that displace oneself [+*gen* indicating separation]
κατηγορία, -ας, ἡ	accusation
καυστηριάζω	brand; sear
κεῖμαι	be lying/reclining; exist for, be set for
κενοφωνία, -ας, ἡ	empty talk, prattle
κῆρυξ, κήρυκος, ὁ	herald, proclaimer
κοινωνέω	have a share, take part in; share

▷ List 25 — 1×

κοινωνικός, -ή, -όν	given to sharing, liberal
κοσμέω	put in order, arrange, prepare; adorn, make attractive
κράτος, -ους, τό	strength, might, power; rule, sovereignty
κρύπτω	(*intrans mid*) hide (oneself), be hidden ▸
κτίζω	create
κτίσμα, -ατος, τό	that which is created, creation
κυριεύω	lord over, rule (over) (+*gen obj*)
κωλύω	hinder, prevent
λογομαχία, -ας, ἡ	dispute about words
λοιδορία, -ας, ἡ	verbal abuse, insult

▷ List 26 — 1×

Μακεδονία, -ας, ἡ	Macedonia
μακροθυμία, -ας, ἡ	patience; forbearance
μαργαρίτης, -ου, ὁ	pearl
μαρτυρία, -ας, ἡ	[the act of giving] testimony; evidence
μαρτύριον, -ίου, τό	testimony, witness, proof
ματαιολογία, -ας, ἡ	empty/idle talk
μελετάω	pursue, practice; set one's mind on, think about
μεσίτης, -ου, ὁ	mediator, arbitrator
μετάλημψις, -ήμψεως, ἡ	participation, partaking
μέχρι	(*conj*) until; (*prep* +*gen*) until; as far as; to the point of

▷ List 27 1×

μηκέτι	no longer
μητρολῴας, -ου, ὁ	one who kills his or her mother
μισθός, -οῦ, ὁ	pay, wages; recompense, reward
μονόω	(*pass*) be left alone, abandoned
ναυαγέω	suffer shipwreck
νεότης, -ητος, ἡ	youth
νεόφυτος, -ον	newly planted; newly converted
νίπτω	(*act*) wash (something); (*mid*) wash (oneself)
νοέω	understand; consider, think about
νομίζω	think, suppose, believe

▷ List 28 1×

νομίμως	lawfully
νομοδιδάσκαλος, -άλου, ὁ	teacher of the law
νοσέω	have an unhealthy interest (in), have a morbid craving (for)
νοῦς, νοός, ὁ	mind; understanding, intellect; thought ▷
ξενοδοχέω	show hospitality
ὀδύνη, -ης, ἡ	pain; grief, distress
οἰκεῖος, -εία, -ον	in/of the house, (*subst pl*) household members
οἰκέω	(*intrans*) dwell, live; (*trans*) inhabit
οἰκοδεσποτέω	manage one's household
οἰκονομία, -ας, ἡ	management, administration; arrangement, plan

▷ List 29 1×

ὄλεθρος, ὀλέθρου, ὁ	destruction
ὁμολογέω	acknowledge; declare, confess
ὁμολογουμένως	most certainly, undeniably
ὀνειδισμός, -οῦ, ὁ	reproach, insult; disgrace
ὀπίσω	behind, back; (*prep +gen*) behind; after [temporal or spatial]
ὀργή, -ῆς, ἡ	anger; wrath
ὅσιος, -ία, -ον	devout, pious, holy
παιδεύω	educate, instruct, give guidance; discipline, correct
παράβασις, -άσεως, ἡ	transgression, violation
παραδέχομαι	receive, accept

▷ List 30 1×

παραθήκη, -ης, ἡ	deposit
παράκλησις, -ήσεως, ἡ	encouragement, exhortation; comfort, consolation
παρακολουθέω	follow faithfully [instruction] (*+dat obj*)
παρατίθημι	(*act*) set/put before; (*mid*) demonstrate; commend, entrust
πάροινος, -ον	addicted to wine
παρρησία, -ας, ἡ	plainness; openness; boldness
πατρολῴας, -ου, ὁ	one who kills his or her father
πειρασμός, -οῦ, ὁ	test, trial; temptation
περίεργος, -ον	(*subst*) meddlesome person, busybody; magic
περιέρχομαι	go about

▶

▷ List 31 1×

περιπείρω	pierce through, impale
περιποιέω	(*mid*) keep/save for oneself; acquire, obtain
πλάνος, -ον	deceitful; (*subst*) deceiver
πλάσσω	form, mold ▷
πλέγμα, -ατος, τό	braided hair
πλήκτης, -ου, ὁ	brawler, violent person
πλούσιος, -ία, -ον	rich, wealthy; rich (in), abounding (in)
πλουσίως	richly, abundantly
πλοῦτος, πλούτου, ὁ/τό	wealth, riches; abundance
πολυτελής, -ές	very costly/valuable

▷ List 32 1×

Πόντιος, -ίου, ὁ	Pontius
πόρνος, -ου, ὁ	sexually immoral person, fornicator
πραϋπάθεια/πραϋπαθία, -είας/ίας, ἡ	gentleness, gentle disposition
πρέπω	(*impers*) it is fitting/appropriate/right
πρεσβυτέριον, -ίου, τό	council of elders
πρόγονος, -ον	born before; (*subst pl*) parents, forebears; ancestors
προκοπή, -ῆς, ἡ	progress, advancement
πρόκριμα, -ίματος, τό	prejudgment, discrimination
προνοέω	give careful thought to; care/provide for (+*gen obj*)
πρόσκλισις, -ίσεως, ἡ	partiality

▷ List 33 1×

πρότερος, -έρα, -ον	former, earlier; [*neut sg* as *adv*] before, formerly
πυκνός, -ή, -όν	frequent, numerous
ῥητῶς	explicitly, distinctly
ῥίζα, -ης, ἡ	root; shoot [from a root]
σκέπασμα, -άσματος, τό	covering
σπαταλάω	live luxuriously/indulgently
στόμαχος, -άχου, ὁ	stomach
στρατεία, -ας, ἡ	war campaign, (*pl*) warfare
στρατεύω	(*mid*) serve in the army; wage war
στῦλος, στύλου, ὁ	pillar, column [metaphorically, a thing/person that provides support]

▷ List 34 1×

σωματικός, -ή, -όν	bodily
σώφρων, σῶφρον	sensible, prudent; self-controlled
ταχέως	quickly, without delay; soon; (*comp*) τάχιον more quickly
τάχος, -ους, τό	ἐν τάχει quickly; soon
τεκνογονέω	bear/have children
τεκνογονία, -ας, ἡ	childbearing
τεκνοτροφέω	raise children
τιμάω	honor; set a price
τύπος, -ου, ὁ	pattern, model, example
ὑβριστής, -οῦ, ὁ	violent/insolent/arrogant person

▷ List 35 1×

ὑδροποτέω	abstain from alcohol, be a teetotaler
Ὑμέναιος, -αίου, ὁ	Hymeneus
ὑπεροχή, -ῆς, ἡ	superiority; authority
ὑπερπλεονάζω	abound exceedingly
ὑπόκρισις, -ίσεως, ἡ	pretense, hypocrisy
ὑπομονή, -ῆς, ἡ	endurance, perseverance, steadfastness
ὑπόνοια, -οίας, ἡ	suspicion, conjecture
ὑποτίθημι	(*mid*) instruct, demonstrate
ὑποτύπωσις, -ώσεως, ἡ	pattern, model
ὕστερος, -έρα, -ον	latter, last

▷ List 36 1×

ὑψηλοφρονέω	be haughty/arrogant
φανερός, -ά, -όν	visible, plain, evident, known
φεύγω	flee; escape; avoid ➢
φθόνος, -ου, ὁ	envy
φιλαργυρία, -ας, ἡ	love of money
φιλόξενος, -ον	loving strangers, hospitable
φιμόω	muzzle; silence
φλύαρος, -ον	foolish, chatty
χάριν	(+*gen* preceding or following) because of, for the sake of
χάρισμα, -ίσματος, τό	(gracious) gift

▹ List 37 1×

χείρων, -ον	worse
χρυσίον, -ου, τό	gold; objects of gold [e.g., jewelry, money] <NA/UBS, SBL only>
χρυσός, -οῦ, ὁ	gold; objects of gold [e.g., jewelry, money] <TH only>
ψευδολόγος, -ον	lying, (*subst pl*) liars
ψεύδομαι	lie, speak falsely
ψευδώνυμος, -ον	falsely called
ψεύστης, -ου, ὁ	liar

2 TIMOTHY

▷ List 1	4 to 3×	
ἀνθίστημι	resist, oppose, withstand (+*dat obj*)	▸
ἀρνέομαι	deny; refuse; disown	
διδασκαλία, -ας, ἡ	teaching, instruction [activity or content]	
ἔλεος, ἐλέους, τό	compassion, mercy	
ἐπαισχύνομαι	be ashamed (of)	
ἐπιθυμία, -ας, ἡ	desire, longing; lust, craving	
ἐπιφάνεια, -είας, ἡ	appearing, appearance	
μανθάνω	learn	▸
προκόπτω	advance, progress	
ῥύομαι	save, rescue, deliver	▸

▷ List 2	3 to 2×	
ἀθλέω	compete [as an athlete]	
αἰτία, -ας, ἡ	cause, reason; accusation, charge	
ἀκοή, -ῆς, ἡ	hearing, listening; ear; news, rumor, report, message	
ἀπολείπω	(*act*) leave behind; abandon; (*mid*) remain	▸
ἀποστρέφω	(*act*) turn (something) away (from something); put back, return; (*mid*) turn away from, reject	▸
διάβολος, -ον	slanderous; (*subst*) adversary; devil	
διακονία, -ας, ἡ	service, serving; (ministerial) service, ministry	
διαμαρτύρομαι	[generally more emphatic than similar words] bear witness, attest; warn, exhort (+*dat obj*)	
σπουδάζω	strive, make every effort (to), be eager (to)	
φυλάσσω	guard, protect	

▹ List 3 — 2×

διωγμός, -οῦ, ὁ	persecution
ἐγκαταλείπω	leave behind; forsake, abandon ▸
ἐνδυναμόω	(*trans act*) strengthen; (*intrans mid*) become strong
ἐνοικέω	live/dwell in
ἐπίγνωσις, -ώσεως, ἡ	knowledge
εὔχρηστος, -ον	useful
Ἔφεσος, -έσου, ἡ	Ephesus
ἐφίστημι	stand by/near; attack (+*dat obj*); [with reference to events] (*pf*) be at hand/ impending ▸
καθαρός, -ά, -όν	clean; pure; innocent
κακοπαθέω	suffer hardship; endure hardship

▹ List 4 — 2×

μακροθυμία, -ας, ἡ	patience; forbearance
οἷος, οἵα, οἷον	such as, of what sort
Ὀνησίφορος, -όρου, ὁ	Onesiphorus
παραθήκη, -ης, ἡ	deposit
πλανάω	(*act*) lead astray, deceive; (*mid*) wander, go astray, be misled
πληροφορέω	fulfill completely
πρόθεσις, -έσεως, ἡ	setting forth, presentation; purpose
σκεῦος, σκεύους, τό	object, thing; vessel, container
συγκακοπαθέω	join in suffering
Τιμόθεος, -έου, ὁ	Timothy

▷ List 5 — 2 to 1×

ἁγιάζω	consecrate, make holy; regard as holy
ἀγωγή, -ῆς, ἡ	conduct, way of life
ἀγών, -ῶνος, ὁ	(athletic) contest; struggle
ἀγωνίζομαι	exert effort, strive; struggle, fight
ἀδιάλειπτος, -ον	unceasing, constant
ἀδικία, -ας, ἡ	injustice, unrighteousness; wrongdoing, misdeed
ἀδόκιμος, -ον	unqualified, disqualified; worthless
αἰχμαλωτίζω	put into captivity, make captive, capture
ὑγιαίνω	be well; (*attr ptc*) correct, sound [describing Christian instruction or teaching]
ὑπομένω	stay behind; endure, stand firm

▷ List 6 — 1×

ἀκαίρως	untimely, inopportunely
ἀκρατής, -ές	without self-control
Ἀκύλας, Ἀκύλα, ὁ	Aquila
ἀλαζών, -όνος, ὁ	boaster
Ἀλέξανδρος, -άνδρου, ὁ	Alexander
ἅλυσις, ἁλύσεως, ἡ	chain, [extended sense] imprisonment
ἀναζωπυρέω	rekindle
ἀναλαμβάνω	lift up; get ▷
ἀνάλυσις	departure
ἀναμιμνῄσκω	(*trans act*) remind; (*intrans mid*) remember ▷

▷ **List 7**	**1×**
ἀνανήφω	sober up, come to one's senses
ἀνατρέπω	overturn; ruin, subvert
ἀναψύχω	refresh
ἀνεξίκακος, -ον	enduring evil, long-suffering
ἀνεπαίσχυντος, -ον	having no cause for shame, with nothing to be ashamed of
ἀνέχω	(*mid +gen/acc obj*) bear with, tolerate, put up with
ἀνήμερος, -ον	savage, wild
ἄνοια, ἀνοίας, ἡ	folly, foolishness
ἀνόσιος, -ον	unholy, profane
ἀντιδιατίθημι	(*mid*) oppose

▷ **List 8**	**1×**
Ἀντιόχεια, -είας, ἡ	Antioch
ἀνυπόκριτος, -ον	without pretense, genuine, sincere
ἀπαίδευτος, -ον	uneducated
ἀπειθής, -ές	disobedient
ἀπιστέω	not believe; be unfaithful
ἀπόκειμαι	lay/put away [for safekeeping], reserve
ἀπολογία, -ας, ἡ	defense [a speech or the act of making a defense]
ἀποτρέπω	turn away from, avoid
ἀργυροῦς, -ᾶ, -οῦν	made of silver
ἀρέσκω	please (+*dat obj*)

➤

▷ List 9 1×

ἄρτιος, -ία, -ον	fit, suitable, complete
ἀσέβεια, -είας, ἡ	ungodliness
ἀσθενέω	be sick; be weak
Ἀσία, -ας, ἡ	Asia
ἄσπονδος, -ον	implacable, irreconcilable
ἄστοργος, -ον	lacking affection, unfeeling
ἀστοχέω	miss the mark; fail, stray/deviate (from)
ἀτιμία, -ας, ἡ	dishonor, disgrace
ἀφθαρσία, -ας, ἡ	incorruptibility, immortality
ἀφιλάγαθος, -ον	not loving the good

▷ List 10 1×

ἀφίστημι	(*trans*) draw away, incite; (*intrans*) withdraw, depart; keep away ▷
ἀχάριστος, -ον	ungrateful
β′	2 [in the book title ΠΡΟΣ ΤΙΜΟΘΕΟΝ Β "2 Timothy"]
βέβηλος, -ον	profane, worldly, impure
βελτίων, -ον	better; (*adv*) very well
βιβλίον, -ου, τό	scroll; document
βίος, -ου, ὁ	life, manner of living; livelihood, means of living
βλάσφημος, -ον	slanderous, defaming, reviling
βρέφος, -ους, τό	infant, baby
γάγγραινα, -αίνης, ἡ	gangrene

▷ List 11 1×

Γαλατία, -ας, ἡ	Galatia
γεωργός, -οῦ, ὁ	farmer, cultivator
γόης, -ητος, ὁ	cheat, charlatan
γονεύς, -έως, ὁ	parent
γράμμα, -ατος, τό	letter [of the alphabet]; document, writing, letter
γυναικάριον, -ίου, τό	little woman [pejorative], weak woman
δάκρυον, -ύου, τό	tear(drop)
Δαλματία, -ας, ἡ	Dalmatia
δέησις, δεήσεως, ἡ	entreaty; prayer, petition
δειλία, -ας, ἡ	cowardice, timidity

▷ List 12 1×

δέσμιος, -ίου, ὁ	prisoner
δεσμός, -οῦ, ὁ	(*sg*) binding, impediment; (*pl*) bonds, chains, [extended sense] imprisonment
δεσπότης, -ου, ὁ	master, lord
Δημᾶς, Δημᾶ, ὁ	Demas
διακονέω	serve
διδακτικός, -ή, -ον	skillful in teaching
διδαχή, -ῆς, ἡ	teaching [activity or content]
δόκιμος, -ον	approved
δρόμος, -ου, ὁ	race; course, [extended sense] mission, assignment
δυνατός, -ή, -όν	able, capable, strong, powerful; possible

▷ **List 13**		1×
ἔκδηλος, -ον	quite evident, obvious	
ἐκκαθαίρω	cleanse; clean out, clear away	
ἐκλεκτός, -ή, -όν	chosen, elect	
ἐκτρέπω	(*mid*) turn away/aside from	▷
ἐλεγμός, -οῦ, ὁ	reproving, refutation	
ἐλέγχω	expose; reprove; convict, accuse	
ἐμπλέκω	(*mid*) be entangled in	
ἐνδείκνυμι	(*mid*) show, demonstrate, exhibit	▷
ἐνδύνω	slip in	
ἐνίστημι	(*fut mid*) will come/arrive	▷

▷ **List 14**		1×
ἐξαρτίζω	complete; ready, equip	
ἐπανόρθωσις, -ώσεως, ἡ	correction, improvement	
ἐπίθεσις, -έσεως, ἡ	laying on	
ἐπικαλέω	(*mid*) call upon, invoke, appeal	▷
ἐπιποθέω	long for, strongly desire	
ἐπισωρεύω	heap up, accumulate	
ἐπιτιμάω	rebuke	
ἐπουράνιος, -ον	heavenly	
Ἔραστος, Ἐράστου, ὁ	Erastus	
ἐργάτης, -ου, ὁ	worker, laborer; doer	

▷ List 15	1×
Ἑρμογένης, -ους, ὁ	Hermogenes
εὐαγγελιστής, -οῦ, ὁ	proclaimer of good news, evangelist
Εὔβουλος, -ούλου, ὁ	Eubulus
εὐκαίρως	timely, at an opportune time
Εὐνίκη, -ης, ἡ	Eunice
εὐσέβεια, -είας, ἡ	devoutness, piety
εὐσεβῶς	devoutly, piously
ζήτησις, -ήσεως, ἡ	investigation; discussion; controversy
ζωγρέω	catch alive, capture
ἡμέτερος, -τέρα, -ον	our

▷ List 16	1×
ἤπιος, -ία, -ον	gentle, kind
θεμέλιος, -ίου, ὁ	foundation
θεόπνευστος, -ον	God-breathed
Θεσσαλονίκη, -ης, ἡ	Thessalonica
Ἰαμβρῆς, ὁ (*gen* unattested)	Jambres
Ἰάννης, -ου, ὁ	Jannes
ἱερός, -ά, -όν	sacred, holy
ἱκανός, -ή, -όν	sufficient; able, qualified
Ἰκόνιον, -ίου, τό	Iconium
κακοῦργος, -ον	(*subst*) criminal

▷ List 17 1×

Κάρπος, -ου, ὁ	Carpus
καταργέω	make ineffective, nullify; set aside, eliminate
καταστροφή, -ῆς, ἡ	(total) destruction, ruin
καταφθείρω	destroy; corrupt ▷
κενοφωνία, -ας, ἡ	empty talk, prattle
κήρυγμα, -ύγματος, τό	proclamation
κῆρυξ, κήρυκος, ὁ	herald, proclaimer
Κλαυδία, -ας, ἡ	Claudia
κλῆσις, κλήσεως, ἡ	call, calling, invitation
κνήθω	(*mid-pass*) itch

▷ List 18 1×

κοπιάω	be weary/tired; labor, toil
Κόρινθος, -ίνθου, ἡ	Corinth
Κρήσκης, Κρήσκεντος, ὁ	Crescens
κριτής, -οῦ, ὁ	judge
λατρεύω	serve, worship [the carrying out of religious duties] (+*dat obj*)
λέων, λέοντος, ὁ	lion
λίαν	very (much), exceedingly
Λίνος, -ου, ὁ	Linus
λογομαχέω	fight over words
Λουκᾶς, Λουκᾶ, ὁ	Luke

▷ List 19 1×

Λύστρα, -ας, ἡ/τά	Lystra ▶
Λωΐς, -ΐδος, ἡ	Lois
μάλιστα	most of all, especially
μάμμη, -ης, ἡ	grandmother
Μᾶρκος, Μάρκου, ὁ	Mark
μαρτύριον, -ίου, τό	testimony, witness, proof
μάρτυς, μάρτυρος, ὁ	witness
μάχη, -ης, ἡ	battle; quarrel, dispute
μάχομαι	fight; quarrel, dispute
μεμβράνα, -ης, ἡ	parchment

▷ List 20 1×

μέντοι (*postp*)	nevertheless, however
μεταλαμβάνω	have/receive a share, partake (+*gen obj*) ▶
μετάνοια, -οίας, ἡ	change of mind and heart, repentance
μέχρι	(*conj*) until; (*prep* +*gen*) until; as far as; to the point of
μηδέποτε	never
μήποτε	(*conj*) so that . . . not; (*interr*) whether (perhaps)
Μίλητος, -ήτου, ἡ	Miletus
μιμνήσκομαι/ μιμνῄσκομαι	(+*gen obj*) remember; be mindful of ▶
μνεία, -ας, ἡ	remembrance, memory; mention
μνημονεύω	remember (+*gen/acc obj*)

▷ List 21 1×

μόρφωσις, -ώσεως, ἡ	embodiment, form, shape
μῦθος, μύθου, ὁ	story, tale, myth
μωρός, -ά, -όν	foolish, stupid
νεωτερικός, -ή, -όν	youthful
νήφω	be sober/temperate
νοέω	understand; consider, think about
νομή, -ῆς, ἡ	pasture; spreading
νομίμως	lawfully
νοῦς, νοός, ὁ	mind; understanding, intellect; thought ▹
ξύλινος, -ίνη, -ον	wooden

▷ List 22 1×

ὀνομάζω	name, call; utter, mention
ὀρθοτομέω	cut a straight path; handle rightly
ὀστράκινος, -ίνη, -ον	earthen, (made of) clay
παγίς, -ίδος, ἡ	snare, trap
πάθημα, -ήματος, τό	suffering; emotion, passion
παιδεία, -ας, ἡ	instruction, discipline, training
παιδεύω	educate, instruct, give guidance; discipline, correct
παραγίνομαι	come, arrive, be present ▹
παραιτέομαι	request; excuse oneself; reject, refuse
παρακολουθέω	(+*dat obj*) follow faithfully [instruction]; pay close attention to; accompany

▹ List 23 1×

παρατίθημι	(*mid*) demonstrate; commend, entrust
περιΐστημι	(*intrans mid*) avoid, shun
πιστόω	(*mid-pass*) be confident/convinced
ποικίλος, -η, -ον	(*pl*) of various kinds
πολλάκις	often, many times
Πούδης, Πούδεντος, ὁ	Pudens
πραγματεία, -ας, ἡ	activity, occupation, (*pl*) affairs, matters
πραΰτης, -ητος, τό	humility, gentleness
Πρίσκα, -ης, ἡ	Prisca
πρόγονος, -ον	born before; (*subst pl*) parents, forebears; ancestors

▹ List 24 1×

προδότης, -ου, ὁ	traitor, betrayer
προπετής, -ές	rash, reckless
Ῥώμη, -ης, ἡ	Rome
σοφίζω	make wise
σπένδω	pour (something) out as a drink offering
σπουδαίως	with haste; eagerly; earnestly, diligently
στερεός, -ά, -όν	firm, solid; steadfast
στέφανος, -άνου, ὁ	wreath, crown
στεφανόω	crown (someone)
στρατεύω	(*mid*) serve in the army; wage war

▷ List 25 1×

στρατιώτης, -ου, ὁ	soldier
στρατολογέω	recruit (into military service)
συζάω	live together/with (+*dat obj*)
συμβασιλεύω	reign together with (+*dat obj*)
συναποθνῄσκω	die with (+*dat obj*) ▶
συνείδησις, -ήσεως, ἡ	consciousness, awareness; conscience
σύνεσις, -έσεως, ἡ	understanding, comprehension [mental faculty]; insight [content of what is understood]
σφραγίς, -ῖδος, ἡ	signet, seal; seal [the impression left by a signet]
σωρεύω	(*act*) heap/pile up; (*pass*) be heaped/laden with (something)
σωτήρ, -ῆρος, ὁ	savior, deliverer

▷ List 26 1×

σωφρονισμός, -οῦ, ὁ	the exercise of good judgment, self-control, self-discipline
ταχέως	quickly, without delay; soon
τελέω	complete, finish; carry out (completely), accomplish; pay
Τίτος, -ου, ὁ	Titus
τρόπος, -ου, ὁ	manner, way, ὅν τρόπον in the manner in which, (just) as
Τρόφιμος, -ίμου, ὁ	Trophimus
Τρῳάς, -άδος, ἡ	Troas
τυγχάνω	happen upon, obtain, attain (+*gen obj*) ▶
τυφόω	(*mid*) be conceited/arrogant
Τυχικός, -οῦ, ὁ	Tychicus

▷ List 27 1×

Ὑμέναιος, -αίου, ὁ	Hymeneus	
ὑπερήφανος, -ον	arrogant, proud, haughty	
ὑπομιμνῄσκω/ ὑπομιμνήσκω	remind, bring up	▸
ὑπόμνησις, -ήσεως, ἡ	reminding, reminder; remembrance	
ὑπομονή, -ῆς, ἡ	endurance, perseverance, steadfastness	
ὑποτύπωσις, -ώσεως, ἡ	pattern, model	
ὑποφέρω	endure	▸
φαιλόνης, -ου, ὁ	cloak	
φεύγω	flee; escape; avoid	▸
φιλάργυρος, -ον	loving money	

▷ List 28 1×

φίλαυτος, -ον	loving oneself, selfish
φιλήδονος, -ον	loving pleasure
Φίλητος, -ήτου, ὁ	Philetus
φιλόθεος, -ον	loving God, devout
Φύγελος, -έλου, ὁ	Phygellus
φωτίζω	(*trans*) illuminate, give light to; bring to light, make known
χαλεπός, -ή, -όν	hard to deal with, difficult; dangerous
χαλκεύς, -έως, ὁ	metalworker
χάρισμα, -ίσματος, τό	(gracious) gift
χειμών, -ῶνος, ὁ	bad weather, storm; winter, χειμῶνος in winter

▷ List 29 1×

χείρων, -ον	worse
χρήσιμος, -ίμη, -ον	useful, advantageous
χρυσοῦς, -ῆ, -οῦν	golden
ὠφέλιμος, -ον	useful, helpful, beneficial

TITUS

▹ LIST 1	6 TO 2×
ἀνέγκλητος, -ον	irreproachable, blameless
ἀντιλέγω	[+*dat* of person] argue (against), contradict; oppose
ἀνυπότακτος, -ον	not made subject, [of people] rebellious
διδασκαλία, -ας, ἡ	teaching, instruction [activity or content]
ἐλέγχω	expose; reprove; convict, accuse
καθαρός, -ά, -όν	clean; pure; innocent
σωτήρ, -ῆρος, ὁ	savior, deliverer
σώφρων, σῶφρον	sensible, prudent; self-controlled
ὑγιαίνω	be well; (*attr ptc*) correct, sound [describing Christian instruction or teaching]
ὑποτάσσω	subject, subordinate ▸

▹ LIST 2	2×
ἀπειθής, -ές	disobedient
ἀρνέομαι	deny; refuse; disown
βλασφημέω	slander, speak disrespectfully about, revile
ἐνδείκνυμι	(*mid*) show, demonstrate, exhibit
ἐπιθυμία, -ας, ἡ	desire, longing; lust, craving
ἐπιταγή, -ῆς, ἡ	command; authority
ἐπιφαίνω	(*act*) give light; (*mid*) appear
λείπω	be lacking/deficient
μιαίνω	stain, defile, taint ▸
νέος, -α, -ον	new; young ▸

▷ List 3 — 2 to 1×

ἁγνός, -ή, -όν	pure
ἀδόκιμος, -ον	unqualified, disqualified; worthless
ἀεί	always, constantly
αἱρετικός, -ή, -όν	divisive, factious
αἰσχροκερδής, -ές	shamelessly greedy
νομικός, -οῦ, ὁ	relating to/about law(s); (*subst*) legal expert, lawyer
προΐστημι	(+*gen obj*) lead, manage, be at the head of; show concern for
Τίτος, -ου, ὁ	Titus
χάριν	(+*gen* preceding or following) because of, for the sake of
ὡσαύτως	in the same way, likewise

▷ List 4 — 1×

αἰσχρός, -ά, -όν	shameful, disgraceful
αἰτία, -ας, ἡ	cause, reason; accusation, charge
ἄκαρπος, -ον	unfruitful; useless
ἀκατάγνωστος, -ον	not to be condemned, beyond reproach
ἀληθής, -ές	true, trustworthy; real
ἄμαχος, -ον	noncombative, peaceable
ἀναγκαῖος, -αία, -ον	necessary, important
ἀνακαίνωσις, -ώσεως, ἡ	renewal
ἀνατρέπω	overturn; ruin, subvert
ἀνόητος, -ον	unintelligent, senseless, foolish

▷ List 5 1×

ἀνομία, -ας, ἡ	lawlessness [condition or action]
ἀντέχω	(*mid +gen obj*) cling/be devoted to
ἀνωφελής, -ές	unprofitable, useless
ἄπιστος, -ον	unbelieving; unbelievable
ἀπολείπω	(*act*) leave behind; abandon; (*mid*) remain
Ἀπολλῶς, Ἀπολλῶ, ὁ	Apollos
ἀποστρέφω	(*act*) turn (something) away (from something); put back, return; (*mid*) turn away from, reject
ἀποτόμως	severely, sharply
ἀργός, -ή, -όν	idle, having nothing to do; lazy; useless
Ἀρτεμᾶς, Ἀρτεμᾶ, ὁ	Artemas

▷ List 6 1×

ἀσέβεια, -είας, ἡ	ungodliness
ἀσωτία, -ας, ἡ	recklessness, dissipation, debauchery
αὐθάδης, -ες	self-willed, arrogant
αὐτοκατάκριτος, -ον	self-condemned
ἀφθορία, -ας, ἡ	freedom from corruption, integrity
ἀψευδής, -ές	without deceit
βδελυκτός, -ή, -όν	detestable, abominable
βούλομαι	want, desire; intend, plan
γαστήρ, γαστρός, ἡ	belly; womb
γενεαλογία, -ας, ἡ	genealogy

▹ List 7 1×

γνήσιος, -ία, -ον	legitimate, true [validity of family membership]; genuine
δεσπότης, -ου, ὁ	master, lord
διαβεβαιόομαι	speak confidently, insist, maintain strongly
διάβολος, -ον	slanderous; (*subst*) adversary; devil
διάγω	spend one's life, live
διατάσσω	(*act/mid*) instruct, direct ▹
διδαχή, -ῆς, ἡ	teaching [activity or content]
δικαιόω	justify, consider right/righteous, make righteous; vindicate, put in the right
δικαίως	[juridical] justly, fairly; [of character] uprightly, justly
δουλεύω	be a slave; slave (for), serve (+*dat obj*)

▹ List 8 1×

δουλόω	enslave
δυνατός, -ή, -όν	able, capable, strong, powerful; possible
ἐγκρατής, -ές	self-controlled, disciplined
ἐκλεκτός, -ή, -όν	chosen, elect
ἐκστρέφω	turn (something) out, pull (something) out; [figurative] change entirely, distort ▹
ἐκχέω/ἐκχύν(ν)ω	pour out
ἔλεος, ἐλέους, τό	compassion, mercy
ἐναντίος, -α, -ον	opposite, facing; opposed, contrary
ἐντρέπω	(*mid*) be ashamed; have regard for, respect ▹
ἐπαγγέλλομαι	promise

▷ List 9 — 1×

ἐπίγνωσις, -ώσεως, ἡ	knowledge
ἐπιδιορθόω	(*mid*) set in order, resolve
ἐπιεικής, -ές	reasonable, fair, yielding
ἐπίσκοπος, -όπου, ὁ	overseer, guardian
ἐπιστομίζω	bridle, silence
ἐπιφάνεια, -είας, ἡ	appearing, appearance
ἔρις, -ιδος, ἡ	strife, contention
ἕτοιμος, -οίμη, -ον	ready
εὐάρεστος, -ον	pleasing
εὐσέβεια, -είας, ἡ	devoutness, piety

▷ List 10 — 1×

εὐσεβῶς	devoutly, piously
ζηλωτής, -οῦ, ὁ	enthusiast, loyalist; zealot
Ζηνᾶς, Ζηνᾶ, ὁ	Zenas
ζήτησις, -ήσεως, ἡ	investigation; discussion; controversy
ἡδονή, -ῆς, ἡ	pleasure
ἡμέτερος, -τέρα, -ον	our, οἱ ἡμέτεροι our people
ἱεροπρεπής, -ές	reverent
Ἰουδαϊκός, -ή, -όν	Judean, Jewish
καθαρίζω	cleanse, make clean
καθίστημι/καθιστάνω	appoint, put in charge

➤

▷ List 11 1×

κακία, -ας, ἡ	wickedness; malice; trouble, misfortune
καλοδιδάσκαλος, -ον	teaching what is good
κατάστημα, -ήματος, τό	behavior, demeanor
κατηγορία, -ας, ἡ	accusation
κέρδος, -ους, τό	gain, profit
κήρυγμα, -ύγματος, τό	proclamation
κληρονόμος, -ου, ὁ	heir; beneficiary, heir
κοινός, -ή, -όν	common, shared
κοσμέω	put in order, arrange, prepare; adorn, make attractive
κοσμικός, -ή, -όν	earthly; worldly

▷ List 12 1×

Κρής, Κρητός, ὁ	Cretan
Κρήτη, -ης, ἡ	Crete
λουτρόν, -οῦ, τό	bath, washing
λυτρόω	(*mid*) release [by payment of ransom], redeem, ransom
μάλιστα	most of all, especially
μανθάνω	learn
μαρτυρία, -ας, ἡ	[the act of giving] testimony; evidence
ματαιολόγος, -ον	(*subst*) empty/idle talker
μάταιος, -αία, -ον	empty, idle, vain, useless
μάχη, -ης, ἡ	battle; quarrel, dispute

▶

▷ List 13 1×

μῦθος, μύθου, ὁ	story, tale, myth
μωρός, -ά, -όν	foolish, stupid
νηφάλιος, -ία, -ον	temperate, self-controlled
Νικόπολις, -όλεως, ἡ	Nicopolis
νοσφίζω	put aside for oneself, keep back, steal
νουθεσία, -ας, ἡ	instruction, warning, admonition
νοῦς, νοός, ὁ	mind; understanding, intellect; thought ▸
οἰκονόμος, -ου, ὁ	household manager/steward; administrator, manager
οἰκουργός, -όν	working at home, carrying out household duties
οἶνος, οἴνου, ὁ	wine

▷ List 14 1×

ὁμολογέω	acknowledge; declare, confess
ὀργίλος, -η, -ον	quick-tempered, hotheaded
ὅσιος, -ία, -ον	devout, pious, holy
παιδεύω	educate, instruct, give guidance; discipline, correct
παλιγγενεσία, -ας, ἡ	renewal, rebirth, restoration
παραιτέομαι	request; excuse oneself; reject, refuse
παραχειμάζω	spend the winter
παρέχω	(*mid*) show oneself to be
πάροινος, -ον	addicted to wine
πειθαρχέω	obey

▷ List 15 1×

περιΐστημι	(*intrans mid*) avoid, shun
περιούσιος, -ον	special
περιτομή, -ῆς, ἡ	circumcision; one who is circumcised
περιφρονέω	despise, treat with contempt (+*gen obj*)
πλανάω	(*act*) lead astray, deceive; (*mid*) wander, go astray, be misled
πλήκτης, -ου, ὁ	brawler, violent person
πλουσίως	richly, abundantly
ποικίλος, -η, -ον	(*pl*) of various kinds
ποτέ (*encl*)	when, at some time; formerly, once
πραΰτης, -ητος, τό	humility, gentleness

▷ List 16 1×

πρέπω	(*impers*) it is fitting/appropriate/right
πρεσβύτης, -ου, ὁ	old/elderly man
πρεσβῦτις, -ύτιδος, ἡ	old/elderly woman
προπέμπω	send (someone) on their way [with assistance]
προσδέχομαι	receive, welcome; wait for, await, expect
προσέχω	pay attention/attend to (+*dat obj*)
σεμνός, -ή, -όν	worthy of reverence/respect
σεμνότης, -ητος, ἡ	dignity, solemnity
σπουδάζω	strive, make every effort (to), be eager (to)
σπουδαίως	with haste; eagerly; earnestly, diligently

▷ List 17	1×
στυγητός, -ή, -όν	loathsome, hated
συνείδησις, -ήσεως, ἡ	consciousness, awareness; conscience
σωτήριος, -ον	bringing salvation/deliverance
σωφρονέω	be of sound mind; be sensible/self-controlled
σωφρονίζω	encourage, urge
σωφρόνως	sensibly, showing self-control
τύπος, -ου, ὁ	pattern, model, example
Τυχικός, -οῦ, ὁ	Tychicus
ὑγιής, -ές	whole, healthy; wholesome, sound
ὑπομιμνῄσκω/ ὑπομιμνήσκω	remind, bring up ▷

▷ List 18	1×
ὑπομονή, -ῆς, ἡ	endurance, perseverance, steadfastness
φαῦλος, φαύλη, φαῦλον	bad; low-grade
φθόνος, -ου, ὁ	envy
φιλάγαθος, -ον	loving what is good
φίλανδρος, -ον	loving one's husband
φιλανθρωπία, -ας, ἡ	loving humanity, benevolence, kindness
φιλέω	love, like; kiss
φιλόξενος, -ον	loving strangers, hospitable
φιλότεκνος, -ον	loving one's children
φρεναπάτης, -ου, ὁ	deceiver

▷ List 19 1×

φροντίζω	give thought to, consider intently, be concerned about (+*gen obj*)
χρηστότης, -ητος, ἡ	kindness, goodness
ψεύστης, -ου, ὁ	liar
ὠφέλιμος, -ον	useful, helpful, beneficial

PHILEMON

▷ List 1 — 3 to 1×

ἀδελφή, -ῆς, ἡ	sister
ἀδικέω	(*trans*) wrong; injure
ἀναπαύω	(*trans act*) give rest, refresh; (*intrans mid*) rest
δέσμιος, -ίου, ὁ	prisoner
δεσμός, -οῦ, ὁ	(*sg*) binding, impediment; (*pl*) bonds, chains, [extended sense] imprisonment
νυνί	now, at this time
προσευχή, -ῆς, ἡ	prayer
σπλάγχνον, -ου, τό	[always *pl*] entrails; seat of emotion [similar to English's "heart"]; compassion, affection
συνεργός, -όν	helpful, contributing; [only *subst* in NT] fellow worker
Φιλήμων, -ονος, ὁ	Philemon

▷ List 2 — 1×

ἅμα	at the same time
ἀνάγκη, -ης, ἡ	necessity, constraint, pressure; distress, anguish
ἀναπέμπω	send up (to one in a higher position); send back
ἀνήκω	(*subst ptc*) what is proper/right
ἀπέχω	(*trans act*) receive in full
ἀποτίνω	make compensation, pay in full
Ἀπφία, -ας, ἡ	Apphia
Ἀρίσταρχος, -άρχου, ὁ	Aristarchus
Ἄρχιππος, -ίππου, ὁ	Archippus
ἄχρηστος, -ον	useless

▷ List 3 1×

βούλομαι	want, desire; intend, plan
γνώμη, -ης, ἡ	judgment, opinion; purpose, intent, will
Δημᾶς, Δημᾶ, ὁ	Demas
διακονέω	(+*dat obj*) serve; care for; wait on; administer
ἑκούσιος, -ία, -ον	voluntary
ἐλλογέω/ἐλλογάω	charge [to someone's account]
ἐλπίζω	hope (for); expect ▹
ἐμαυτοῦ, -ῆς	myself, my (own) [when *gen*]
ἐνεργής, -ές	effective, active
Ἐπαφρᾶς, Ἐπαφρᾶ, ὁ	Epaphras

▷ List 4 1×

ἐπίγνωσις, -ώσεως, ἡ	knowledge
ἐπιτάσσω	command, order (+*dat obj*)
εὐχαριστέω	thank, give thanks, be thankful
εὔχρηστος, -ον	useful
κατέχω	hold fast/to; hold back, restrain ▹
κοινωνία, -ας, ἡ	(close) fellowship; participation, sharing; generosity
κοινωνός, -οῦ, ὁ/ἡ	companion, partner, sharer
Λουκᾶς, Λουκᾶ, ὁ	Luke
μάλιστα	most of all, especially
Μᾶρκος, Μάρκου, ὁ	Mark

▷ List 5 — 1×

μνεία, -ας, ἡ	remembrance, memory; mention
ναί	yes
ξενία, -ας, ἡ	hospitality; guest room
Ὀνήσιμος, -ίμου, ὁ	Onesimus
ὀνίνημι	(*mid*) have profit/benefit/delight [+*gen* indicating source] ▸
ὀφείλω	owe, be indebted to; be obligated, ought; have to
παράκλησις, -ήσεως, ἡ	encouragement, exhortation; comfort, consolation
παρρησία, -ας, ἡ	plainness; openness; boldness
πόσος, -η, -ον	[*interr* or *exclam*] how much?, how great?; how much?, how many?
ποτέ (*encl*)	when, at some time; formerly, once

▷ List 6 — 1×

πρεσβύτης, -ου, ὁ	old/elderly man
προσλαμβάνω	(*mid*) take to oneself; receive, welcome ▸
προσοφείλω	still owe
σός, σή, σόν	your, yours
συναιχμάλωτος, -ώτου, ὁ	fellow prisoner
συστρατιώτης, -ου, ὁ	fellow soldier
τάχα	perhaps
Τιμόθεος, -έου, ὁ	Timothy
ὑπακοή, -ῆς, ἡ	obedience
χαρίζομαι	give graciously/freely; forgive

▷ **List 7** 1×

χωρίζω	(*act*) divide, separate; (*mid*) separate oneself, leave, depart

HEBREWS

▷ LIST 1	17 TO 8×
ἅπαξ	once; once and for all
διαθήκη, -ης, ἡ	will, testament; covenant
ἐπεί	since, because; for otherwise
θυσία, -ας, ἡ	sacrifice, offering
ἱερεύς, -έως, ὁ	priest
κατάπαυσις, -αύσεως, ἡ	(place of) rest
κρείττων, κρεῖττον / κρείσσων, κρεῖσσον	better, superior [rank or value]; [*neut acc sg* as *adv*] better
Μελχισέδεκ/ Μελχισεδέκ, ὁ (*indecl*)	Melchizedek
σκηνή, -ῆς, ἡ	tent, dwelling, tabernacle
τελειόω	complete, finish; bring (something) to its goal/conclusion; perfect

▷ LIST 2	7 TO 5×
ἁγιάζω	consecrate, make holy; regard as holy
δῶρον, δώρου, τό	gift [general or votive]
ἐπουράνιος, -ον	heavenly
ἡγέομαι	consider, regard; lead, (*subst pres ptc*) leader, ruler
κατασκευάζω	prepare; build, construct
λατρεύω	serve, worship [the carrying out of religious duties] (+*dat obj*)
μέτοχος, -ον	sharing in, partaking of; (*subst*) companion, partner
ὅθεν	from where; as a result of which, consequently
ὀμνύω	make an oath, swear
τάξις, -εως, ἡ	order [sequence]; order, arrangement; orderliness

▶

▷ List 3 — 5 to 4×

ἀδύνατος, -ον	powerless, disabled; impossible
Αἴγυπτος, -ύπτου, ἡ	Egypt
ἀνάγκη, -ης, ἡ	necessity, constraint, pressure; distress, anguish
ἀναφέρω	lead/take up; offer up [cultic term]; take up (a burden), bear
ἀσθένεια, -είας, ἡ	sickness, disease; weakness
πειράζω	test; tempt
προσφορά, -ᾶς, ἡ	sacrificing, offering [activity]; sacrifice, offering [item brought]
συνείδησις, -ήσεως, ἡ	consciousness, awareness; conscience
τοσοῦτος, -αύτη, -οῦτο(ν)	so many; so much/great; such
ὑποτάσσω	subject, subordinate ▷

▷ List 4 — 4×

βέβαιος, -αία, -ον	steadfast, steady; firm, reliable, certain
δέκατος, -άτη, -ον	tenth, (*subst*) a tenth (part)
διατίθημι	(*mid*) arrange (as one likes), draw up; make a will
διηνεκής, -ές	continuous, εἰς τὸ διηνεκές for all time, continually
ἐνιαυτός, -οῦ, ὁ	year
ἐπαγγέλλομαι	promise
Ἰσαάκ, ὁ (*indecl*)	Isaac
καθαρίζω	cleanse, make clean ▷
κληρονομέω	(*intrans*) be an heir; (*trans*) acquire, obtain
μήποτε	(*conj*) so that . . . not; (*adv*) never

▹ List 5 4×

μιμνήσκομαι/ μιμνῄσκομαι	(+*gen obj*) remember; be mindful of ▸
ὁρκωμοσία, -ας, ἡ	(swearing of an) oath
παιδεία, -ας, ἡ	instruction, discipline, training
παρρησία, -ας, ἡ	plainness; openness; boldness
πολλάκις	often, many times
ῥάβδος, -ου, ἡ	rod, staff, scepter
ῥαντίζω	sprinkle; purify ▸
σκληρύνω	harden
τράγος, -ου, ὁ	male goat
ὑπομένω	stay behind; endure, stand firm

▹ List 6 3×

Ἀαρών, ὁ (*indecl*)	Aaron
ἀληθινός, -ή, -όν	true, trustworthy; real
ἀλλότριος, -ία, -ον	another's; foreign; (*subst*) stranger; foreign enemy
ἀντιλογία, -ας, ἡ	dispute; opposition
ἀπολείπω	(*mid*) remain
βραχύς, -εῖα, -ύ	[*neut* as *adv*] for a short time, διὰ βραχέως briefly
γεύομαι	taste, partake (+*gen/acc obj*)
διάφορος, -ον	different, various; (*comp*) διαφορώτερος, -έρα, -ον better, more excellent
ἐπιλαμβάνομαι	take/lay hold of (+*gen obj*)
ἐπιλανθάνομαι	(+*gen/acc obj*) forget; neglect, ignore ▸

▹ List 7 3×

εὐαρεστέω	(*act*) please, be pleasing; (*mid*) be pleased
εὐδοκέω	be well pleased; determine, resolve
ἐφάπαξ	once for all
ἥκω	be present, have come
Ἰακώβ, ὁ (*indecl*)	Jacob
ἱερωσύνη, -ης, ἡ	priestly office, priesthood
ἰσχυρός, -ά, -όν	strong, mighty [of living beings]; strong, powerful, violent, forcible [pertaining to strength or impact]
καθίστημι/καθιστάνω	appoint, put in charge; make, cause to be
καίπερ	although
καταβολή, -ῆς, ἡ	foundation, [technical term] sowing of seed, begetting

▹ List 8 3×

καταπαύω	(*trans*) cause to rest; (*intrans*) rest, stop
καταπέτασμα, -άσματος, τό	curtain
καταρτίζω	restore, put in order; prepare, make ready
κατέχω	hold fast/to ▹
κληρονόμος, -ου, ὁ	heir; beneficiary, heir
κομίζω	(*act*) bring; (*mid*) receive
μάχαιρα, -αίρης, ἡ	dagger, short sword
μεσίτης, -ου, ὁ	mediator, arbitrator
μετάθεσις, -έσεως, ἡ	change in position/location, removal; change
μετάνοια, -οίας, ἡ	change of mind and heart, repentance

▹ List 9 3×

μετατίθημι	(*trans*) transfer, move to a new place; change, alter
μετέχω	(+*gen obj*) share, have a share in; partake of
μέχρι	(+*gen*) until; as far as; to the point of
μισθαποδοσία, -ας, ἡ	recompense, payment [positive or negative]
μνημονεύω	remember (+*gen/acc obj*)
ὁμολογία, -ας, ἡ	profession, confession
ὀνειδισμός, -οῦ, ὁ	reproach, insult; disgrace
ὀφείλω	owe, be indebted to; be obligated, ought; have to
πάθημα, -ήματος, τό	suffering; emotion, passion
παιδεύω	educate, instruct, give guidance; discipline, correct

▹ List 10 3×

παλαιόω	(*trans act*) make old/obsolete; (*intrans mid*) become old [often with the connotation of becoming useless]
παραιτέομαι	request; excuse oneself; reject, refuse
παράκλησις, -ήσεως, ἡ	encouragement, exhortation; comfort, consolation
παρεμβολή, -ῆς, ἡ	(fortified) camp; barracks; battle line, army
πλανάω	(*act*) lead astray, deceive; (*mid*) wander, go astray, be misled
πρᾶγμα, πράγματος, τό	deed, act, matter, thing, occurrence
πρόκειμαι	be set before
πρότερος, -έρα, -ον	former, earlier; [*neut sg* as *adv*] before, formerly
πρωτότοκος, -ον	firstborn [literal or figurative]
σαλεύω	shake; disturb, upset

▷ List 11 — 3 to 2×

Ἄβελ, ὁ (*indecl*)	Abel
ἀθέτησις, -ήσεως, ἡ	annulment; setting aside, removal
ἀκοή, -ῆς, ἡ	hearing, listening; ear; news, rumor, report, message
ἀμελέω	not care (for), disregard (+*gen obj*)
ὑπόδειγμα, -είγματος, τό	example, pattern; sketch, outline [to be copied]
ὑπόστασις, -άσεως, ἡ	substantial nature, essence; undertaking; confidence; plan
ὑστερέω	(*intrans act*) miss out on, fall short of; (*intrans mid*) be in need
φοβερός, -ά, -όν	terrifying
χρηματίζω	warn [revelation of a divine message]
ὥσπερ	(just) as

▷ List 12 — 2×

ἀμετάθετος, -ον	unchangeable
ἀμίαντος, -ον	undefiled, pure
ἀναστρέφω	(*act*) return, go back; (*mid*) conduct oneself, live
ἀνομία, -ας, ἡ	lawlessness [condition or action]
ἀντί	(+*gen*) instead of, in place of
ἀξιόω	consider worthy
ἀπείθεια, -είας, ἡ	disobedience
ἀπειθέω	disobey, be disobedient, resist (+*dat obj*)
ἀπιστία, -ας, ἡ	unbelief; unfaithfulness
ἀπολύτρωσις, -ώσεως, ἡ	release, liberation, deliverance, redemption

▷ List 13 — 2×

ἀρχηγός, -οῦ, ὁ	founder, originator
ἄφεσις, ἀφέσεως, ἡ	release; forgiveness (of)
βαπτισμός, -οῦ, ὁ	baptism, (ceremonial) plunging/washing
βεβαιόω	confirm, establish; guarantee [legal term]
βιβλίον, -ου, τό	scroll; document
βρῶμα, βρώματος, τό	food
γάλα, -ακτος, τό	milk
γυμνάζω	train, practice, discipline
δάκρυον, -ύου, τό	tear(drop)
δεκατόω	(*act*) receive/collect a tithe/tenth; (*mid*) pay a tithe/tenth

▷ List 14 — 2×

δέσμιος, -ίου, ὁ	prisoner
δηλόω	make clear, disclose, reveal, explain
διακονέω	(+*dat obj*) serve; care for; wait on; administer
διάνοια, -οίας, ἡ	mind, understanding; thought, disposition
διδαχή, -ῆς, ἡ	teaching [activity or content]
δικαίωμα, -ώματος, τό	ordinance, requirement; righteous/just act
διότι	because, since; for; because of this
ἐάνπερ	if in fact, if indeed
ἕβδομος, -όμη, -ον	seventh
ἐγγύς	near [spatial or temporal]; (*prep* +*gen/dat*) near

▷ **List 15**		2×
ἐγκαινίζω	inaugurate	▷
ἐγκαταλείπω	leave behind; forsake, abandon	▷
ἐκδέχομαι	wait (for), expect, anticipate	
ἐκζητέω	seek out	
ἐκλύω	(*mid-pass*) become weary/weak, give out/up	
ἐκφεύγω	escape; flee	▷
ἐλαττόω	make lower/inferior, diminish	
ἐμφανίζω	(*trans act*) make visible; make known/clear; (*intrans mid*) appear	
ἐνδείκνυμι	(*mid*) show, demonstrate, exhibit	▷
ἐντέλλω	(*mid*) command, instruct	

▷ **List 16**		2×
ἐπαισχύνομαι	be ashamed (of)	
ἔπειτα	then, next	
ἐπιγράφω	write on, inscribe	
ἐπιζητέω	seek after, search for; seek, want	
ἐπιτελέω	finish; complete, accomplish, fulfill (a duty)	
ἐπιτυγχάνω	obtain, attain (+*gen/acc obj*)	▷
εὐλάβεια, -είας, ἡ	reverence, awe/fear of God	
εὐλογία, -ας, ἡ	praise; blessing; gift	
ἐχθρός, -ά, -όν	hated; hostile; (*subst*) enemy	
Ἠσαῦ, ὁ (*indecl*)	Esau	

▷ List 17 2×

θεμέλιος, -ίου, ὁ	foundation
θιγγάνω	touch (+*gen obj*) ▶
θυσιαστήριον, -ίου, τό	altar
Ἰωσήφ, ὁ (*indecl*)	Joseph
κακουχέω	mistreat, torment, injure
καταλείπω	(*trans act*) leave (behind); (*intrans mid-pass*) remain, be left behind
κατανοέω	look at, observe; consider [something one is looking at]; think about, contemplate
κιβωτός, -οῦ, ἡ	boat, ark; chest, ark [of the covenant]
κληρονομία, -ας, ἡ	inheritance; property, possession
κτίσις, -εως, τό	creation [act or product]

▷ List 18 2×

λατρεία, -ας, ἡ	cultic service, worship
λειτουργία, -ας, ἡ	service [cultic or generic]
λειτουργός, -οῦ, ὁ	minister, [cultic] servant
Λευ(ε)ί(ς), Λευ(ε)ί, ὁ (freq. *indecl*)	Levi
μάρτυς, μάρτυρος, ὁ	witness
μεγαλωσύνη, -ῆς, ἡ	majesty, the Majesty [as a term for God]
μερισμός, -οῦ, ὁ	division, separation; distribution, apportionment
μεταλαμβάνω	have/receive a share, partake (+*gen obj*) ▶
μήτε	[continuing a previous *neg*] and not, neither, nor
μόσχος, -ου, ὁ	calf, young bull

▷ List 19 2×

νομοθετέω	(*act*) enact by law; (*mid*) receive laws, be furnished with laws
νυνί	now, at this time
νωθρός, -ά, -όν	sluggish, lazy
ξένος, -η, -ον	strange, foreign; (*subst*) stranger, foreigner
οἰκουμένη, -ης, ἡ	the inhabited world; the (Roman) empire
ὁλοκαύτωμα, -ώματος, τό	whole burnt offering
ὁμοιότης, -ητος, ἡ	likeness, καθ᾽ ὁμοιότητα in the same way
ὁμολογέω	acknowledge; declare, confess
ὀργή, -ῆς, ἡ	anger; wrath
ὅρκος, -ου, ὁ	oath

▷ List 20 2×

ὀσφῦς, -ύος, ἡ	waist, loins
οὐδέποτε	never
οὔπω	not yet
παράβασις, -άσεως, ἡ	transgression, violation
παραπικρασμός, -οῦ, ὁ	provocation, rebellion
πάρειμι	be present/here, have come
πεῖρα, πείρας, ἡ	attempt; experience
περίκειμαι	(+*dat obj*) surround; (+*acc obj*) have around oneself, be surrounded by, wear
περισσός, -ή, -όν	extraordinary, remarkable; abundant, superfluous; (*comp*) περισσότερος, -έρα, -ον greater, better, excessive; [*neut* of *comp* as *adv*] even more
περισσοτέρως	(*comp*) (even) more; (*superl*) especially

▷ List 21	2×
πληθύνω	increase, multiply (something), make (someone) numerous
πληροφορία, -ας, ἡ	assurance, certainty
ποικίλος, -η, -ον	(*pl*) of various kinds
πόρνος, -ου, ὁ	sexually immoral person, fornicator
πόσος, -η, -ον	[*interr* or *exclam*] how much?, how great?; how much?, how many?
ποτέ (*encl*)	when, at some time; formerly, once
πού (*encl*)	somewhere
πρέπω	(*impers*) it is fitting/appropriate/right
προσδέχομαι	receive, welcome; wait for, await, expect
προσέχω	(+*dat obj*) look after, pay attention/attend to; devote/apply oneself to ▸

▷ List 22	2×
προσοχθίζω	be angry (with)
Σαλήμ, ἡ (*indecl*)	Salem
σκιά, -ᾶς, ἡ	shadow, [extended sense] outline, (mere) representation
στερεός, -ά, -όν	firm, solid; steadfast
στεφανόω	crown (someone)
συμπαθέω	sympathize with ▸
συναντάω	meet (+*dat obj*)
ταῦρος, ταύρου, ὁ	bull
ταχέως	quickly, without delay; soon; (*comp*) τάχιον more quickly
τέλειος, -εία, -ον	complete, perfect, mature [of character or behavior]; (*comp*) τελειότερος, -έρα, -ον more perfect

▷ List 23 2×

τεσσεράκοντα/ τεσσαράκοντα (*indecl*)	forty
τροφή, -ῆς, ἡ	nourishment, food
τυγχάνω	happen upon, meet with, obtain, attain (+*gen obj*) ▸
ὑπακούω	obey
ὑπομονή, -ῆς, ἡ	endurance, perseverance, steadfastness
ὑποπόδιον, -ίου, τό	footstool
ὑψηλός, -ή, -όν	high, tall; exalted, proud, haughty
φυλή, -ῆς, ἡ	tribe; people group
φωτίζω	(*trans*) illuminate, light up; enlighten, give light to
χεῖλος, χείλους, τό	lip; χεῖλος τῆς θαλάσσης shore

▷ List 24 2 to 1×

ἀγαλλίασις, -άσεως, ἡ	great joy, extreme gladness
ἀγενεαλόγητος, -ον	without genealogy, of unrecorded descent
ἁγιασμός, -οῦ, ὁ	holiness, consecration
ἁγιότης, -ητος, ἡ	holiness
ἄγκυρα, -ύρας, ἡ	anchor
ἀγνοέω	not know, be uninformed/ignorant; not understand; ignore, disregard
ἀγνόημα, -ήματος, τό	sin committed in ignorance
χειροποίητος, -ον	made by hand
χρυσοῦς, -ῆ, -οῦν	golden
ὠφελέω	help, benefit, be of use to (+*dat/acc obj*)

▷ List 25 1×

ἀγρυπνέω	stay alert, be watchful
ἀγών, -ῶνος, ὁ	(athletic) contest; struggle
ἀδικία, -ας, ἡ	injustice, unrighteousness; wrongdoing, misdeed
ἄδικος, -ον	unjust, unrighteous
ἀδόκιμος, -ον	unqualified, disqualified; worthless
ἀεί	always, constantly
ἀθετέω	nullify, invalidate; reject
ἄθλησις, -ήσεως, ἡ	contest, struggle
αἴγειος, -εία, -ον	of a goat
Αἰγύπτιος, -ία, -ον	(*subst*) Egyptian

▷ List 26 1×

αἱματεκχυσία, -ας, ἡ	shedding of blood
αἴνεσις, -έσεως, ἡ	praise
αἱρέω	(*mid*) choose; prefer ➤
αἰσθητήριον, -ίου, τό	faculty, capacity to understand
αἰσχύνη, -ης, ἡ	shame, dishonor; [sense/experience of] shame; shameful deed
αἰτία, -ας, ἡ	cause, reason; accusation, charge
αἴτιος, -ία, -ον	(*subst*) cause, reason; ground [for legal action]
ἄκακος, -ον	innocent, guileless; simple, naïve
ἄκανθα, ἀκάνθης, ἡ	thorn; thornbush
ἀκατάλυτος, -ον	indestructible, endless

▷ List 27 1×

ἀκλινής, -ές	unwavering, firm
ἀκροθίνιον, -ίου, τό	spoils, plunder
ἄκρον, -ου, τό	high point, top; extreme limit, end
ἀλλάσσω	change, alter; exchange ▷
ἀλυσιτελής, -ές	unprofitable
ἄμεμπτος, -ον	blameless, faultless
ἀμήτωρ, ἀμήτορος	motherless
ἄμμος, -ου, ἡ	sand
ἄμωμος, -ον	unblemished; blameless
ἀναγκαῖος, -αία, -ον	necessary, important

▷ List 28 1×

ἀνάγω	lead/bring up
ἀναδέχομαι	receive, accept
ἀναθεωρέω	look at carefully; consider, reflect on
ἀναιρέω	do away with, destroy, kill
ἀνακαινίζω	renew, restore
ἀνακάμπτω	go back, return
ἀναλογίζομαι	consider carefully
ἀναμιμνῄσκω	(*trans act*) remind; (*intrans mid*) remember
ἀνάμνησις, -ήσεως, ἡ	reminder, remembrance
ἀναρίθμητος, -ον	innumerable

▷ List 29 1×

ἀνασταυρόω	crucify (again)
ἀναστροφή, -ῆς, ἡ	conduct, way of life
ἀνατέλλω	(*trans*) cause to rise; (*intrans*) rise, come up ▸
ἀνέχω	(*mid +gen/acc obj*) bear with, tolerate, put up with
ἀνίημι	let go, loose ▸
ἀνορθόω	set straight, straighten up
ἀνταγωνίζομαι	struggle against
ἀνταποδίδωμι	give/pay back [favorable or unfavorable actions]
ἀντικαθίστημι	(*intrans*) be set against, oppose, resist ▸
ἀντίτυπος, -ον	corresponding, (*subst*) antitype, representation

▷ List 30 1×

ἀνυπότακτος, -ον	not made subject, [of people] rebellious
ἄνω	above; up(ward)
ἀνώτερος, -έρα, -ον	[*neut sg* as *adv*] higher; preceding, earlier, above [*comp* of ἄνω]
ἀνωφελής, -ές	unprofitable, useless
ἀόρατος, -ον	invisible
ἀπαλλάσσω	set free, deliver
ἀπαράβατος, -ον	permanent
ἀπάτη, -ης, ἡ	deception, deceit
ἀπάτωρ, -ορος	fatherless
ἀπαύγασμα, -άσματος, τό	radiance, effulgence; reflection

▷ List 31	1×
ἄπειρος, -ον	inexperienced, unacquainted (with)
ἀπεκδέχομαι	await
ἀποβάλλω	throw away ➤
ἀποβλέπω	look/gaze intently at; pay attention to
ἀπογράφω	register (someone), enter (someone/something) into a list ➤
ἀποδεκατόω	collect a tenth/tithe
ἀποδοκιμάζω	reject as unworthy/unfit
ἀποκαθίστημι/ ἀποκαθιστάνω	restore, reestablish ➤
ἀπόκειμαι	lay/put away [for safekeeping]; (*impers*) it is appointed
ἀπόλαυσις, -αύσεως, ἡ	enjoyment

▷ List 32	1×
ἀποστρέφω	(*mid*) turn away from, reject
ἀποτίθημι	(*mid*) put away, lay aside
ἀπώλεια, -είας, ἡ	destruction; waste
ἀρκέω	(*mid*) be content/satisfied
ἁρμός, -οῦ, ὁ	joint
ἀρνέομαι	deny; refuse; disown
ἁρπαγή, -ῆς, ἡ	seizure, plundering
ἀσάλευτος, -ον	unshakable
ἀσθενής, -ές	weak; sick, ill
ἀστεῖος, -εία, -ον	beautiful; well-bred

▷ List 33 1×

ἄστρον, -ου, τό	star
ἀσφαλής, -ές	certain, sure, dependable, safe
ἀφαιρέω	remove, take away
ἀφανής, -ές	unseen, hidden
ἀφανισμός, -οῦ, ὁ	disappearance
ἀφιλάργυρος, -ον	not loving money
ἀφίστημι	withdraw, depart; keep away
ἀφομοιόω	(*pf mid*) be like/similar
ἀφοράω	fix one's eyes (on); determine, see
Βαράκ, ὁ (*indecl*)	Barak

▷ List 34 1×

βεβαίωσις, -ώσεως, ἡ	confirmation, guarantee
βέβηλος, -ον	profane, worldly, impure
βλαστάνω	produce (growth), make grow
βοήθεια, -είας, ἡ	help, aid
βοηθέω	help, come to the aid of (+*dat obj*)
βοηθός, -όν	helping, (*subst*) helper
βοτάνη, -ης, ἡ	plant, vegetation
βουλή, -ῆς, ἡ	intention, motive; decision, plan, purpose
βούλομαι	want, desire; intend, plan
βρῶσις, βρώσεως, ὁ	food; eating, consumption

▷ List 35 1×

γάμος, -ου, ὁ	wedding celebration; marriage
Γεδεών, ὁ (*indecl*)	Gideon
γενεαλογέω	trace genealogically
γεωργέω	cultivate
γηράσκω	grow old
γνόφος, -ου, ὁ	darkness
γόνυ, γόνατος, τό	knee
γυμνός, -ή, -όν	naked, bare, [figurative] uncovered; inadequately dressed; lightly dressed
δάμαλις, -άλεως, ἡ	heifer, young cow
δέησις, δεήσεως, ἡ	entreaty; prayer, petition

▷ List 36 1×

δείκνυμι	show, make known; explain ▷
δέος, -ους, τό	awe
δέρμα, -ατος, τό	skin, hide
δεσμός, -οῦ, ὁ	(*sg*) binding, impediment; (*pl*) bonds, chains, [extended sense] imprisonment
δημιουργός, -οῦ, ὁ	craftsperson, maker, builder
δήπου	of course, surely
διαβαίνω	cross, go through ▷
διάβολος, -ον	slanderous; (*subst*) adversary; devil
διακονία, -ας, ἡ	service, serving; (ministerial) service, ministry
διάκρισις, -ίσεως, ἡ	differentiation, distinction

JAMES

▷ List 1	5 to 3×
ἀκροατής, -οῦ, ὁ	hearer
ἄνωθεν	from above
βούλομαι	want, desire; intend, plan
κριτής, -οῦ, ὁ	judge
πειράζω	test; tempt
πλούσιος, -ία, -ον	rich, wealthy; rich (in), abounding (in)
ποιητής, -οῦ, ὁ	doer
πτωχός, -ή, -όν	poor
τέλειος, -εία, -ον	complete, perfect, mature [of character or behavior]
φονεύω	murder

▷ List 2	3×
δαμάζω	subdue, tame
δείκνυμι	show, make known; explain ▸
διακρίνω	(*mid*) make a distinction [among oneself and others]; dispute, contest, contend (with) ▸
δικαιόω	justify, consider right/righteous, make righteous; vindicate, put in the right
ἔλεος, ἐλέους, τό	compassion, mercy
ἐσθής, -ῆτος, ἡ	clothing
καλῶς	well, appropriately, effectively; correctly
καταλαλέω	disparage, speak evil of
λείπω	(*mid*) be lacking/deficient
μακροθυμέω	be patient

▹ List 3 — 3 to 2×

ἄγε	come!, come on! (*interj*) [*pres impv* of ἄγω]
ἀκατάστατος, -ον	unstable, unsettled
ἄνθος, -ους, τό	flower
ἀντιτάσσω	(*mid +dat obj*) oppose, resist
ἀποκυέω	give birth to
αὔριον	next day, tomorrow; soon, shortly
μέλος, -ους, τό	member [of the human body], limb; member [of a group]
μήτε	[continuing a previous *neg*] and not, neither, nor
πταίω	stumble, [extended sense] make a mistake
ὑπομονή, -ῆς, ἡ	endurance, perseverance, steadfastness

▹ List 4 — 2×

βραδύς, -εῖα, -ύ	slow
βρέχω	wet; send rain; (*impers*) it rains
γένεσις, -έσεως, ἡ	birth; existence
γλυκύς, γλυκεῖα, γλυκύ	sweet
δίψυχος, -ον	double-minded, wavering
ἐλευθερία, -ας, ἡ	freedom, liberty
ἐνιαυτός, -οῦ, ὁ	year
ἔοικα	be like, resemble [old *pf* of εἴκω]
ἐπαγγέλλομαι	promise
ἔπειτα	then, next

▷ List 5 2×

ἐπιθυμία, -ας, ἡ	desire, longing; lust, craving
ἐπιστρέφω	(*trans*) turn, redirect
ἐριθεία, -ᾶς, ἡ	selfish ambition
ζῆλος, ζήλου/ζήλους, ὁ/τό	zeal; jealousy
ἡδονή, -ῆς, ἡ	pleasure
ἡλίκος, -η, -ον	such, what size [context indicates whether it is "how great" or "how small"]
θρησκεία, -ας, ἡ	religion, religious service
ἰός, ἰοῦ, ὁ	poison; rust
καθίστημι/καθιστάνω	(*intrans mid*) make oneself, become
κατακαυχάομαι	boast against, exult over (+*gen obj*)

▷ List 6 2×

κατανοέω	look at, observe; consider [something one is looking at]; think about, contemplate
καυχάομαι	boast (about)
λαμπρός, -ά, -όν	bright, shining
μεστός, -ή, -όν	full
μετάγω	direct, steer
μοιχεύω	commit adultery
ναί	yes
ὀργή, -ῆς, ἡ	anger; wrath
ὄφελος, ὀφέλους, τό	benefit, gain, good
παραβάτης, -ου, ὁ	transgressor

▷ List 7 2×

παρουσία, -ας, ἡ	presence; arrival, coming
πειρασμός, -οῦ, ὁ	test, trial; temptation
πικρός, -ή, -όν	bitter (taste), [figurative] bitter attitude, embittered
πλανάω	(*act*) lead astray, deceive; (*mid*) wander, go astray, be misled
πλησίον	(+*gen*) near; (*subst*) neighbor
πόθεν	from where?, how is it that?
πραΰτης, -ητος, τό	humility, gentleness
ταπεινός, -ή, -όν	humble; lowly
ὑπομένω	stay behind; endure, stand firm
φίλος, -η, -ον	friendly; (*subst*) friend

▷ List 8 2 to 1×

ἁγνίζω	purify
ἁγνός, -ή, -όν	pure
ἀδελφή, -ῆς, ἡ	sister
ἀδιάκριτος, -ον	impartial
ἀδικία, -ας, ἡ	injustice, unrighteousness; wrongdoing, misdeed
ἀκαταστασία, -ας, ἡ	instability, disorder; turmoil, disturbance
φλογίζω	set on fire
φύσις, -εως, τό	nature [inherent/basic qualities, features, or character]
χαλιναγωγέω	bridle, control
χόρτος, -ου, ὁ	grass

▷ List 9 1×

ἀλαζονεία, -ας, ἡ	arrogance
ἀλείφω	anoint
ἁλυκός, -ή, -όν	salty
ἀμάω	reap, cut [grain], mow
ἀμίαντος, -ον	undefiled, pure
ἄμπελος, -έλου, ἡ	vine, grapevine
ἀνάπτω	kindle
ἀναστροφή, -ῆς, ἡ	conduct, way of life
ἀνατέλλω	(*trans*) cause to rise; (*intrans*) rise, come up
ἀναφέρω	lead/take up; offer up [cultic term]

▷ List 10 1×

ἀνέλεος, -ον	merciless
ἀνεμίζω	(*pass*) be driven by the wind
ἄνεμος, ἀνέμου, ὁ	wind
ἀνθίστημι	resist, oppose, withstand (+*dat obj*) ▷
ἀνθρώπινος, -ίνη, -ον	human
ἀντί	(+*gen*) instead of, in place of
ἀνυπόκριτος, -ον	without pretense, genuine, sincere
ἀπαρχή, -ῆς, ἡ	firstfruits
ἅπας, ἅπασα, ἅπαν	whole, all; (*subst*) everyone, all, everything
ἀπατάω	deceive, mislead

▷ List 11	1×
ἀπείραστος, -ον	unable to be tempted
ἁπλῶς	sincerely, without reservation
ἀποσκίασμα, -άσματος, τό	shadow
ἀποστερέω	steal, defraud
ἀποτελέω	(*act*) finish, complete; (*mid*) come to completion, be fully formed
ἀποτίθημι	(*mid*) put away, lay aside
ἀργός, -ή, -όν	idle, having nothing to do; lazy; useless
ἄργυρος, -ύρου, ὁ	silver [metal]; silver money
ἀσθενέω	be sick; be weak
ἄσπιλος, -ον	spotless; without fault

▷ List 12	1×
ἀτιμάζω	dishonor, shame
ἀτμίς, -ίδος, ἡ	mist, vapor
αὐχέω	boast
ἀφανίζω	(*trans act*) destroy; (*intrans mid*) disappear, vanish
βασιλικός, -ή, -όν	royal
βλαστάνω	produce (growth), make grow
βλασφημέω	slander, speak disrespectfully about, revile
βοή, -ῆς, ἡ	cry, shout
βρύω	gush forth (with)
γέεννα, γεέννης, ἡ	Gehenna, Valley of Hinnom

▷ List 13 1×

γέλως, -ωτος, ὁ	laughter
γεωργός, -οῦ, ὁ	farmer, cultivator
γυμνός, -ή, -όν	naked, bare, [figurative] uncovered; inadequately dressed; lightly dressed
δαιμονιώδης, -ες	demonic
δαπανάω	spend (money)
δέησις, δεήσεως, ἡ	entreaty; prayer, petition
δελεάζω	lure, entice
διάβολος, -ον	slanderous; (*subst*) adversary; devil
διαλογισμός, -οῦ, ὁ	reasoning, thought
διασπορά, -ᾶς, ἡ	dispersion

▷ List 14 1×

διότι	because, since; for; because of this
δοκίμιον, -ίου, τό	testing; genuineness
δόκιμος, -ον	approved
δόσις, -εως, ἡ	giving; gift
δυνατός, -ή, -όν	able, capable, strong, powerful; possible
δώρημα, -ήματος, τό	gift
εἰρηνικός, -ή, -όν	peaceable
εἶτα	then, next; furthermore
ἐκδέχομαι	wait (for), expect
ἐκλέγομαι	choose; select

▷ **List 15**	1×
ἐκπίπτω	fall off ▷
ἐλαία, -ας, ἡ	olive tree; olive
ἔλαιον, ἐλαίου, τό	olive oil
ἐλαύνω	drive/propel along
ἐλάχιστος, -ίστη, -ον	least, smallest [in status, value, or size]
ἐλέγχω	expose; reprove; convict, accuse
ἕλκω	draw, pull; draw, attract
ἐμπορεύομαι	(*intrans*) engage in business
ἔμφυτος, -ον	implanted
ἐνάλιος, -ον	of the sea, (*subst pl*) sea creatures

▷ **List 16**	1×
ἔνειμι	be in(side) ▷
ἐνεργέω	(*intrans*) be at work/active; (*trans*) work, produce
ἔνοχος, -ον	subject to, held in; (held) liable (for), guilty (of), deserving of
ἐντεῦθεν	from here
ἕξ (*indecl*)	six
ἐξέλκω	draw/drag away
ἐξομολογέω	(*mid*) confess, admit; profess, acknowledge
ἐπέρχομαι	come (up)on, approach
ἐπιβλέπω	look at intently; pay close attention to
ἐπίγειος, -ον	earthly

▷ List 17 1×

ἐπιεικής, -ές	reasonable, fair, yielding
ἐπιθυμέω	long for, desire (+*gen/acc obj*)
ἐπικαλέω	call, name ▸
ἐπιλανθάνομαι	(+*gen/acc obj*) forget; neglect, ignore
ἐπιλησμονή, -ῆς, ἡ	forgetfulness
ἐπιποθέω	long for, strongly desire
ἐπισκέπτομαι	visit; look after
ἐπίσταμαι	understand; know
ἐπιστήμων, -ον	learned, intelligent
ἐπιστολή, -ῆς, ἡ	letter

▷ List 18 1×

ἐπιτήδειος, -εία, -ον	necessary
ἐπιτυγχάνω	obtain, attain (+*gen/acc obj*) ▸
ἐργάτης, -ου, ὁ	worker, laborer; doer
ἑρπετόν, -οῦ, τό	reptile
ἔσοπτρον, ἐσόπτρου, τό	mirror
εὐθέως	immediately
εὐθυμέω	be cheerful/in good spirits
εὐθύνω	make straight; steer, (*subst ptc*) pilot
εὐλογία, -ας, ἡ	praise; blessing; gift
εὐπειθής, -ές	compliant, obedient

▷ List 19 1×

εὐπρέπεια, -είας, ἡ	beauty
εὐχή, -ῆς, ἡ	prayer
εὔχομαι	pray (for); wish (for)
ἐφήμερος, -ον	for the day, daily
ἔχθρα, -ας, ἡ	enmity, hatred
ἐχθρός, -ά, -όν	hated; hostile; (*subst*) enemy
ζηλόω	be zealous for; be jealous
ἡγέομαι	consider, regard
Ἠλίας, Ἠλίου, ὁ	Elijah
ἥλιος, -ίου, ὁ	sun

▷ List 20 1×

θανατηφόρος, -ον	deadly
θερίζω	reap, harvest
θερμαίνω	(*mid*) warm oneself
θησαυρίζω	store (up), save
θρῆσκος/θρησκός, -ον/όν	religious
θύρα, -ας, ἡ	door; entrance
θυσιαστήριον, -ίου, τό	altar
ἰάομαι	heal; restore
ἵππος, -ου, ὁ	horse
Ἰσαάκ, ὁ (*indecl*)	Isaac

▷ List 21 — 1×

ἰσχύω	be strong/powerful/able; prevail
Ἰώβ, ὁ (*indecl*)	Job
καθαρίζω	cleanse, make clean
καθαρός, -ά, -όν	clean; pure; innocent
κακία, -ας, ἡ	wickedness; malice; trouble, misfortune
κακοπάθεια/κακοπαθία, -είας/ίας, ἡ	suffering; perseverance [in suffering]
κακοπαθέω	suffer hardship
κακῶς	badly, ill; wrongly, wickedly
καλύπτω	cover; hide, conceal
κάμνω	be weary; be ill

▷ List 22 — 1×

καταδικάζω	condemn, pronounce guilty
καταδυναστεύω	oppress
κατάρα, -ας, ἡ	curse
καταράομαι	curse
κατεργάζομαι	do; produce, bring about
κατέρχομαι	come/go down
κατήφεια, -είας, ἡ	dejection, despondency
κατιόω	(*mid*) become rusty
κατοικίζω	cause to dwell/settle
καύσων, -ωνος, ὁ	scorching heat

▹ List 23 1×

καύχησις, -ήσεως, ἡ	boasting
κενός, -ή, -όν	empty, fruitless; in vain, for nothing
κενῶς	in vain, to no purpose
κερδαίνω	gain ➢
κληρονόμος, -ου, ὁ	heir; beneficiary, heir
κλύδων, -ωνος, ὁ	rough water, wave, surge
κρίμα, -ατος, τό	judgment [process of evaluation]; judgment [end result], judicial verdict
κριτήριον, -ίου, τό	law court; lawsuit
κτίσμα, -ατος, τό	that which is created, creation
μακαρίζω	consider blessed/fortunate

▹ List 24 1×

μακροθυμία, -ας, ἡ	patience; forbearance
μαραίνω	(*mid*) die out, wither, disappear
μαρτύριον, -ίου, τό	testimony, witness, proof
μάταιος, -αία, -ον	empty, idle, vain, useless
μάχη, -ης, ἡ	battle; quarrel, dispute
μάχομαι	fight; quarrel, dispute
μέντοι (*postp*)	nevertheless, however
μεταστρέφω	change, alter; distort, twist <TH only> ➢
μετατρέπω	turn (something) around; change (something) <NA/UBS, SBL only> ➢
μήν, μηνός, ὁ	month

▷ List 25 1×

μήτι	not
μισθός, -οῦ, ὁ	pay, wages; recompense, reward
μοιχαλίς, -ίδος, ἡ	adulteress
νομοθέτης, -ου, ὁ	lawgiver
ξηραίνω	(*trans act*) dry (up/out); (*intrans mid*) become dry; wither
ὅδε, ἥδε, τόδε	this
οἰκτίρμων, -ον	compassionate, merciful
οἴομαι	think, suppose, expect
ὁλόκληρος, -ον	complete, whole
ὀλολύζω	cry with a loud voice

▷ List 26 1×

ὀμνύω	make an oath, swear
ὁμοιοπαθής, -ές	with the same nature (as), like
ὁμοίως	likewise, in the same way
ὁμοίωσις, -ώσεως, ἡ	likeness
ὀνειδίζω	revile, mock, insult; reprimand, reproach
ὀπή, -ῆς, ἡ	opening
ὁποῖος, -οία, -ον	of what sort, what kind of; as
ὅρκος, -ου, ὁ	oath
ὁρμή, -ῆς, ἡ	impulse
ὀρφανός, -ή, -όν	without parents, (*subst*) orphan

▷ List 27	1×
οὖς, ὠτός, τό	ear; hearing, understanding
ὄψιμος, -ον	late in the season, (*subst*) late/spring rain
παρακύπτω	stoop down (and look); look into [figuratively]
παραλλαγή, -ῆς, ἡ	change, variation
παραλογίζομαι	deceive
παραμένω	stay; continue, persevere [in a state or condition]
παρέρχομαι	pass by; pass [of time]; pass away, disappear ▷
πενθέω	(*intrans*) grieve, mourn
πένθος, -ου, ὁ	grief, mourning
περιπίπτω	fall into, encounter (+*dat obj*) ▷

▷ List 28	1×
περισσεία, -ας, ἡ	surplus, abundance
πετεινόν, -οῦ, τό	bird
πηγή, -ῆς, ἡ	spring; well
πηδάλιον, -ίου, τό	rudder
πλάνη, -ης, ἡ	error, deceit
πλῆθος, πλήθους, τό	multitude, a great quantity
πλοῦτος, πλούτου, ὁ/τό	wealth, riches; abundance
ποίησις, -ήσεως, ἡ	doing, what one does
ποικίλος, -η, -ον	(*pl*) of various kinds
ποῖος, ποία, ποῖον	of what kind?; which?, what?

▷ List 29 — 1×

πολεμέω	wage war, fight
πόλεμος, -έμου, ὁ	war; battle, fight
πολύσπλαγχνος, -ον	very compassionate
πορεία, -ας, ἡ	journey; way of life, pursuit
πόρνη, -ης, ἡ	sex worker
πρᾶγμα, πράγματος, τό	deed, act, matter, thing, occurrence
πρόϊμος, -ον	early in the season, (*subst*) early/winter rain
προσευχή, -ῆς, ἡ	prayer
προσκαλέω	(*mid*) invite, call to, summon
προσωπολημπτέω	show partiality/favoritism

▷ List 30 — 1×

προσωπολημψία, -ας, ἡ	partiality
Ῥαάβ, ἡ (*indecl*)	Rahab
ῥιπίζω	blow here and there
ῥυπαρία, -ας, ἡ	filth, [extended sense] defilement, moral filth
ῥυπαρός, -ά, -όν	filthy, dirty
Σαβαώθ (*indecl*)	[Heb.] Sabaoth, of armies/hosts
σήπω	(*pf*) be decayed, have become rotted
σητόβρωτος, -ον	moth-eaten
σκληρός, -ά, -όν	hard, harsh
σοφός, -ή, -όν	wise; skillful

▹ List 31 1×

σπαταλάω	live luxuriously/indulgently	
σπιλόω	stain, defile	
στενάζω	sigh, groan, [extended sense] complain	
στέφανος, -άνου, ὁ	wreath, crown	
στηρίζω	set, establish; strengthen/make more firm [inwardly]	▸
στρατεύω	(*mid*) serve in the army; wage war	
συκῆ, -ῆς, ἡ	fig tree	
σῦκον, σύκου, τό	fig	
συλλαμβάνω	capture, seize; conceive	▸
συνεργέω	work together with	

▹ List 32 1×

σφαγή, -ῆς, ἡ	slaughter
ταλαιπωρέω	be miserable, experience distress
ταλαπωρία, -ας, ἡ	misery, distress
ταπεινόω	bring low; humble [positive], humiliate [negative]
ταπείνωσις, -ώσεως, ἡ	humiliation; low status, humble station
ταχύς, ταχεῖα, ταχύ	quick
τελειόω	complete, finish; bring (something) to its goal/conclusion; perfect
τελέω	complete, finish; carry out (completely), accomplish; pay
τηλικοῦτος, -αύτη, -ο	so great/large
τίκτω	give birth to, bear, [inanimate] produce

▷ List 33 1×

τίμιος, -ία, -ον	valuable, precious
τρέφω	nourish, feed, support
τροπή, -ῆς, ἡ	turning
τροφή, -ῆς, ἡ	nourishment, food
τροχός, -οῦ, ὁ	wheel [figuratively used to refer to the course of life]
τρυφάω	live indulgently, revel
ὑετός, -οῦ, ὁ	rain
ὕλη, -ης, ἡ	forest
ὑπερήφανος, -ον	arrogant, proud, haughty
ὑπόδειγμα, -είγματος, τό	example, pattern

▷ List 34 1×

ὑποδέχομαι	welcome, receive into one's house
ὑποπόδιον, -ίου, τό	footstool
ὑποτάσσω	subject, subordinate ▷
ὕψος, -ους, τό	height [dimension or position]; high position
ὑψόω	lift up; exalt
φαίνω	(*act*) shine; (*mid*) appear
φαῦλος, φαύλη, φαῦλον	bad; low-grade
φεύγω	flee; escape; avoid
φθόνος, -ου, ὁ	envy
φιλία, -ας, ἡ	friendship, affection, fondness

▷ List 35 1×

φορέω	bear constantly/regularly; [of clothing] wear
φρίσσω	shudder [from fear]
φυλή, -ῆς, ἡ	tribe; people group
χαλινός, -οῦ, ὁ	bit, bridle
χήρα, -ας, ἡ	widow
χορτάζω	(*trans act*) fill, feed; (*intrans mid*) eat one's fill; be satisfied
χρή	(*impers*) it ought
χρυσοδακτύλιος, -ον	wearing a gold ring
χρυσός, -οῦ, ὁ	gold; objects of gold [e.g., jewelry, money]
χώρα, -ας, ἡ	land; region; country

▷ List 36 1×

ψάλλω	sing, make music
ψεύδομαι	lie, speak falsely
ψυχικός, -ή, -όν	[that which pertains to ψυχή] natural, worldly
ὦ	(*interj*) O [address]; oh!
ὥσπερ	(just) as

1 PETER

▷ List 1	6 to 3×
ἀγαθοποιέω	do good to [+*acc* of person]; do good/what is right
ἀγαλλιάω	exult, rejoice; be overjoyed
ἀναστροφή, -ῆς, ἡ	conduct, way of life
ἀπειθέω	disobey, be disobedient, resist (+*dat obj*)
ἀποκαλύπτω	reveal, disclose ▷
ἀποκάλυψις, -ύψεως, ἡ	revelation, disclosure
ἐκλεκτός, -ή, -όν	chosen, elect
ἐπιθυμία, -ας, ἡ	desire, longing; lust, craving
πάθημα, -ήματος, τό	suffering; emotion, passion
ὑποτάσσω	subject, subordinate ▷

▷ List 2	3×
ἄφθαρτος, -ον	incorruptible, immortal, undecaying
διακονέω	(+*dat obj*) serve; care for; wait on; administer
διότι	because, since; for; because of this
δόλος, -ου, ὁ	deceit, cunning, craftiness
κακοποιός, -όν	(*subst*) evildoer
νήφω	be sober/temperate
ὁμοίως	likewise, in the same way
ποτέ (*encl*)	when, at some time; formerly, once
συνείδησις, -ήσεως, ἡ	consciousness, awareness; conscience
ὑπακοή, -ῆς, ἡ	obedience

▷ List 3 — 3 to 2×

ἀδελφότης, -ητος, ἡ	brotherhood, family of believers
ἀναγεννάω	cause to be born again, give a new birth
ἀναφέρω	lead/take up; offer up [cultic term]
ἄνευ	(+*gen*) without
ἄνθος, -ους, τό	flower
ἀντί	(+*gen*) instead of, in place of
ἀποδοκιμάζω	reject as unworthy/unfit
χόρτος, -ου, ὁ	grass
χρυσίον, -ου, τό	gold; objects of gold [e.g., jewelry, money]
ἄρτι	(just) now

▷ List 4 — 2×

ἐλεέω	have compassion (on), show mercy to
ἐλπίζω	hope (for); expect
ἔντιμος, -ον	honored, distinguished; valuable, precious
ἔπαινος, ἐπαίνου, ὁ	praise, recognition, commendation
ἐποπτεύω	watch, observe
ἕτοιμος, -οίμη, -ον	ready
ἱεράτευμα, -εύματος, τό	priesthood
κακία, -ας, ἡ	wickedness; malice; trouble, misfortune
καταισχύνω	put to shame
καταλαλέω	disparage, speak evil of

▷ List 5 — 2×

κομίζω	(*act*) bring; (*mid*) receive
κράτος, -ους, τό	strength, might, power; rule, sovereignty
λοιδορία, -ας, ἡ	verbal abuse, insult
ξενίζω	(*trans act*) astonish, surprise; (*intrans mid*) be astonished, surprised
παρεπίδημος, -ον	(*subst*) sojourner
παύω	(*trans act*) make stop/cease; (*intrans mid*) stop, cease
πειρασμός, -οῦ, ὁ	test, trial; temptation
πνευματικός, -ή, -όν	spiritual
ποικίλος, -η, -ον	(*sg*) manifold; (*pl*) of various kinds
ποίμνιον, -ίου, τό	flock

▷ List 6 — 2 to 1×

α′	1 [in the book title ΠΕΤΡΟΥ Α "1 Peter"]
ἀγαθοποιΐα, -ας, ἡ	doing what is good
ἀγαθοποιός, -όν	(*subst*) one who does good
ἁγιάζω	consecrate, make holy; regard as holy
ἁγιασμός, -οῦ, ὁ	holiness, consecration
ποῖος, ποία, ποῖον	of what kind?; which?, what?
προσευχή, -ῆς, ἡ	prayer
τιμάω	honor; set a price
ὑπομένω	stay behind; endure, stand firm
φθαρτός, -ή, -όν	perishable

▹ List 7 1×

ἁγνίζω	purify
ἄγνοια, -οίας, ἡ	ignorance
ἁγνός, -ή, -όν	pure
ἀγνωσία, -ας, ἡ	ignorance
ἄδικος, -ον	unjust, unrighteous
ἀδίκως	unjustly, undeservedly
ἄδολος, -ον	unadulterated, pure
ἀεί	always, constantly
ἀθέμιτος, -ίτου, ὁ	lawless; disgusting, wanton
αἰσχροκερδῶς	greedily

▹ List 8 1×

αἰσχύνω	(*mid*) be ashamed
ἀκρογωνιαῖος, -αία, -ον	at the extreme angle/corner, (*subst*) foundation, cornerstone
ἀληθής, -ές	true, trustworthy; real
ἀλλοτριεπίσκοπος, -όπου, ὁ	[the meaning of this word is not agreed upon, but posited glosses include] meddler, busybody; spy, informer, revolutionist
ἀμαράντινος, -ίνη, -ον	unfading
ἀμάραντος, -ον	unfading
ἀμίαντος, -ον	undefiled, pure
ἀμνός, -οῦ, ὁ	lamb
ἄμωμος, -ον	unblemished; blameless
ἀναγγέλλω	report; disclose, announce

▷ List 9 — 1×

ἀναγκαστῶς	under compulsion
ἀναζώννυμι	bind/gird up
ἀναπαύω	(*intrans mid*) rest
ἀναστρέφω	(*act*) return, go back; (*mid*) conduct oneself, live ➢
ἀνάχυσις, -ύσεως, ἡ	flood, excess
ἀνεκλάλητος, -ον	inexpressible
ἀνθίστημι	resist, oppose, withstand (+*dat obj*)
ἀνθρώπινος, -ίνη, -ον	human
ἀντίδικος, -ίκου, ὁ	[legal] adversary, opponent, accuser
ἀντιλοιδορέω	revile in return

▷ List 10 — 1×

ἀντιτάσσω	(*mid +dat obj*) oppose, resist
ἀντίτυπος, -ον	corresponding, (*subst*) antitype, representation
ἀνυπόκριτος, -ον	without pretense, genuine, sincere
ἅπαξ	once; once and for all
ἀπειλέω	threaten, warn
ἀπεκδέχομαι	await
ἀπέχω	(*intrans mid*) abstain from, keep away from
ἀπιστέω	not believe; be unfaithful
ἀπογίνομαι	die
ἀπόθεσις, -έσεως, ἡ	removal

▷ List 11	1×
ἀπολογία, -ας, ἡ	defense [a speech or the act of making a defense]
ἀπονέμω	assign, render, show
ἀποτίθημι	(*mid*) put away, lay aside
ἀπροσωπολήμτως	impartially
ἀργύριον, -ίου, τό	silver; money
ἀρετή, -ῆς, ἡ	excellence [often referring to character or civic performance], virtue
ἀρκετός, -ή, -όν	sufficient, adequate, enough
ἀρτιγέννητος, -ον	newborn
ἀρχιποίμην, -ενός, ὁ	chief shepherd
ἀσεβής, -ές	ungodly

▷ List 12	1×
ἀσέλγεια, -είας, ἡ	licentiousness, excessive sensuality
ἀσθενής, -ές	weak; sick, ill; (*comp*) ἀσθενέστερος, -έρα, -ον
Ἀσία, -ας, ἡ	Asia
ἄσπιλος, -ον	spotless; without fault
ἀσωτία, -ας, ἡ	recklessness, dissipation, debauchery
αὐξάνω/αὔξω	(*trans*) make grow/increase; (*intrans*) grow, increase
ἄφρων, -ον	senseless, foolish
Βαβυλών, -ῶνος, ἡ	Babylon
βάπτισμα, -ίσματος, τό	baptism, (ceremonial) plunging/washing
βασίλειος, -ον	royal

▷ List 13	1×
Βιθυνία, -ας, ἡ	Bithynia
βιόω	spend one's life, live
βλασφημέω	slander, speak disrespectfully about, revile
βούλημα, -ήματος, τό	purpose, intent, will
βρέφος, -ους, τό	infant, baby
γάλα, -ακτος, τό	milk
Γαλατία, -ας, ἡ	Galatia
γένος, -ους, τό	people group, family; offspring, descendant; kind, class
γεύομαι	taste, partake (*+gen/acc obj*)
γνῶσις, γνώσεως, ἡ	knowledge [understanding/comprehension or that which is known]

▷ List 14	1×
γογγυσμός, -οῦ, ὁ	discreet talk; murmuring, grumbling
γρηγορέω	be (fully) awake/alert; be watchful/on the alert
γυναικεῖος, -εία, -ον	feminine, (*subst*) wife
γωνία, -ας, ἡ	corner
δέησις, δεήσεως, ἡ	entreaty; prayer, petition
δεσπότης, -ου, ὁ	master, lord
δηλόω	make clear, disclose, reveal, explain
διάβολος, -ον	slanderous; (*subst*) adversary; devil
διάνοια, -οίας, ἡ	mind, understanding; thought, disposition
διασπορά, -ᾶς, ἡ	dispersion

▹ List 15 1×

διασῴζω	bring safely through, preserve; save, rescue ▸
δικαίως	[juridical] justly, fairly; [of character] uprightly, justly
δοκιμάζω	examine, evaluate; determine, put to the test; approve
δοκίμιον, -ίου, τό	testing; genuineness
ἐγκομβόομαι	put on, clothe oneself
ἐγκόπτω	hinder
εἰδωλολατρία, -ας, ἡ	image worship, idolatry
ἐκδίκησις, -ήσεως, ἡ	carrying out of justice; vengeance; punishment
ἐκζητέω	seek out
ἐκκλίνω	avoid, turn away/aside (from)

▹ List 16 1×

ἑκουσίως	willingly, voluntarily
ἐκπίπτω	fall off ▸
ἐκτενής, -ές	earnest, steadfast
ἐκτενῶς	earnestly, steadfastly
ἔλεος, ἐλέους, τό	compassion, mercy
ἐλευθερία, -ας, ἡ	freedom, liberty
ἐλεύθερος, -έρα, -ον	free
ἐμπλοκή, -ῆς, ἡ	braiding
ἐναντίον	(+*gen*) in front of, before; (*adv*) τοὐναντίον instead, on the contrary
ἔνδυσις, -ύσεως, ἡ	putting on, wearing

▹ List 17 1×

ἔννοια, -οίας, ἡ	way of thinking, thought
ἐξαγγέλλω	proclaim, make known
ἐξεραυνάω	search out, examine
ἔξωθεν	(from) outside; (*prep* +*gen*) outside
ἐπακολουθέω	follow close upon/after (+*dat obj*)
ἐπερώτημα, -ήματος, τό	pledge
ἐπηρεάζω	mistreat, disparage
ἐπιεικής, -ές	reasonable, fair, yielding
ἐπιθυμέω	long for, desire (+*gen/acc obj*)
ἐπικαλέω	(*mid*) call upon, invoke, appeal

▹ List 18 1×

ἐπικάλυμμα, -ύμματος, τό	covering
ἐπίλοιπος, -ον	remaining
ἐπιμαρτυρέω	bear witness, attest
ἐπιποθέω	long for, strongly desire
ἐπιρίπτω	throw (upon)
ἐπισκοπέω	oversee, look after, care for
ἐπισκοπή, -ῆς, ἡ	visitation; oversight
ἐπίσκοπος, -όπου, ὁ	overseer, guardian
ἐπιστολή, -ῆς, ἡ	letter
ἐπιστρέφω	(*intrans act/mid*) return, go/come back; turn (around); change (one's thinking or behavior) ▸

▷ List 19 1×

ἐπιτελέω	finish; complete, accomplish, fulfill (a duty)
ἐραυνάω	search, examine
ἑτοίμως	readily
εὐλογητός, -ή, -όν	blessed, praised
εὐλογία, -ας, ἡ	praise; blessing; gift
εὐπρόσδεκτος, -ον	acceptable
εὔσπλαγχνος, -ον	tenderhearted, compassionate
ζηλωτής, -οῦ, ὁ	enthusiast, loyalist; zealot
ζωοποιέω/ζῳοποιέω	give life to, make alive
ἡγεμών, ἡγεμόνος, ὁ	leader; governor

▷ List 20 1×

ἡσύχιος, -ον	quiet, well-ordered, at rest
θανατόω	put to death
θαυμαστός, -ή, -όν	marvelous, wonderful, remarkable
θεμελιόω	lay a foundation, found, establish
θρίξ, τριχός, ἡ	hair
θυσία, -ας, ἡ	sacrifice, offering
ἰάομαι	heal; restore
ἰσχύς, -ύος, ἡ	strength
ἴχνος, -ους, ὁ	footstep
καθαρός, -ά, -όν	clean; pure; innocent

▷ List 21	1×
καθό	how; insofar as, to the degree that
κακοποιέω	do what is evil
κακόω	harm, mistreat; spoil, corrupt
καλύπτω	cover; hide, conceal
Καππαδοκία, -ας, ἡ	Cappadocia
καταβολή, -ῆς, ἡ	foundation
κατακυριεύω	dominate, lord (over) (+*gen obj*)
καταλαλιά, -ᾶς, ἡ	slander
καταπίνω	swallow (up), gulp (down), [extended sense] devour ▶
καταρτίζω	restore, put in order; prepare, make ready

▷ List 22	1×
κατασκευάζω	prepare; build, construct
κατεργάζομαι	do; produce, bring about
κερδαίνω	gain ▶
κιβωτός, -οῦ, ἡ	boat, ark; chest, ark [of the covenant]
κλέος, -ους, τό	fame, good reputation
κλέπτης, -ου, ὁ	thief
κληρονομέω	(*intrans*) be an heir; (*trans*) acquire, obtain
κληρονομία, -ας, ἡ	inheritance; property, possession
κλῆρος, κλήρου, ὁ	lot; allotment, share
κοινωνέω	have a share, take part in; share

▷ List 23 1×

κοινωνός, -οῦ, ὁ/ἡ	companion, partner, sharer
κολαφίζω	strike, beat [with one's fists]
κοσμέω	put in order, arrange, prepare; adorn, make attractive
κραταιός, -ά, -όν	strong, mighty
κρείττων, κρεῖττον / κρείσσων, κρεῖσσον	better, superior [rank or value]
κρίμα, -ατος, τό	judgment [process of evaluation]; judgment [end result], judicial verdict
κρυπτός, -ή, -όν	hidden, secret
κτίσις, -εως, τό	creation [act or product]
κτίστης, -ου, ὁ	creator
κῶμος, κώμου, ὁ	unseemly/excessive partying, carousal

▷ List 24 1×

λέων, λέοντος, ὁ	lion
λογικός, -ή, -όν	rational, reasonable
λόγιον, -ίου, τό	saying, oracle
λοιδορέω	revile
λυπέω	(*act*) cause grief/sorrow; (*mid*) grieve, be sad/distressed
λύπη, -ης, ἡ	grief, sadness; pain
λυτρόω	(*mid*) release [by payment of ransom], redeem, ransom
μακροθυμία, -ας, ἡ	patience; forbearance
Μᾶρκος, Μάρκου, ὁ	Mark
μάρτυς, μάρτυρος, ὁ	witness

▷ List 25 1×

μάταιος, -αία, -ον	empty, idle, vain, useless
μέλει	(*impers*) it is a concern to/of interest to [*3sg* of μέλω]
μέριμνα, -ίμνης, ἡ	anxiety, worry
μηκέτι	no longer
μόλις	scarcely, barely, with difficulty; rarely
μώλωψ, -ωπος, ὁ	bruise, welt, wound
νέος, -α, -ον	new; young
Νῶε, ὁ (*indecl*)	Noah
ξένος, -η, -ον	strange, foreign; (*subst*) stranger, foreigner
ξηραίνω	(*mid*) become dry; wither

▷ List 26 1×

ξύλον, -ου, τό	wood; tree
οἰκέτης, -ου, ὁ	(house) slave
οἰκονόμος, -ου, ὁ	household manager/steward; administrator, manager
οἰνοφλυγία, -ας, ἡ	drunkenness
ὀκτώ (*indecl*)	eight
ὁμόφρων, -ον	like-minded, united
ὀνειδίζω	revile, mock, insult; reprimand, reproach
ὁπλίζω	(*mid*) ready oneself, arm/equip oneself
ὀσφῦς, -ύος, ἡ	waist, loins
οὖς, ὠτός, τό	ear; hearing, understanding

▹ **List 27**	1×
παρακύπτω	stoop down (and look); look into [figuratively]
παρατίθημι	(*act*) set/put before; (*mid*) demonstrate; commend, entrust
παρέρχομαι	pass by; pass [of time]; pass away, disappear ▹
παροικία, -ας, ἡ	sojourn, temporary stay
πάροικος, -οίκου, ὁ	foreign, alien; (*subst*) stranger; (resident) foreigner
πατροπαράδοτος, -ον	handed down from one's ancestors, inherited
περιέχω	contain
περίθεσις, -έσεως, ἡ	putting on, wearing
περιποίησις, -ήσεως, ἡ	keeping safe, preservation; possessing, possession
πέτρα, -ας, ἡ	rock [formation or piece]

▹ **List 28**	1×
πλανάω	(*act*) lead astray, deceive; (*mid*) wander, go astray, be misled
πλῆθος, πλήθους, τό	multitude, a great quantity
πληθύνω	(*trans act*) increase, multiply; (*intrans mid*) increase, grow, multiply
ποιμαίνω	shepherd, tend ▹
ποιμήν, ποιμένος, ὁ	shepherd
πολυτελής, -ές	very costly/valuable
πολύτιμος, -ον	highly valued; (*comp*) πολυτιμότερος, -έρα, -ον more precious
Πόντος, -ου, ὁ	Pontus
πότος, -ου, ὁ	drinking party, carousal
πραΰς, πραεῖα, πραΰ	gentle, meek

▷ List 29 1×

πραΰτης, -ητος, τό	humility, gentleness
πρόβατον, -άτου, τό	sheep
προγινώσκω	know beforehand ▸
πρόγνωσις, -ώσεως, ἡ	foreknowledge; predetermination
προθύμως	eagerly
προμαρτύρομαι	bear witness to beforehand
προσάγω	bring forward/to [into someone's presence] ▸
πρόσκομμα, -κόμματος, τό	stumbling; obstacle
προσκόπτω	(*intrans*) stumble
πρότερος, -έρα, -ον	former, earlier

▷ List 30 1×

προφητεύω	prophesy [disclose divine will]; foretell; reveal
πτόησις, -ήσεως, ἡ	fear, terror
πύρωσις, -ώσεως, ἡ	fiery trial, proving by fire
ῥαντισμός, -οῦ, ὁ	sprinkling
ῥύπος, -ου, ὁ	dirt
σαρκικός, -ή, -όν	material, physical, fleshly; worldly, (merely) human
Σάρρα, -ας, ἡ	Sarah
σθενόω	strengthen
Σιλουανός, -οῦ, ὁ	Silvanus
Σιών, ἡ (*indecl*)	Zion

▷ LIST 31 1×

σκάνδαλον, -άλου, τό	trap; cause of sin ["stumbling block"]; offense
σκεῦος, σκεύους, τό	object, thing; vessel, container
σκολιός, -ά, -όν	crooked, bent, [extended sense] perverse, unjust
σκότος, -ους, τό	darkness [literal or figurative]
σπορά, -ᾶς, ἡ	seed
στερεός, -ά, -όν	firm, solid; steadfast
στέφανος, -άνου, ὁ	wreath, crown
στηρίζω	set, establish; strengthen/make more firm [inwardly] ➢
στρατεύω	(*mid*) serve in the army; wage war
συγκληρονόμος, -ον	(*subst*) co-heir

▷ LIST 32 1×

συμβαίνω	(*impers*) it happens/comes about
συμπαθής, -ές	sympathetic
συμπρεσβύτερος, -έρου, ὁ	fellow elder
συνεκλεκτός, -ή, -όν	(*subst*) one chosen together with
συνοικέω	live with (+*dat obj*)
συντρέχω	run together with, [figurative] join with (in conduct/behavior)
συσχηματίζω	form (something) [according to a pattern], model, conform
σωφρονέω	be of sound mind; be sensible/self-controlled
ταπεινός, -ή, -όν	humble; lowly
ταπεινοφροσύνη, -ῆς, ἡ	humility

▹ List 33 1×

ταπεινόφρων, -ον	humble
ταπεινόω	bring low; humble [positive], humiliate [negative]
ταράσσω	agitate, disturb [physically, mentally, or spiritually] ▹
τελείως	completely, perfectly
τίμιος, -ία, -ον	valuable, precious
τύπος, -ου, ὁ	pattern, model, example
ὑπακούω	obey
ὑπερέχω	surpass, be superior; have power/authority over
ὑπερήφανος, -ον	arrogant, proud, haughty
ὑπογραμμός, -οῦ, ὁ	model, pattern, example

▹ List 34 1×

ὑπόκρισις, -ίσεως, ἡ	pretense, hypocrisy
ὑπολιμπάνω	leave behind
ὑποφέρω	endure
ὑψόω	lift up; exalt
φαίνω	(*act*) shine; (*mid*) appear
φθόνος, -ου, ὁ	envy
φιλαδελφία, -ας, ἡ	brotherly/sisterly love
φιλάδελφος, -ον	having love for one's siblings
φίλημα, -ήματος, τό	kiss
φιλόξενος, -ον	loving strangers, hospitable

▷ **List 35**	**1×**
φιμόω	muzzle; silence
φονεύς, -έως, ὁ	murderer
φρουρέω	keep watch; guard, protect
χάρισμα, -ίσματος, τό	(gracious) gift
χεῖλος, χείλους, τό	lip
χορηγέω	supply, provide (generously)
χρηστός, -ή, -όν	serviceable; good; kind
χριστιανός, -οῦ, ὁ	one who follows/belongs to Christ, Christian
ὠρύομαι	roar

2 PETER

▷ LIST 1	5 TO 3 ×
ἀποφεύγω	escape (from) (+*gen/acc obj*) ▸
ἀπώλεια, -είας, ἡ	destruction; waste
ἀρετή, -ῆς, ἡ	excellence [often referring to character or civic performance], virtue
ἀσέλγεια, -είας, ἡ	licentiousness, excessive sensuality
ἐπίγνωσις, -ώσεως, ἡ	knowledge
ἐπιθυμία, -ας, ἡ	desire, longing; lust, craving
εὐσέβεια, -είας, ἡ	devoutness, piety
ἡγέομαι	consider, regard
σωτήρ, -ῆρος, ὁ	savior, deliverer
φθορά, -ᾶς, ἡ	corruption, decay, ruin, destruction

▷ LIST 2	3 TO 2 ×
ἀδικία, -ας, ἡ	injustice, unrighteousness; wrongdoing, misdeed
ἄθεσμος, -ον	lawless
ἀναστροφή, -ῆς, ἡ	conduct, way of life
βλασφημέω	slander, speak disrespectfully about, revile
γνῶσις, γνώσεως, ἡ	knowledge [understanding/comprehension or that which is known]
ἐξακολουθέω	follow (+*dat obj*)
ἐπιστολή, -ῆς, ἡ	letter
παρουσία, -ας, ἡ	presence; arrival, coming
προσδοκάω	wait (for), expect
σπουδάζω	strive, make every effort (to), be eager (to)

▷ List 3 2×

ἀσεβής, -ές	ungodly
ἀστήρικτος, -ον	unstable
βέβαιος, -αία, -ον	steadfast, steady; firm, reliable, certain; (*comp*) βεβαιότερος, -έρα, -ον
δελεάζω	lure, entice
διεγείρω	wake (someone) up, stir (someone) up
δωρέομαι	bestow
ἐγκράτεια, -είας, ἡ	self-control
ἔκπαλαι	long ago; for a long time
ἐπάγγελμα, -έλματος, τό	promise [the act of promising or the content of what is promised]
ἐπάγω	bring (up)on

▷ List 4 2×

ἐπιχορηγέω	provide, supply, furnish
ζόφος, -ου, ὁ	darkness, gloom [of the netherworld]
ἡττάομαι	succumb (to), be defeated (by)
θεῖος, θεία, θεῖον	divine
καυσόω	(*mid*) burn; (*pass*) be burned up
λανθάνω	escape notice [+*acc* of party who is unaware of or ignores the matter in question]
μισθός, -οῦ, ὁ	pay, wages; recompense, reward
πάρειμι	be present/here, have come
πλάνη, -ης, ἡ	error, deceit
πλεονεξία, -ας, ἡ	greed; greedy act, extortion

▷ List 5 — 2×

ποτέ (*encl*)	when; formerly; (+*neg*) never
προφητεία, -ας, ἡ	prophetic activity; prophecy [the gift]; prophecy [an utterance]
ῥύομαι	save, rescue, deliver
σκήνωμα, -ώματος, τό	habitation
στοιχεῖον, -είου, τό	(basic) element, (fundamental) part, elemental force/spirit; celestial body
ταχινός, -ή, -όν	soon, imminent, swift
ὑπόμνησις, -ήσεως, ἡ	reminding, reminder; remembrance
ὑπομονή, -ῆς, ἡ	endurance, perseverance, steadfastness
φείδομαι	spare (+*gen obj*); refrain (from)
φθέγγομαι	speak, utter

▷ List 6 — 2 to 1×

ἀγνοέω	not know, be ignorant; not understand
ἀγοράζω	buy
ἀδικέω	(*trans*) wrong; injure <NA/UBS, SBL only>
ἄδικος, -ον	unjust, unrighteous
ἀεί	always, constantly
αἵρεσις, -έσεως, ἡ	faction, sect; (factional) opinion, dogma
ἄκαρπος, -ον	unfruitful; useless
φιλαδελφία, -ας, ἡ	brotherly/sisterly love
φυλάσσω	(*act*) guard, protect; (*mid*) be on one's guard, look out, beware
χίλιοι, -αι, -α	a thousand

▷ List 7 1×

ἀκατάπαυστος, -ον	unceasing
ἀκοή, -ῆς, ἡ	hearing, listening
ἀληθής, -ές	true, trustworthy; real
ἄλογος, -ον	without reason, irrational
ἅλωσις, ἁλώσεως, ἡ	capture, catching
ἀμαθής, -ές	ignorant
ἀμώμητος, -ον	without blemish, blameless
ἀναστρέφω	(*act*) return, go back; (*mid*) conduct oneself, live
ἀνατέλλω	(*trans*) cause to rise; (*intrans*) rise, come up
ἄνομος, -ον	lawless

▷ List 8 1×

ἄνυδρος, -ον	waterless
ἀπάτη, -ης, ἡ	deception, deceit
ἀπόθεσις, -έσεως, ἡ	removal
ἀργέω	be idle
ἀργός, -ή, -όν	idle, having nothing to do; lazy; useless
ἀρνέομαι	deny; refuse; disown
ἀρχαῖος, -αία, -ον	old, ancient
ἀσεβέω	live in an ungodly manner, act impiously
ἄσπιλος, -ον	spotless; without fault
αὐθάδης, -ες	self-willed, arrogant

▷ List 9 1×

αὐξάνω/αὔξω	(*trans*) make grow/increase; (*intrans*) grow, increase
αὐχμηρός, -ά, -όν	gloomy, dark, bleak
ἄφωνος, -ον	silent; speechless [incapable of speech]
β′	2 [in the book title ΠΕΤΡΟΥ Β "2 Peter"]
Βαλαάμ, ὁ (*indecl*)	Balaam
βασανίζω	torment, torture
βλάσφημος, -ον	slanderous, defaming, reviling
βλέμμα, -ατος, τό	seeing
βόρβορος, -όρου, ὁ	mud, mire
Βοσόρ, ὁ (*indecl*)	Bosor

▷ List 10 1×

βούλομαι	want, desire; intend, plan
βραδύνω	delay, be slow
βραδύτης, -ητος, ἡ	slowness
γνωρίζω	make known, inform; know
Γόμορρα, -όρρας/όρρων, ἡ/τά	Gomorrah
γυμνάζω	train, practice, discipline
δεσπότης, -ου, ὁ	master, lord
δηλόω	make clear, disclose, reveal, explain
διαμένω	remain, persist
διάνοια, -οίας, ἡ	mind, understanding; thought, disposition

▷ List 11 1×

διαυγάζω	shine through, [of the day] dawn
δουλόω	enslave
δυσνόητος, -ον	hard to understand
ἐγκατοικέω	live/dwell (among)
εἰλικρινής, -ές	pure, sincere
εἴσοδος, -όδου, ἡ	entrance [location or activity]; reception, welcome
ἑκάστοτε	always, at any time
ἐκλογή, -ῆς, ἡ	choice, election
ἐκπίπτω	fall off; fall from (+*gen obj*) ➢
ἐλαύνω	drive/propel along

▷ List 12 1×

ἔλεγξις, ἐλέγξεως, ἡ	rebuke
ἐλευθερία, -ας, ἡ	freedom, liberty
ἐμπαιγμονή, -ῆς, ἡ	mocking, mockery
ἐμπαίκτης, -ου, ὁ	mocker
ἐμπλέκω	(*mid*) be entangled in ➢
ἐμπορεύομαι	(*intrans*) engage in business; (*trans*) exploit
ἐντρυφάω	delight in, [negative sense] revel, carouse
ἐξέραμα, -άματος, τό	vomit
ἔξοδος, -όδου, ὁ	departure [euphemism for death]
ἐπαγγέλλομαι	promise

▹ **List 13**	1×
ἐπίλυσις, -ύσεως, ἡ	interpretation
ἐπιστρέφω	(*intrans act/mid*) return, go/come back; change (one's thinking or behavior)
ἐπόπτης, -ου, ὁ	eyewitness
εὐδοκέω	be well pleased; determine, resolve
εὐθύς, -εῖα, -ύ	straight; proper, right
εὐσεβής, -ές	godly, devout
ζῷον/ζῶον, -ου, τό	animal
ἡδονή, -ῆς, ἡ	pleasure
ἥκω	be present, have come
θησαυρίζω	store (up), save, reserve

▹ **List 14**	1×
ἰσότιμος, -ον	of equal honor/privilege; of equal value
ἰσχύς, -ύος, ἡ	strength
καθαρισμός, -οῦ, ὁ	cleansing
καθίστημι/καθιστάνω	appoint; make, cause to be
καίπερ	although
καλῶς	well, appropriately, effectively; correctly
κατακλύζω	deluge, inundate
κατακλυσμός, -οῦ, ὁ	deluge, flood
κατακρίνω	condemn
καταλείπω	leave (behind); cause to be left over ▸

▷ List 15 1×

καταπονέω	oppress, distress
κατάρα, -ας, ἡ	curse
καταστροφή, -ῆς, ἡ	(total) destruction, ruin
καταφρονέω	despise, look down on, disregard (+*gen obj*)
κῆρυξ, κήρυκος, ὁ	herald, proclaimer
κλέπτης, -ου, ὁ	thief
κλῆσις, κλήσεως, ἡ	call, calling, invitation
κοιμάω	(*mid*) sleep, fall asleep; die
κοινωνός, -οῦ, ὁ/ἡ	companion, partner, sharer
κολάζω	punish

▷ List 16 1×

κομίζω	(*mid*) receive <TH only>
κρείττων, κρεῖττον / κρείσσων, κρεῖσσον	better, superior [rank or value]
κρίμα, -ατος, τό	judgment [process of evaluation]; judgment [end result], judicial verdict
κτίσις, -εως, τό	creation [act or product]
κυλισμός, -οῦ, ὁ	rolling, wallowing
κυριότης, -ητος, ἡ	lordship, dominion, ruling power
κύων, κυνός, ὁ	dog [also, of persons, used as an invective]
κωλύω	hinder, prevent
λαγχάνω	receive [as a portion], obtain [by lot] ▷
λαῖλαψ, λαίλαπος, ἡ	furious storm

▹ List 17	1×
λήθη, -ης, ἡ	forgetfulness
λούω	wash
λύχνος, -ου, ὁ	lamp
Λώτ, ὁ (*indecl*)	Lot
μακροθυμέω	be patient
μακροθυμία, -ας, ἡ	patience; forbearance
μάλιστα	most of all, especially
ματαιότης, -ητος, ἡ	futility, purposelessness
μεγαλειότης, -ητος, ἡ	magnificence, grandeur, majesty
μεγαλοπρεπής, -ές	magnificent, majestic

▹ List 18	1×
μεστός, -ή, -όν	full
μετάνοια, -οίας, ἡ	change of mind and heart, repentance
μίασμα, -άσματος, τό	polluting deed; defilement [resulting from an action]
μιασμός, -οῦ, ὁ	corruption, defilement
μιμνήσκομαι/ μιμνῄσκομαι	(+*gen obj*) remember; be mindful of ➤
μνήμη, -ης, ἡ	remembrance, recollection
μοιχαλίς, -ίδος, ἡ	adulteress
μῦθος, μύθου, ὁ	story, tale, myth
μυωπάζω	be nearsighted
μῶμος, μώμου, ὁ	blemish

▷ List 19 1×

νυστάζω	be drowsy, doze
Νῶε, ὁ (*indecl*)	Noah
ὄγδοος, ὀγδόη, ὄγδοον	eighth
ὁμίχλη, -ης, ἡ	mist, fog
ὄντως	really, truly, actually
ὀπίσω	behind, back; (*prep* +*gen*) behind; after [temporal or spatial]
πάλαι	long ago, formerly
παρανομία, -ας, ἡ	transgression
παραφρονία, -ας, ἡ	madness, irrationality
παρεισάγω	bring in, introduce

▷ List 20 1×

παρεισφέρω	apply (beside), bring to bear ➢
παρέρχομαι	pass by; pass [of time]; pass away, disappear ➢
παροιμία, -ας, ἡ	illustration, figure of speech; proverb
πειρασμός, -οῦ, ὁ	test, trial; temptation
πηγή, -ῆς, ἡ	spring; well
πλανάω	(*act*) lead astray, deceive; (*mid*) wander, go astray, be misled
πλαστός, -ή, -όν	fabricated, made-up
πλεονάζω	(*intrans*) increase, abound; (*trans*) (cause to) increase
πληθύνω	(*trans act*) increase, multiply; (*intrans mid*) grow, multiply
πλουσίως	richly, abundantly

▷ List 21 — 1×

ποταπός, -ή, -όν	what sort of?, what kind of?
προγινώσκω	know beforehand
προλέγω	tell beforehand/in advance
προσέχω	look after, pay attention/attend to (+*dat obj*)
προφητικός, -ή, -όν	prophetic
πταίω	stumble
πυρόω	burn (up), set on fire [literal or metaphorical]
ῥοιζηδόν	with a rushing noise
σειρά, -ᾶς, ἡ	cord, rope, chain <NA/UBS, SBL only>
σ(ε)ιρός, -οῦ, ὁ	pit <TH only>

▷ List 22 — 1×

σκότος, -ους, τό	darkness [literal or figurative]
Σόδομα, -όμων, τά	Sodom
σοφίζω	(*act*) make wise; (*mid*) devise craftily, (*attr mid-pass ptc*) craftily devised
σπεύδω	(*trans*) make hurry, hasten
σπίλος, -ου, ὁ	spot, blemish
σπουδή, -ῆς, ἡ	haste; zeal, eagerness, diligence
στηριγμός, -οῦ, ὁ	firmness, steadiness
στηρίζω	set, establish; strengthen/make more firm [inwardly] ▸
στρεβλόω	twist, distort
συμβαίνω	(*impers*) it happens/comes about ▸

▹ List 23 1×

Συμεών, ὁ (*indecl*)	Simeon
συναπάγω	lead away with/together
συνευωχέομαι	feast together (with)
συνίστημι/συνιστάνω/ συνιστάω	(*intrans pf*) stand with/by; exist; come together
ταρταρόω	hurl into Tartarus
τεφρόω	burn/reduce to ashes
τήκω	(*mid*) melt
τίμιος, -ία, -ον	valuable, precious
τοιόσδε, τοιάδε, τοιόνδε	such as this
τολμητής, -οῦ, ὁ	bold, daring

▹ List 24 1×

τρέμω	tremble [in fear and awe]
τρυφή, -ῆς, ἡ	indulgence, reveling, wantonness
ὑπέρογκος, -ον	bombastic, high-sounding
ὑπόδειγμα, -είγματος, τό	example, pattern
ὑποζύγιον, -ίου, τό	donkey
ὑπομιμνῄσκω/ ὑπομιμνήσκω	remind, bring up ▹
ὑποστρέφω	return, turn back
ὗς, ὑός, ἡ	sow
φαίνω	(*act*) shine; (*mid*) appear
φθείρω	corrupt, ruin, destroy ▹

▷ List 25 1×

φυσικός, -ή, -όν	natural [in accordance with nature]
φύσις, -εως, τό	nature [inherent/basic qualities, features, or character]
φωσφόρος, -ον	(*subst*) Morning Star [Venus]
χείρων, -ον	worse
χωρέω	hold, have room for; go, reach
ψευδοδιδάσκαλος, -άλου, ὁ	false teacher
ψευδοπροφήτης, -ου, ὁ	false prophet

1 JOHN

▷ **List 1**	**6 to 4×**
ἀληθινός, -ή, -όν	true, trustworthy; real
ἀντίχριστος, -ίστου, ὁ	antichrist, one opposed to the Messiah
διάβολος, -ον	slanderous; (*subst*) adversary; devil
κοινωνία, -ας, ἡ	(close) fellowship; participation, sharing; generosity
μαρτυρία, -ας, ἡ	[the act of giving] testimony; evidence
νικάω	(*trans*) overcome, defeat, conquer; (*intrans*) prevail, be victorious
ὁμολογέω	acknowledge; declare, confess
σκοτία, -ας, ἡ	darkness [literal or figurative]
τεκνίον, -ου, τό	little child
ψεύστης, -ου, ὁ	liar

▷ **List 2**	**4 to 2×**
ἀγγελία, -ας, ἡ	message, announcement; instruction
ἀδικία, -ας, ἡ	injustice, unrighteousness; wrongdoing, misdeed
ἀρνέομαι	deny; refuse; disown
ἐπιθυμία, -ας, ἡ	desire, longing; lust, craving
θεάομαι	see, look at
ὀφείλω	owe, be indebted to; be obligated, ought; have to
παρρησία, -ας, ἡ	plainness; openness; boldness; (*adv*) plainly, openly, boldly
πλανάω	(*act*) lead astray, deceive; (*mid*) wander, go astray, be misled
τελειόω	complete, finish; bring (something) to its goal/conclusion; perfect
χρῖσμα, χρίσματος, τό	anointing

▷ List 3 — 2×

ἀληθής, -ές	true, trustworthy; real
ἀνθρωποκτόνος, -ου, ὁ	murderer
ἀνομία, -ας, ἡ	lawlessness [condition or action]
βίος, -ου, ὁ	life, manner of living; livelihood, means of living
ἡμέτερος, -τέρα, -ον	our
ἱλασμός, -οῦ, ὁ	atoning sacrifice
καθαρίζω	cleanse, make clean
καταγινώσκω	condemn (+*gen obj*)
νεανίσκος, -ου, ὁ	young man
παλαιός, -ά, -όν	old

▷ List 4 — 2 to 1×

αʹ	1 [in the book title ΙΩΑΝΝΟΥ Α "1 John"]
ἁγνίζω	purify
ἁγνός, -ή, -όν	pure
αἰσχύνω	(*mid*) be ashamed
αἴτημα, -ήματος, τό	request
ἀλαζονεία, -ας, ἡ	arrogance
ἀληθῶς	truly, actually
παράγω	go along, pass by; go away
σφάζω	slay, slaughter
ψεῦδος, ψεύδους, τό	lie, falsehood

▶

▹ List 5	1×
ἀναγγέλλω	report; disclose, announce
ἅπτω	(*mid +gen obj*) touch, hold, cling to
ἀρεστός, -ή, -όν	pleasing
ἄρτι	(just) now
βαρύς, -εῖα, -ύ	heavy; burdensome; weighty, serious
διάνοια, -οίας, ἡ	mind, understanding; thought, disposition
δοκιμάζω	examine, evaluate; determine, put to the test
εἴδωλον, -ώλου, τό	idol, cultic image
ἐπαγγέλλομαι	promise
ἐπιστολή, -ῆς, ἡ	letter

▹ List 6	1×
ἥκω	be present, have come
ἰσχυρός, -ά, -όν	strong, mighty
Κάϊν, ὁ (*indecl*)	Cain
κεῖμαι	be lying/reclining; exist, be set
κλείω	shut, close
κόλασις, -άσεως, ἡ	punishment
μεταβαίνω	go, move ▹
μονογενής, -ές	only; unique
νίκη, -ης, ἡ	victory
ὅθεν	from where; as a result of which, consequently

▷ List 7	1×
οὔπω	not yet
παράκλητος, -ήτου, ὁ	helper, intercessor, advocate
παρουσία, -ας, ἡ	presence; arrival, coming
πλάνη, -ης, ἡ	error, deceit
ποταπός, -ή, -όν	of what sort/kind, how great
πώποτε	at any time, ever
σκάνδαλον, -άλου, τό	trap; cause of sin ["stumbling block"]; offense
σκότος, -ους, τό	darkness [literal or figurative]
σπλάγχνον, -ου, τό	[always *pl*] entrails; seat of emotion [similar to English's "heart"]; compassion, affection
σωτήρ, -ῆρος, ὁ	savior, deliverer

▷ List 8	1×
τέλειος, -εία, -ον	complete, perfect
τυφλόω	blind
φαίνω	(*act*) shine; (*mid*) appear
φανερός, -ά, -όν	visible, plain, evident, known
φυλάσσω	guard, protect
χάριν	(+*gen* preceding or following) because of, for the sake of
ψεύδομαι	lie, speak falsely
ψευδοπροφήτης, -ου, ὁ	false prophet
ψηλαφάω	touch

2 JOHN

▹ List 1	3 to 1×
ἀδελφή, -ῆς, ἡ	sister
ἀντίχριστος, -ίστου, ὁ	antichrist, one opposed to the Messiah
ἀπολαμβάνω	receive ▹
β′	2 [in the book title ΙΩΑΝΝΟΥ Β "2 John"]
βούλομαι	want, desire; intend, plan
διδαχή, -ῆς, ἡ	teaching [activity or content]
ἐκλεκτός, -ή, -όν	chosen, elect
ἔλεος, ἐλέους, τό	compassion, mercy
κυρία, -ας, ἡ	lady, mistress
πλάνος, -ον	deceitful; (*subst*) deceiver

▹ List 2	1×
ἐλπίζω	hope (for); expect
ἐπιστολή, -ῆς, ἡ	letter
κοινωνέω	have a share, take part in; share
λίαν	very (much), exceedingly
μέλας, μέλαινα, μέλαν	black; (*neut subst*) ink ▹
μισθός, -οῦ, ὁ	pay, wages; recompense, reward
ὁμολογέω	acknowledge; declare, confess
πλήρης, -ες (freq. *indecl*)	full, filled; full, complete
προάγω	(*intrans*) go before, precede [spatially or temporally]
χάρτης, -ου, ὁ	papyrus, paper

3 JOHN

▷ List 1 — 2 to 1×

ἀγαθοποιέω	do good/what is right
ἀληθής, -ές	true, trustworthy; real
ἀξίως	worthily, in a manner worthy of
ἀρκέω	(*mid*) be content/satisfied
βούλομαι	want, desire; intend, plan
γ′	3 [in the book title ΙΩΑΝΝΟΥ Γ "3 John"]
Γάϊος, Γαΐου, ὁ	Gaius
ἐπιδέχομαι	welcome
εὐοδόω	prosper, succeed, go well
φίλος, -η, -ον	friendly; (*subst*) friend

▷ List 2 — 1×

Δημήτριος, -ίου, ὁ	Demetrius
Διοτρέφης, -ους, ὁ / Διοτρεφής, -οῦς, ὁ	Diotrephes
ἐθνικός, -ή, -όν	gentile, (*subst*) gentile
ἐλπίζω	hope (for); expect
ἐπιστολή, -ῆς, ἡ	letter
εὐθέως	immediately
εὔχομαι	pray (for); wish (for)
κακοποιέω	do what is evil
κάλαμος, -άμου, ὁ	reed, stalk; reed pen
καλῶς	well, appropriately, effectively; correctly

▹ List 3 1×

κωλύω	hinder, prevent
λίαν	very (much), exceedingly
μαρτυρία, -ας, ἡ	[the act of giving] testimony; evidence
μέλας, μέλαινα, μέλαν	black; (*neut subst*) ink ▸
μιμέομαι	imitate
ξένος, -η, -ον	strange, foreign; (*subst*) stranger, foreigner; host
ὀφείλω	owe, be indebted to; be obligated, ought; have to
προπέμπω	send (someone) on their way [with assistance]
συνεργός, -όν	helpful, contributing; [only *subst* in NT] fellow worker
ὑγιαίνω	be well

▹ List 4 1×

ὑπολαμβάνω	lift/take up; support
ὑπομιμνῄσκω/ ὑπομιμνήσκω	remind, bring up
φιλοπρωτεύω	love to be first/in charge
φλυαρέω	talk nonsense; disparage

JUDE

▷ List 1	3 to 1×
ἀγαλλίασις, -άσεως, ἡ	great joy, extreme gladness
ἅπαξ	once; once and for all
ἀσέβεια, -είας, ἡ	ungodliness
ἀσεβής, -ές	ungodly
βλασφημέω	slander, speak disrespectfully about, revile
διακρίνω	(*act*) separate; evaluate; make a distinction; judge; (*mid*) dispute, contend (with)
ἐλεάω	have compassion (on), show mercy to [later byform of ἐλεέω]
ἔλεος, ἐλέους, τό	compassion, mercy
ἐπιθυμία, -ας, ἡ	desire, longing; lust, craving
ζόφος, -ου, ὁ	darkness, gloom [of the netherworld]

▷ List 2	1×
ἄγριος, -ία, -ον	wild [not cultivated], [extended sense] uncontrolled
Ἀδάμ, ὁ (*indecl*)	Adam
ἀθετέω	nullify, invalidate; reject
Αἴγυπτος, -ύπτου, ἡ	Egypt
ἀΐδιος, -ον	eternal
αἰσχύνη, -ης, ἡ	shame, dishonor; [sense/experience of] shame; shameful deed
ἄκαρπος, -ον	unfruitful; useless
ἄλογος, -ον	without reason, irrational
ἄμωμος, -ον	unblemished; blameless
ἀνάγκη, -ης, ἡ	necessity, constraint, pressure; distress, anguish

▷ List 3 1×

ἄνεμος, ἀνέμου, ὁ	wind
ἀντιλογία, -ας, ἡ	opposition, rebellion
ἄνυδρος, -ον	waterless
ἀποδιορίζω	mark by dividing/separating, [extended sense] cause divisions
ἀπολείπω	(*act*) leave behind; abandon; (*mid*) remain ▷
ἄπταιστος, -ον	without stumbling
ἀρνέομαι	deny; refuse; disown
ἁρπάζω	seize; take away, snatch
ἀρχάγγελος, -έλου, ὁ	archangel
ἀσεβέω	live in an ungodly manner, act impiously

▷ List 4 1×

ἀσέλγεια, -είας, ἡ	licentiousness, excessive sensuality
ἀστήρ, -έρος, ὁ	(luminous) celestial body, star
ἀφόβως	without fear
Βαλαάμ, ὁ (*indecl*)	Balaam
βλασφημία, -ας, ἡ	slander, defamation, reviling
βούλομαι	want, desire; intend, plan
γογγυστής, -οῦ, ὁ	grumbler
Γόμορρα, -όρρας/όρρων, ἡ/τά	Gomorrah
δεῖγμα, δείγματος, τό	example
δένδρον, -ου, τό	tree

▷ List 5 1×

δεσμός, -οῦ, ὁ	(*sg*) binding, impediment; (*pl*) bonds, chains, [extended sense] imprisonment
δεσπότης, -ου, ὁ	master, lord
διάβολος, -ον	slanderous; (*subst*) adversary; devil
διαλέγομαι	converse, address, discuss; dispute, argue
δίκη, -ης, ἡ	punishment, justice
δίς	twice
ἕβδομος, -όμη, -ον	seventh
ἐκπορνεύω	engage in sexual sin
ἐκριζόω	uproot
ἐκχέω/ἐκχύν(ν)ω	pour out

▷ List 6 1×

ἐλέγχω	expose; reprove; convict, accuse
ἐμπαίκτης, -ου, ὁ	mocker
ἐνυπνιάζομαι	dream
Ἑνώχ/Ἐνώχ, ὁ (*indecl*)	Enoch
ἐπαγωνίζομαι	contend, struggle
ἐπαφρίζω	cause to foam up
ἐπίσταμαι	understand; know
ἐπιστολή, -ῆς, ἡ	letter
ἐπιτιμάω	rebuke (+*dat obj*)
ἐπιφέρω	bring/pronounce (a charge) ▸

▷ List 7 1×

ἐποικοδομέω	build (up)on
ζῷον/ζῶον, -ου, τό	animal
Κάϊν, ὁ (*indecl*)	Cain
κατενώπιον	(+*gen*) before, opposite, in front of
κλητός, -ή, -όν	called, invited
κοινός, -ή, -όν	common, shared
Κόρε, ὁ (*indecl*)	Korah
κράτος, -ους, τό	strength, might, power; rule, sovereignty
κρίμα, -ατος, τό	judgment [process of evaluation]; judgment [end result], judicial verdict
κῦμα, κύματος, τό	wave

▷ List 8 1×

κυριότης, -ητος, ἡ	lordship, dominion, ruling power
μεγαλωσύνη, -ῆς, ἡ	majesty
μεμψίμοιρος, -ον	malcontent, discontented
μέντοι (*postp*)	nevertheless, however
μετατίθημι	(*trans*) transfer, move to a new place; change, alter
μιαίνω	stain, defile, taint
μιμνήσκομαι/ μιμνῄσκομαι	(+*gen obj*) remember; be mindful of
μισθός, -οῦ, ὁ	pay, wages; recompense, reward
Μιχαήλ, ὁ (*indecl*)	Michael
μυριάς, -άδος, ἡ	ten thousand, (*pl*) myriads

▷

▷ **List 9**	1×
νεφέλη, -ης, ἡ	cloud
οἰκητήριον, -ίου, τό	dwelling, abode
ὁμοίως	likewise, in the same way
ὀπίσω	behind, back; (*prep +gen*) behind; after [temporal or spatial]
πάλαι	long ago, formerly
παραφέρω	carry away
παρεισδύ(ν)ω	slip in secretly
πλάνη, -ης, ἡ	error, deceit
πλανήτης, -ου, ὁ	wanderer, (*adj*) wandering
πληθύνω	(*trans act*) increase, multiply; (*intrans mid*) increase, grow, multiply

▷ **List 10**	1×
ποιμαίνω	shepherd, tend
προγράφω	write beforehand/in advance ➢
πρόκειμαι	be set forth, displayed
προλέγω	tell beforehand/in advance
προσδέχομαι	receive, welcome; wait for, await, expect
προφητεύω	prophesy [disclose divine will]; foretell; reveal
σκληρός, -ά, -όν	hard, harsh
σκότος, -ους, τό	darkness [literal or figurative]
Σόδομα, -όμων, τά	Sodom
σπιλάς, -άδος, ἡ	rock, reef [hidden under the surface of the sea]

▷ List 11 1×

σπιλόω	stain, defile
σπουδή, -ῆς, ἡ	haste; zeal, eagerness, diligence
συνευωχέομαι	feast together (with)
σωτήρ, -ῆρος, ὁ	savior, deliverer
τολμάω	dare, bring oneself (to), have the courage (to)
τρόπος, -ου, ὁ	manner, way
ὑπέρογκος, -ον	bombastic, high-sounding
ὑπέχω	undergo/suffer (punishment) [legal term]
ὑπομιμνῄσκω/ ὑπομιμνήσκω	(*trans act*) remind, bring up; (*intrans mid*) remember ▷
φθείρω	corrupt, ruin, destroy

▷ List 12 1×

φθινοπωρινός, -ή, -όν	in late autumn
φυλάσσω	guard, protect
φυσικῶς	naturally, by nature
χάριν	(+*gen* preceding or following) because of, for the sake of
χιτών, -ῶνος, τό	tunic
ψυχικός, -ή, -όν	[that which pertains to ψυχή] natural, worldly
ὠφέλεια, -είας, ἡ	gain, advantage, benefit

REVELATION

▹ List 1 — 29 to 16×

ἀρνίον, -ου, τό	lamb, sheep
βιβλίον, -ου, τό	scroll; document
ζῷον/ζῶον, -ου, τό	animal; living being/creature
ἵππος, -ου, ὁ	horse
λευκός, -ή, -όν	white; bright, shining
νικάω	(*trans*) overcome, defeat, conquer; (*intrans*) prevail, be victorious
πληγή, -ῆς, ἡ	blow, striking, beating; wound; plague
τέσσαρες, -α	four
φυλή, -ῆς, ἡ	tribe; people group
χιλιάς, -άδος, ἡ	a thousand

▹ List 2 — 15 to 11×

ἀδικέω	(*intrans*) do wrong, be in the wrong; (*trans*) wrong; injure
ἀστήρ, -έρος, ὁ	(luminous) celestial body, star
δράκων, -οντος, ὁ	dragon, serpent
ἥλιος, -ίου, ὁ	sun
καπνός, -οῦ, ὁ	smoke
μετανοέω	repent
περιβάλλω	(*trans act*) clothe, put on; (*trans mid*) clothe/put on oneself; (*intrans mid*) be wearing/clothed
σφραγίς, -ῖδος, ἡ	signet, seal; seal [the impression left by a signet]
φιάλη, -ης, ἡ	bowl
χρυσοῦς, -ῆ, -οῦν	golden

▸

▷ List 3 — 11 to 9×

ἀληθινός, -ή, -όν	true, trustworthy; real
ἀριθμός, -οῦ, ὁ	number, total
βροντή, -ῆς, ἡ	thunder
δέκα (*indecl*)	ten
ἐκχέω/ἐκχύν(ν)ω	pour out
εἰκών, εἰκόνος, ἡ	image, likeness [crafted or non-crafted]
θυμός, -οῦ, ὁ	desire, passion; anger, wrath
κέρας, -ατος, τό	horn; horn-shaped corner
πυλών, -ῶνος, ὁ	gateway
σαλπίζω	blow a trumpet

▷ List 4 — 9 to 8×

ἐκπορεύομαι	go/come out
θυσιαστήριον, -ίου, τό	altar
ἰσχυρός, -ά, -όν	strong, mighty [of living beings]; strong, powerful, violent, forcible [pertaining to strength or impact]
μαρτυρία, -ας, ἡ	[the act of giving] testimony; evidence
μέτωπον, -ώπου, τό	forehead
οἶνος, οἴνου, ὁ	wine
οὖς, ὠτός, τό	ear; hearing, understanding
παντοκράτωρ, παντοκράτορος, ὁ	[of God] the Almighty
πόλεμος, -έμου, ὁ	war; battle, fight
χίλιοι, -αι, -α	a thousand

▹ List 5 — 8 to 7×

ἄβυσσος, ἀβύσσου, ἡ	abyss
βασιλεύω	reign, rule, be king
γέμω	be full (of something) [+*gen/acc* of thing]
πλανάω	(*act*) lead astray, deceive; (*mid*) wander, go astray, be misled
ποταμός, -οῦ, ὁ	river, stream
σατανᾶς, σατανᾶ, ὁ	[Heb.] Satan
στέφανος, -άνου, ὁ	wreath, crown
σφάζω	slay, slaughter ▹
σφραγίζω	seal; seal up; mark with a seal; certify
τελέω	complete, finish; carry out (completely), accomplish; pay

▹ List 6 — 7×

δείκνυμι	show, make known; explain ▹
δρέπανον, -άνου, τό	sickle
λυχνία, -ας, ἡ	lampstand
νεφέλη, -ης, ἡ	cloud
ξύλον, -ου, τό	wood; object made of wood [e.g., club, stocks, cross]; tree
ὅδε, ἥδε, τόδε	this; τάδε λέγει thus says, this is what (someone) says
ὀξύς, ὀξεῖα, ὀξύ	sharp
πορνεία, -ας, ἡ	sexual immorality, fornication
προφητεία, -ας, ἡ	prophetic activity; prophecy [the gift]; prophecy [an utterance]
σεισμός, -οῦ, ὁ	shaking, shock, commotion [earthquake, storm]

▷ List 7 — 7 to 6×

ἀγοράζω	buy
Βαβυλών, -ῶνος, ἡ	Babylon
βασανισμός, -οῦ, ὁ	torture; torment
εἴκοσι (*indecl*)	twenty
ἥκω	be present, have come
θεῖον, θείου, τό	sulfur
καθαρός, -ά, -όν	clean; pure; innocent
τέταρτος, -άρτη, -ον	fourth, (*subst neut*) the fourth part, a fourth of
ὑπομονή, -ῆς, ἡ	endurance, perseverance, steadfastness
χάραγμα, -άγματος, τό	mark, brand

▷ List 8 — 6×

κλείω	shut, close
λέων, λέοντος, ὁ	lion
λίμνη, -ης, ἡ	lake
μήν, μηνός, ὁ	month
ὀργή, -ῆς, ἡ	anger; wrath
πολεμέω	wage war, fight
ῥομφαία, -ας, ἡ	sword
σάλπιγξ, σάλπιγγος, ἡ	trumpet; trumpet call
ταχύς, ταχεῖα, ταχύ	quick; [*neut sg* as *adv*] soon, quickly, without delay
τεῖχος, τείχους, τό	wall

▹ List 9 — 6 to 5×

ἀκάθαρτος, -ον	impure, unclean [cultic or moral]
βασανίζω	torment, torture
βλασφημία, -ας, ἡ	slander, defamation, reviling
βύσσινος, -ίνη, -ον	made of fine linen
διάβολος, -ον	slanderous; (*subst*) adversary; devil
ἕβδομος, -όμη, -ον	seventh
ἕκτος, -η, -ον	sixth
καίω	kindle, light; burn (up)
τεσσεράκοντα/ τεσσαράκοντα (*indecl*)	forty
τίμιος, -ία, -ον	valuable, precious; costly

▹ List 10 — 5×

κατακαίω	burn completely, burn up/down	▸
κατεσθίω	devour, consume	▸
λαμπρός, -ά, -όν	bright, shining; (*subst pl*) splendor; clear, transparent	
μαργαρίτης, -ου, ὁ	pearl	
μάρτυς, μάρτυρος, ὁ	witness	
μετρέω	measure; measure out, apportion	
οὐρά, -ᾶς, ἡ	tail	
ὄφις, -εως, ὁ	snake, serpent	
πέτομαι	fly	
πηγή, -ῆς, ἡ	spring; well	

▷ List 11 — 5 to 4×

ᾅδης/ἅδης, -ου, ὁ	Hades
ἀλληλουϊά/ἀλληλούϊα	[Heb.] praise Yahweh, hallelujah
ἀστραπή, -ῆς, ἡ	lightning
πλουτέω	be rich
πορνεύω	fornicate, commit sexual immorality
πόρνη, -ης, ἡ	sex worker, prostitute
στολή, -ῆς, ἡ	long robe
τίκτω	give birth to, bear, [inanimate] produce ▷
χρυσίον, -ου, τό	gold; objects of gold [e.g., jewelry, money]
ᾠδή, -ῆς, ἡ	song

▷ List 12 — 4×

βλασφημέω	slander, speak disrespectfully about, revile
δένδρον, -ου, τό	tree
ἑκατόν (*indecl*)	one hundred
ἔμπορος, -όρου, ὁ	merchant
θυμίαμα, -άματος, τό	incense
θύρα, -ας, ἡ	door; entrance
ἴασπις, ἰάσπιδος, ἡ	jasper
κλείς, κλειδός, ἡ	key
κόκκινος, -ίνη, -ον	scarlet, (*subst*) scarlet cloth/garment
ληνός, -οῦ, ἡ	winepress

▷ List 13 4×

μάχαιρα, -αίρης, ἡ	dagger, short sword
μήτε	[continuing a previous *neg*] and not, neither, nor
μυστήριον, -ίου, τό	mystery, secret
ναί	yes
νύμφη, -ης, ἡ	bride
πέμπτος, -η, -ον	fifth
πένθος, -ου, ὁ	grief, mourning
πλούσιος, -ία, -ον	rich, wealthy; rich (in), abounding (in)
ποιμαίνω	shepherd, tend ➢
ποτήριον, -ίου, τό	cup

▷ List 14 4×

ῥάβδος, -ου, ἡ	rod, staff, scepter
σελήνη, -ης, ἡ	moon
σιδηροῦς, -ᾶ, -οῦν	(made of) iron
σκηνόω	pitch one's tent, live, dwell
στράτευμα, -εύματος, τό	army, troops
ὑποκάτω	under, below, beneath
φαίνω	(*act*) shine; (*mid*) appear
φεύγω	flee; escape; avoid ➢
φρέαρ, -ατος, τό	well [for water]; pit
χάλαζα, -άζης, ἡ	hail

▹ List 15	3×
ᾄδω	sing
ἀετός, -οῦ, ὁ	eagle
ἄλφα, τό (*indecl*)	alpha
ἀνά	each, apiece; ἀνὰ μέσον in the middle
ἀνατολή, -ῆς, ἡ	rising [of a celestial body]; east
ἄνεμος, ἀνέμου, ὁ	wind
βαστάζω	pick up; carry, bear
βδέλυγμα, -ύγματος, τό	abomination, detestable thing
βιβλαρίδιον, -ίου, τό	little scroll
γνώμη, -ης, ἡ	judgment, opinion; purpose, intent, will

▹ List 16	3×
γρηγορέω	be (fully) awake/alert; be watchful/on the alert
γυμνός, -ή, -όν	naked, bare, [figurative] uncovered; inadequately dressed; lightly dressed
διάδημα, -ήματος, τό	crown
διαφθείρω	destroy; corrupt ▸
διδαχή, -ῆς, ἡ	teaching [activity or content]
διψάω	be thirsty
ἐλεύθερος, -έρα, -ον	free
ἐνδύω	(*act*) dress/clothe (someone); (*mid*) put on, wear
ἐξαλείφω	wipe away/out; destroy
ἑξήκοντα (*indecl*)	sixty

▹ List 17 3×

ἔξωθεν	(from) outside; (*prep* +*gen*) outside
ἐρημόω	make desolate, lay waste, ruin
εὐλογία, -ας, ἡ	praise; blessing; gift
εὐφραίνω	(*intrans mid*) be glad, enjoy oneself, rejoice
ζεστός, -ή, -όν	hot
ἥμισυς, ἡμίσεια, ἥμισυ	half, (*subst*) one-half
θεμέλιος, -ίου, ὁ	foundation
θερίζω	reap, harvest
θρίξ, τριχός, ἡ	hair
Θυάτειρα, -είρων, τά	Thyatira

▹ List 18 3×

θώραξ, -ακος, ὁ	breastplate; chest
ἱερεύς, -έως, ὁ	priest
κάλαμος, -άμου, ὁ	reed, stalk; measuring rod
κεράννυμι	mix ▹
κιθάρα, -ας, ἡ	lyre
κρίμα, -ατος, τό	judgment [process of evaluation]; judgment [end result], judicial verdict
κρύπτω	(*trans act*) hide (something); ▹ (*intrans mid*) hide (oneself), be hidden
κτίζω	create
κυκλόθεν	(*adv*) around, on the outside; (*prep* +*gen*) in a circle, around
κύκλῳ	in a circle; (*prep* +*gen*) around

▷ List 19 3×

λύχνος, -ου, ὁ	lamp
μακρόθεν	from far away, from a distance
μεσουράνημα, -ήματος, τό	midheaven, the sky overhead
μνημονεύω	remember (*+gen/acc obj*)
μυριάς, -άδος, ἡ	ten thousand, (*pl*) myriads
νῆσος, νήσου, ἡ	island
οἰκουμένη, -ης, ἡ	the inhabited world; the (Roman) empire
ὀπίσω	behind, back; (*prep +gen*) behind; after [temporal or spatial]
ὅρασις, -άσεως, ἡ	appearance; vision [in a transcendent mode]
ὄρνεον, -έου, τό	bird

▷ List 20 3×

πατέω	tread, trample
πειράζω	test; tempt
πενθέω	(*intrans*) grieve, mourn
πέντε (*indecl*)	five
πικραίνω	(*trans act*) make bitter; (*intrans mid*) become bitter
πλατεῖα, -είας, ἡ	(wide) road, street
πλάτος, -ους, τό	breadth, width
πόνος, -ου, ὁ	hard work, toil; pain, affliction, distress
προσευχή, -ῆς, ἡ	prayer
πτέρυξ, -υγος, ἡ	wing

▷ List 21 3×

πτῶμα, πτώματος, τό	dead body, corpse
Σάρδεις, -εων, αἱ	Sardis
σκεῦος, σκεύους, τό	object, thing; vessel, container
σκηνή, -ῆς, ἡ	tent, dwelling, tabernacle
σκορπίος, -ου, ὁ	scorpion
σύνδουλος, -ούλου, ὁ	fellow slave
ὑάλινος, -ίνη, -ον	of glass
φλόξ, φλογός, ἡ	flame
φωτίζω	(*intrans*) shine; (*trans*) illuminate, light up
χλωρός, -ά, -όν	yellowish green, (light) green; greenish gray, pale

▷ List 22 3 to 2×

ἀήρ, ἀέρος, ὁ	air
αἰχμαλωσία, -ας, ἡ	captivity
ἀκρίς, -ίδος, ἡ	locust
ἄμμος, -ου, ἡ	sand
ἄμπελος, -έλου, ἡ	vine, grapevine
ἀνάπαυσις, -αύσεως, ἡ	rest, ceasing, respite
ψευδοπροφήτης, -ου, ὁ	false prophet
ψεῦδος, ψεύδους, τό	lie, falsehood
ψυχρός, -ά, -όν	cold
ὦ, τό	omega

▷ List 23 2×

ἀναπαύω	(*trans act*) give rest, refresh; (*intrans mid*) rest	▶
ἀποκάλυψις, -ύψεως, ἡ	revelation, disclosure	
ἀποφέρω	take/carry away, transport, carry	▶
ἀπώλεια, -είας, ἡ	destruction; waste	
ἀρνέομαι	deny; refuse; disown	
ἄρσην, -εν	male	▶
ἄρτι	(just) now <TH ἀπάρτι "just now; from now" instead of ἀπ᾽ ἄρτι>	
ἀρχαῖος, -αία, -ον	old, ancient	
ἀφαιρέω	remove, take away	▶
ἄψινθος, -ίνθου, ὁ/ἡ / ἀψίνθιον, -ίου, τό	wormwood	

▷ List 24 2×

βίβλος, -ου, ἡ	written account, book
γάμος, -ου, ὁ	wedding celebration; marriage
γεμίζω	fill
γλυκύς, γλυκεῖα, γλυκύ	sweet
γόμος, -ου, ὁ	cargo
γωνία, -ας, ἡ	corner
δάκρυον, -ύου, τό	tear(drop)
δεῖπνον, δείπνου, τό	dinner; feast, banquet
δέκατος, -άτη, -ον	tenth, (*subst*) a tenth (part)
δεῦρο	come!, come here!, come on!

▷ List 25 2×

δηνάριον, -ίου, τό	denarius
διακόσιοι, -αι, -α	two hundred
δικαίωμα, -ώματος, τό	ordinance, requirement; righteous/just act
διπλοῦς, διπλῆ, διπλοῦν	double
δίστομος, -ον	double-edged
δωρεάν	freely; without cause
Ἑβραϊστί	in Hebrew/Aramaic
ἐγγύς	near [spatial or temporal]
εἰδωλόθυτος, -ον	(*subst*) meat sacrificed to an idol
εἰδωλολάτρης, -ου, ὁ	image worshiper, idolater

▷ List 26 2×

ἐκδικέω	grant justice; carry out justice, avenge, punish
ἔλαιον, ἐλαίου, τό	olive oil; olive orchard
ἕλκος, -ους, τό	wound, sore
ἕξ (*indecl*)	six
ἑξακόσιοι, -αι, -α	six hundred
ἐπάνω	(*adv*) above, over; more than; (*prep +gen*) above, over
ἐπιστρέφω	(*intrans act/mid*) return; turn (around)
ἐπιτίθημι	lay/put upon
ἔσωθεν	from within/inside; inside, within
Εὐφράτης, -ου, ὁ	Euphrates (River)

▷ List 27 2×

εὐχαριστία, -ας, ἡ	thankfulness, gratitude; thanksgiving
Ἔφεσος, -έσου, ἡ	Ephesus
ἐχθρός, -ά, -όν	hated; hostile; (*subst*) enemy
ζώνη, -ης, ἡ	belt
θαυμαστός, -ή, -όν	marvelous, wonderful, remarkable
ἶρις, ἴριδος, ἡ	rainbow
ἰσχύς, -ύος, ἡ	strength
κάμινος, -ίνου, ἡ	furnace
καταβολή, -ῆς, ἡ	foundation
καῦμα, καύματος, τό	scorching heat

▷ List 28 2×

καυματίζω	scorch, burn
κεῖμαι	be lying/reclining/resting; exist for, be set for
κιθαρῳδός/κιθαρωδός, -οῦ, ὁ	one who plays and sings to the lyre
κινέω	move (something), [with ἐκ] remove
κλέπτης, -ου, ὁ	thief
κοιλία, -ας, ἡ	stomach
κόπος, -ου, ὁ	trouble, hardship; labor, toil
κόπτω	(*trans act*) cut off; (*intrans mid*) beat one's breast in mourning, mourn
κοσμέω	put in order, arrange; adorn, make attractive
κράτος, -ους, τό	strength, might, power; rule, sovereignty

▷ List 29 2×

κρύσταλλος, -άλλου, ὁ	rock crystal; ice
κτίσμα, -ατος, τό	that which is created, creation; creature
λαμπάς, λαμπάδος, ἡ	torch; lamp
Λαοδίκεια, -είας, ἡ	Laodicea
λατρεύω	serve, worship [the carrying out of religious duties] (*+dat obj*)
λιβανωτός, -οῦ, ὁ	censer
λιμός, -οῦ, ὁ/ἡ	hunger; famine
μεγιστάν, -ᾶνος, ὁ	person of high rank, very great/important person
μέλας, μέλαινα, μέλαν	black
μέλι, -ιτος, τό	honey

▷ List 30 2×

μέτρον, -ου, τό	measure [instrument or result of measuring]
μῆκος, μήκους, τό	length
μίγνυμι/μιγνύω	mix, mingle ▸
μισθός, -οῦ, ὁ	pay, wages; recompense, reward
μολύνω	stain, make dirty; defile
Νικολαΐτης, -ου, ὁ	Nicolaitan
νοῦς, νοός, ὁ	mind; understanding, intellect; thought ▸
ξηραίνω	(*mid*) become dry; wither
ὄγδοος, ὀγδόη, ὄγδοον	eighth
ὁμοίως	likewise, in the same way

▷ List 31 2×

ὄπισθεν	(*adv*) on the back, behind
ὀργίζω	(*mid*) be(come) angry
ὅσιος, -ία, -ον	devout, pious, holy
οὔπω	not yet
πατάσσω	strike
Πέργαμος, -άμου, ἡ / Πέργαμον, -άμου, τό	Pergamus/Pergamum
περιζώννυμι/ περιζωννύω	(*act*) gird about; (*mid*) gird oneself ▷
πέτρα, -ας, ἡ	rock [formation or piece]
πλοῦτος, πλούτου, ὁ/τό	wealth, riches; abundance
πλύνω	wash (something)

▷ List 32 2×

πόθεν	from where?, how is it that?
πόρνος, -ου, ὁ	sexually immoral person, fornicator
πορφυροῦς, πορφυρᾶ, πορφυροῦν	purple
προφητεύω	prophesy [disclose divine will]; foretell; reveal
πρωϊνός, -ή, -όν	(of the) early morning
πτωχός, -ή, -όν	poor
πυρόω	burn (up); treat with fire, heat thoroughly
πυρρός, -ά, -όν	fiery red
πύρωσις, -ώσεως, ἡ	burning
ῥίζα, -ης, ἡ	root; shoot [from a root]

▷ List 33 2×

σάκκος, -ου, ὁ	sackcloth
σάρδιον, -ίου, τό	carnelian
σῖτος, σίτου, ὁ	wheat, grain
σκοτόω	(*mid*) be(come) darkened [literal or figurative]
Σμύρνα, -ης, ἡ	Smyrna
στάδιον, -ίου, τό	stade [one-eighth mile]; stadium
στρηνιάω	live indulgently/wantonly
στῦλος, στύλου, ὁ	pillar, column [metaphorically, a thing/person that provides support]
τάχος, -ους, τό	ἐν τάχει quickly; soon
τοσοῦτος, -αύτη, -οῦτο(ν)	so many; so much/great; such

▷ List 34 2×

τρέφω	nourish, feed, support
τρυγάω	pick, gather (ripe fruit)
ὕαλος, ὑάλου, ἡ/ὁ	[something glassy and transparent] crystal; glass
ὑψηλός, -ή, -όν	high, tall; exalted, proud, haughty
φάρμακος, -άκου, ὁ	sorcerer, magician
Φιλαδέλφ(ε)ια, -(ε)ίας, ἡ	Philadelphia
φιλέω	love, like; kiss
φονεύς, -έως, ὁ	murderer
χαλκολίβανον, -άνου, τό	fine brass/bronze
χιλίαρχος, -άρχου, ὁ	commander, captain [of approximately six hundred soldiers]

▷ List 35 — 2 to 1×

Ἀβαδδών, ὁ (*indecl*)	Abaddon
ἀγαλλιάω	exult, rejoice; be overjoyed
ἁγιάζω	consecrate, make holy; regard as holy
ἀδίκημα, -ήματος, τό	injustice, wrongdoing
χοῖνιξ, χοίνικος, ἡ	[dry measure] liter, quart
χόρτος, -ου, ὁ	grass
χρυσός, -οῦ, ὁ	gold; objects of gold [e.g., jewelry, money]
χρυσόω	adorn with gold
ψευδής, -ές	false, lying, (*subst*) liar
ψῆφος, ψήφου, ἡ	pebble, stone

▷ List 36 — 1×

Αἴγυπτος, -ύπτου, ἡ	Egypt
αἰνέω	praise
αἰσχύνη, -ης, ἡ	shame, dishonor; [sense/experience of] shame; shameful deed
ἀκμάζω	become ripe
ἄκρατος, -ον	unmixed, undiluted
ἅλυσις, ἁλύσεως, ἡ	chain
ἀμέθυστος, -ύστου, ἡ	amethyst
ἄμωμον, -ώμου, τό	spice, amomum [Indian spice plant]
ἄμωμος, -ον	unblemished; blameless
ἀναγινώσκω	read (aloud)

APPENDIX

A

ἄγω (*trans*) lead, bring, carry; (*intrans*) go

(*aor act ind*) ἤγαγον; (*pf act ind*) ἀγήοχα

αἱρέω (*mid*) choose; prefer

(*aor mid ind*) εἱλόμην

αἴρω lift up, carry (along/away), take away

(*aor act ind*) ἦρα; (*aor mid-pass ind*) ἤρθην; (*fut act ind*) ἀρῶ;
(*pf act ind*) ἦρκα

αἰώνιος long ago, eternal

There are two occurrences of a distinct feminine form (αἰωνίαν) in the NT.

ἀκούω hear, heed, obey; understand

(*pf act ind*) ἀκήκοα

ἅλας salt

(*neut acc sg*) ἅλα

ἀλλά but, rather

This particle signals a corrective to some element within the reader's mental representation of the discourse, whether that element is explicitly stated or assumed.

ἀλλάσσω change, alter; exchange

(*fut mid-pass ind*) ἀλλαγήσομαι

ἀναβαίνω go up

(*aor act ind*) ἀνέβην; (*fut mid ind*) ἀναβήσομαι [there is no *fut act*];
(*pf act ind*) ἀναβέβηκα

ἀναγινώσκω read (aloud)

(*aor act ind*) ἀνέγνων

ἀναιρέω (*act*) do away with, destroy, kill; (*mid*) take/pick up for oneself, claim

(*aor act ind*) ἀνεῖλον; (*fut act ind*) ἀνελῶ

ἀνακαλύπτω uncover, unveil

(*pf mid-pass ptc*) ἀνακεκαλυμμένος

ἀνακλίνω (*act*) lay down, cause to lie down; cause to recline (at a meal); (*mid*) recline (at a meal)

(*fut mid-pass ind*) ἀνακλιθήσομαι

ἀνακράζω cry out, shout

(*aor act ind*) ἀνέκραξα/ἀνέκραγον

ἀνακρίνω examine closely, inquire into; hear a case, put on trial, investigate

(*aor mid-pass subj*) ἀνακριθῶ

ἀναλαμβάνω lift up; take up/along; get

(*aor act ind*) ἀνέλαβον; (*aor mid-pass ind*) ἀνελήμφθην

ἀναμιμνῄσκω (*trans act*) remind; (*intrans mid*) remember

(*aor mid-pass ind*) ἀνεμνήσθην; (*fut act ind*) ἀναμνήσω

ἀναπαύω give rest, refresh; rest

(*fut mid-pass ind*) ἀναπαήσομαι

ἀναπίπτω recline, lean back

(*aor act ind*) ἀνέπεσον

ἀναστρέφω (*act*) return, go back; (*mid*) conduct oneself, live

(*aor mid-pass ind*) ἀνεστράφην

ἀνατέλλω (*trans*) cause to rise; (*intrans*) rise, come up

(*pf act ind*) ἀνατέταλκα

ἀνατρέφω bring up, care for, raise, rear

(*aor mid-pass ind*) ἀνετράφην; (*pf mid-pass ptc*) ἀνατεθραμμένος

ἀνέρχομαι go/come up

(*aor act ind*) ἀνῆλθον

ἀνέχω (*mid*) bear with, tolerate, put up with; endure

(*impf mid-pass ind*) ἀνειχόμην. In 2 Thess 1:4, the verb is preceded by αἷς, though we would normally expect ἅς or ὧν. This is an instance of case attraction, whereby the case of the relative pronoun has been attracted to the case of its antecedent.

ἀνθίστημι resist, oppose, withstand

(*aor act ind*) ἀντέστην; (*pf act ind*) ἀνθέστηκα

ἀνίημι let go, loose

(*aor act subj*) ἀνῶ; (*pres act ptc nom masc sg*) ἀνιέντες

ἀνίστημι (*trans*) erect, raise (to life); (*intrans*) stand up, rise (from the dead)

(*trans*): (*aor act ind*) ἀνέστησα; (*fut act ind*) ἀναστήσω

(*intrans*): (*pres mid ind*) ἀνίσταμαι; (*root aor act ind*) ἀνέστην; (*fut mid ind*) ἀναστήσομαι

ἀνοίγω (*trans*) open; (*intrans*) be open

(*aor act ind*) ἀνέῳξα/ἠνέῳξα/ἤνοιξα; (*pf act ind*) ἀνέῳγα

ἀντικαθίστημι (*intrans*) be set against, oppose, resist

(*aor act subj*) ἀντικατέστω

ἀντιλέγω argue (against), contradict; oppose

(*aor act ind*) ἀντεῖπον

ἀπάγω lead off, take away, lead astray; bring (before a magistrate/court)

(*aor act ind*) ἀπήγαγον

ἀπέρχομαι go (away), depart

(*aor act ind*) ἀπῆλθον; (*fut mid ind*) ἀπελεύσομαι [there is no *fut act*]; (*pf act ind*) ἀπελήλυθα

ἀποβαίνω move off, disembark; turn out, lead to, result in

(*aor act ind*) ἀπέβην; (*fut mid ind*) ἀποβήσομαι [there is no *fut act*]

ἀποβάλλω throw away

(*aor act subj*) ἀποβάλω

ἀπογράφω register (someone), enter (someone/something) into a list

(*pf mid-pass ptc*) ἀπογεγραμμένος

ἀποθνῄσκω die, face death

(*aor act ind*) ἀπέθανον; (*fut mid ind*) ἀποθανοῦμαι [there is no *fut act*]

ἀποκαθίστημι/ἀποκαθιστάνω restore, reestablish

(*aor mid-pass subj*) ἀποκατασταθῶ

ἀποκαλύπτω reveal, disclose

(*aor mid-pass ind*) ἀπεκαλύφθην; (*fut mid-pass ind*) ἀποκαλυφθήσομαι

ἀποκρίνομαι answer, reply

(*aor mid-pass ind*) ἀπεκρίθην; (*fut mid-pass ind*) ἀποκριθήσομαι

ἀποκρύπτω hide, conceal, keep hidden

(*pf mid-pass ptc*) ἀποκεκρυμμένος

ἀπολαμβάνω receive; recover, get back

(*aor act ind*) ἀπέλαβον; (*fut mid ind*) ἀπολήμψομαι [there is no *fut act*]

ἀπολείπω (*act*) leave behind; abandon; (*mid*) remain

(*aor act ind*) ἀπέλ(ε)ιπον

ἀπόλλυμι (*trans act*) destroy, lose; (*intrans mid*) perish, be ruined/lost

(*aor act ind*) ἀπώλεσα; (*aor mid ind*) ἀπωλόμην; (*fut act ind*) ἀπολέσω/ἀπολῶ; (*fut mid ind*) ἀπολοῦμαι; (*pf act ind*) ἀπολώλεκα/ἀπόλωλα

ἀποπλέω sail away/off

(*aor act ind*) ἀπέπλευσα

ἀποστρέφω (*act*) turn (something) away (from something); put back, return; (*mid*) turn away from, reject

(*aor mid-pass ind*) ἀπεστράφην

ἀποφέρω take /carry away, transport, carry

(*aor act ind*) ἀπήνεγκα

ἀποφεύγω escape (from)

(*aor act ptc*) ἀποφυγών

ἀρέσκω please

(*aor act ind*) ἤρεσα

ἁρπαγμός something used for one's own advantage

This word, which occurs only once in the NT (and is rare in Greek literature), has received much attention, and its meaning is heavily debated. The gloss I have provided represents what I believe to be the correct understanding of the word's use in Philippians based, firstly, on linguistic data and, secondly, on the surrounding linguistic context in Philippians 2. Other suggestions have been argued for, however, and while there is not space to list them here, they should be given due consideration.

ἅρπαξ ravenous, rapacious; (*subst*) robber, swindler

(*masc/fem gen sg*) ἅρπαγος

ἄρσην male

(*gen sg*) ἄρσενος

ἀφαιρέω (*act*) remove, take away; (*mid*) take away, do away with

(*aor act ind*) ἀφεῖλον; (*fut act ind*) ἀφελῶ

ἀφίημι send away; divorce; forgive; leave (behind)

(*aor act ind*) ἀφῆκα; (*aor mid-pass ind*) ἀφέθην; (*fut act ind*) ἀφήσω; (*fut mid-pass ind*) ἀφεθήσομαι; (*aor act impv*) ἄφες; (*aor act subj*) ἀφῶ; (*aor act ptc*) ἀφείς, (*gen*) ἀφέντος

ἀφικνέομαι come to, reach

(*aor mid ind*) ἀφικόμην

ἀφίστημι (*trans*) draw away, incite; (*intrans*) withdraw, depart; keep away

The only *trans* form found in the NT is the *aor act ind 3sg*, ἀπέστησεν. The *intrans* forms found in the NT are as follows: (*root aor act*) ἀπέστην; (*impf mid*) ἀφιστάμην; (*fut mid*) ἀποστήσομαι.

ἀφοράω fix one's eyes (on); determine, see

(*aor act subj*) ἀφίδω

ἀφορίζω separate; set apart

(*fut act ind*) ἀφοριῶ/ἀφορίσω

ἀχρειόω (*mid*) become worthless

(*aor mid-pass ind*) ἠχρεώθην

Β

βάλλω throw, cast; put

(*aor mid-pass ind*) ἐβλήθην; (*fut mid-pass ind*) βληθήσομαι; (*pf act ind*) βέβληκα

βασκαίνω bewitch

(*aor act ind 3sg*) ἐβάσκανεν

Γ

γαμέω marry

(*aor act ptc*) γήμας

γίνομαι be(come), exist, happen, occur; be born/produced

(*aor mid ind*) ἐγενόμην; (*fut mid ind*) γενήσομαι; (*pf act ind*) γέγονα; (*aor mid opt 3sg*) γένοιτο

γινώσκω know, understand, find out, realize

(*aor act ind*) ἔγνων; (*aor mid-pass ind*) ἐγνώσθην; (*fut mid ind*) γνώσομαι [there is no *fut act*]; (*fut mid-pass ind*) γνωσθήσομαι; (*pf act ind*) ἔγνωκα; (*pf mid-pass ind*) ἔγνωσμαι

Δ

δέ but, and, now [non-temporal], [paragraph break]

Crucially, δέ structures the discourse by explicitly segmenting distinct information units. This is not always easily represented in translation.

δείκνυμι show, make known; explain

(*aor act ind*) ἔδειξα; (*fut act ind*) δείξω; (*aor mid-pass ptc*) δειχθείς

δέρω violently mistreat, beat

(*fut mid-pass ind*) δαρήσομαι

δεῦτε come!, come here!, come on!

Serves as the *pl* of δεῦρο.

δή now, then, so

This particle draws the recipient's attention to something important that is assumed to be a part of the common ground or at least prepared for earlier in the text.

διαβαίνω cross, go through

(*aor act ind*) διέβην

διαζώννυμι tie around

(*aor act ind*) διέζωσα; (*pf mid-pass ptc*) διεζωσμένος

διακρίνω (*act*) evaluate; make a distinction; (*mid*) make a distinction [among oneself and others]; dispute, contest, contend (with)

(*aor mid-pass ind*) διακρίθην

διασπείρω (*pass*) be scattered

(*aor mid-pass ind*) διεσπάρην

διαστρέφω turn aside, mislead; make crooked, distort

(*pf mid-pass ptc*) διεστραμμένος

διασῴζω bring safely through, preserve; save, rescue

The *iota* subscript is absent in the other tense-forms.

διατάσσω (*act*) instruct, direct; (*mid*) instruct, direct; make arrangements

(*aor act ind*) διέταξα; (*fut mid ind*) διατάξομαι; (*aor mid-pass ptc*) διαταχθείς/διαταγείς; (*pf mid-pass ptc*) διατεταγμένος; (*pf act inf*) διατεταχέναι

διαφέρω carry through/across; be unlike, differ; differ in worth, surpass, be worth more (than)

(*aor act subj*) διενέγκω

διαφθείρω destroy; corrupt

(*aor mid-pass ind*) διεφθάρην; (*pf mid-pass ptc*) διεφθαρμένος

διδάσκω teach, instruct

(*aor act ind*) ἐδίδαξα; (*aor mid-pass ind*) ἐδιδάχθην; (*fut act ind*) διδάξω

διέρχομαι come/go through

(*aor act ind*) διῆλθον; (*fut act ind*) διελεύσομαι; (*pf act ind*) διελήλυθα

διορύσσω dig through, break in

(*aor mid-pass inf*) διορυγῆναι/διορυχθῆναι

δύο two

(*gen/acc*) δύο, (*dat*) δυσί

E

ἐάω allow, permit, let

(*aor act ind*) εἴασα; (*impf act ind*) εἴων

ἐγγράφω engrave, inscribe, write down (on)

(*pf mid-pass ptc*) ἐνγεγραμμένος

ἐγείρω (*trans act*) wake, rouse, raise; (*intrans mid*) wake/rise up

(*pf mid-pass ind*) ἐγήγερμαι

ἐγκαινίζω inaugurate

(*aor act ind*) ἐνεκαίνισα

ἐγκαλέω accuse, bring charges against

(*impf act ind*) ἐνεκάλουν

ἐγκαταλείπω leave behind; forsake, abandon

(*aor act ind*) ἐγκατέλ(ε)ιπον

εἰμί be; there is/are

(*impf ind*) ἤμην; (*fut ind*) ἔσομαι; (*pres impv*) ἴσθι; (*pres subj*) ὦ; (*pres ptc*) ὤν; (*pres inf*) εἶναι

εἷς, μία, ἕν one, someone, a certain (one)

(*gen*) ἑνός, μιᾶς, ἑνός

εἰσάγω lead/bring in(to)

(*aor act ind*) εἰσήγαγον

εἴσειμι go in(to), enter

[from εἶμι "go/come"] (*pres act ind 3sg*) εἰσίασιν; (*impf act ind 3sg*) εἰσῄει; (*pres act inf*) εἰσιέναι

εἰσέρχομαι enter, come/go into

(*aor act ind*) εἰσῆλθον; (*fut mid ind*) εἰσελεύσομαι [there is no *fut act*]; (*pf act ind*) εἰσελήλυθα

εἰσφέρω lead/bring in

(*aor act ind*) εἰσήνεγκα

ἐκβάλλω expel, throw/send out

(*aor mid-pass ind*) ἐξεβλήθην; (*fut mid-pass ind*) ἐκβληθήσομαι; (*plpf act ind*) ἐκβεβλήκειν

ἐκκόπτω cut off/down; do away with

(*aor mid-pass ind*) ἐξεκόπην; (*fut mid-pass ind*) ἐκκοπήσομαι

ἐκπίπτω fall off; fall from, be deprived of

(*aor act ind*) ἐξέπεσα; (*pf act ind*) ἐκπέπτωκα; (*aor act inf*) ἐκπεσεῖν

ἐκπλέω sail out/away

(*aor act ind*) ἐξέπλευσα

ἐκστρέφω turn (something) out, pull (something) out; [figurative] change entirely, distort

(*pf mid-pass ind*) ἐξέστραπται

ἐκτρέπω (*mid*) turn away/aside from

(*fut mid-pass ind*) ἐκτραπήσομαι

ἐκφέρω carry/bring out; produce

(*aor act ind*) ἐξήνεγκα; (*fut act ind*) ἐξοίσω; (*aor act inf*) ἐξενεγκεῖν

ἐκφεύγω escape; flee

(*aor act ind*) ἐξέφυγον

ἐκχέω/ἐκχύν(ν)ω pour out

(*aor mid-pass ind*) ἐξεχύθην; (*fut act ind*) ἐκχεῶ; (*fut mid-pass ind*) ἐκχυθήσομαι; (*pf mid-pass ind*) ἐκκέχυμμαι

ἕλκω draw, pull; draw, attract

(*aor act ind*) εἵλκυσα; (*impf act ind*) εἷλκον; (*fut act ind*) ἑλκύσω

ἐλπίζω hope (for); expect

(*fut act ind*) ἐλπιῶ; (*pf act ind*) ἤλπικα

ἐμβαίνω embark

(*aor act ind*) ἐνέβην; (*aor act ptc*) ἐμβάς; (*aor act inf*) ἐμβῆναι

ἐμπαίζω mock, ridicule

(*aor act ind*) ἐνέπαιξα; (*aor mid-pass ind*) ἐνεπαίχθην; (*fut act ind*) ἐμπαίξω

ἐμπίπτω fall in(to)

(*aor act subj*) ἐμπέσω

ἐμπλέκω (*mid*) be entangled in

(*aor mid-pass ptc*) ἐμπλακείς

ἐνδείκνυμι (*mid*) show, demonstrate, exhibit

(*aor mid ind*) ἐνεδειξάμην

ἔνειμι be in(side)

(*pres act ind 3sg*) ἔνι

ἐνίστημι (*pf*) be present/here; (*fut*) will come/arrive

(*pf act ptc*) ἐνεστηκώς/ἐνεστώς

ἐντρέπω (*mid*) be ashamed; have regard for, respect

(*aor mid-pass ind*) ἐνετράπην; (*fut mid-pass ind*) ἐντραπήσομαι

ἐξάγω lead/bring out

(*aor act ind*) ἐξήγαγον

ἐξαιρέω (*act*) take out; (*mid*) rescue, deliver, set free

(*aor mid ind*) ἐξειλάμην; (*aor act impv*) ἔξελε

ἔξειμι go out, leave

[from εἶμι "go/come"] (*impf act ind 3sg*) ἐξῄεσαν; (*pres act inf*) ἐξιέναι

ἐξέρχομαι go/come out, go away

(*aor act ind*) ἐξῆλθον; (*fut mid ind*) ἐξελεύσομαι [there is no *fut act*]; (*pf act ind*) ἐξελήλυθα

ἔξεστιν (*impers*) it is right/permitted

(*pres act ptc neut nom sg*) ἐξόν

ἐξηχέω (*intrans mid*) resound, ring out/forth

(*pf mid-pass ind*) ἐξήχημαι

ἐξίστημι/ἐξιστάνω (*trans*) amaze; (*intrans mid*) be amazed

(*trans*): (*aor act*) ἐξέστησα

(*intrans*): (*pres mid*) ἐξίσταμαι; (*root aor act*) ἐξέστην; (*impf mid*) ἐξιστάμην; (*pf act*) ἐξέστακα

Note that the *3pl* of ἐξέστην and ἐξέστησα is the same (ἐξέστησαν).

ἐπαίρω lift up

(*aor act ind*) ἐπῆρα; (*aor mid-pass ind*) ἐπήρθην; (*aor act ptc*) ἐπάρας

ἐπέρχομαι come up(on), approach

(*aor act ind*) ἐπῆλθον; (*fut mid ind*) ἐπελεύσομαι [there is no *fut act*]

ἐπιβαίνω board (a ship); set foot in

(*aor act ind*) ἐπέβην

ἐπιγινώσκω know; learn; recognize

(*aor act ind*) ἐπέγνων; (*aor mid-pass ind*) ἐπεγνώσθην; (*fut mid ind*) ἐπιγνώσομαι [there is no *fut act*]; (*pf act ind*) ἐπέγνωκα

ἐπιδείκνυμι show

(*aor act ind*) ἐπέδειξα

ἐπικαλέω (*act*) call, name; (*mid*) call upon, invoke, appeal

(*aor mid-pass ind*) ἐπεκλήθην; (*pf mid-pass ind*) ἐπικέκλημαι

ἐπιλανθάνομαι forget; neglect, ignore

(*aor mid ind*) ἐπελαθόμην

ἐπιπίπτω fall upon

(*aor act ind*) ἐπέπεσον

ἐπιστηρίζω support, firm up, strengthen

(*aor act ind*) ἐπεστήριξα

ἐπιστρέφω (*intrans act/mid*) return; turn (around); change (one's thinking or behavior); (*trans act*) turn, redirect

(*aor mid-pass ind*) ἐπεστράφην

ἐπιτρέπω permit, give permission, allow

(*aor mid-pass ind*) ἐπετράπην

ἐπιτυγχάνω obtain, attain

(*aor act ind*) ἐπέτυχον

ἐπιφαύσκω shine out

(*fut act ind 3sg*) ἐπιφαύσει

ἐπιφέρω bring/pronounce (a charge)

(*aor act inf*) ἐπενεγκεῖν

ἔρχομαι come, go

(*aor act ind*) ἦλθον; (*fut mid ind*) ἐλεύσομαι [there is no *fut act*]; (*pf act ind*) ἐλήλυθα

ἐσθής clothing

(*dat pl*) ἐσθήσεσι

ἐσθίω eat, consume

(*aor act ind*) ἔφαγον; (*fut mid ind*) φάγομαι [there is no *fut act*]

εὑρίσκω find, discover

(*aor act ind*) εὗρον [Luke 23:2 εὕραμεν for the *1pl*]; (*fut act ind*) εὑρήσω; (*pf act ind*) εὕρηκα

εὐσχήμων noble, dignified, respectable, presentable

(*gen sg*) εὐσχήμονος

ἐφικνέομαι reach, extend (to)

(*aor mid inf*) ἐφικέσθαι

ἐφίστημι stand by/near

(*aor act ind*) ἐπέστησα/ἐπέστην

ἔχω have; be able

(*aor act ind*) ἔσχον; (*fut act ind*) ἕξω; (*pf act ind*) ἔσχηκα

Z

ζώννυμι/ζωννύω gird

(*fut act ind*) ζώσω; (*aor mid impv*) ζῶσαι

Θ

θέλω want, wish

(*aor act ind*) ἠθέλησα; (*impf act ind*) ἤθελον

θιγγάνω touch

(*aor act subj*) θίγω

θλίβω compress, make narrow; press upon; oppress, afflict

(*pf mid-pass ptc*) τεθλιμμένος

θνῄσκω die

(*pf act ind*) τέθνηκα

I

Ἰησοῦς Jesus, Joshua

(*gen/dat*) Ἰησοῦ

ἵστημι (*trans*) set, place, (make) stand; establish; (*intrans*) stand (around)

(*trans*): (*pres act*) ἵστημι; (*aor act*) ἔστησα; (*impf act*) ἵστην; (*fut act*) στήσω

(*intrans*): (*root aor act*) ἔστην; (*aor mid-pass*) ἐστάθην; (*fut mid*) στήσομαι; (*pf act*) ἕστηκα; (*plpf act*) εἱστήκειν

K

καθαιρέω take/bring down; tear down

(*aor act ind*) καθεῖλον; (*fut act ind*) καθελῶ

καθαρίζω cleanse, make clean

(*fut act ind*) καθαριῶ

καθίημι let down, lower

(*aor act ind*) καθῆκα

καθίστημι/καθιστάνω appoint; make, cause to be; bring

(*aor act ind*) κατέστησα; (*aor mid-pass ind*) καθεστάθην; (*fut act ind*) καταστήσω; (*fut mid-pass ind*) κατασταθήσομαι

καλέω call, invite, name

(*aor mid-pass ind*) ἐκλήθην; (*fut mid-pass ind*) κληθήσομαι; (*pf act ind*) κέκληκα

καλύπτω cover; hide, conceal

(*pf mid-pass ptc*) κεκαλυμμένος

καταβαίνω come/go down

(*aor act ind*) κατέβην; (*fut mid ind*) καταβήσομαι [there is no *fut act*]; (*pf act ind*) καταβέβηκα

καταγινώσκω condemn

(*pf mid-pass ptc*) κατεγνωσμένος

κατάγνυμι break, shatter

(*aor act ind*) κατέαξα; (*fut act ind*) κατεάξω

κατάγω (*act*) lead/bring down; (*mid*) put in, land

(*aor act ind*) κατήγαγον

κατακαίω burn completely, burn up/down

(*aor mid-pass ind*) κατεκάην; (*fut act ind*) κατακαύσω

κατακλίνω (*trans act*) cause to recline/sit [for dining]; (*intrans mid*) recline [for dining]

(*aor mid-pass ind*) κατεκλίθην

κατακρίνω condemn

(*aor mid-pass ind*) κατεκρίθην; (*fut mid-pass ind*) κατακριθήσομαι

καταλαμβάνω grasp, attain; seize, secure; overtake; catch; understand, realize

(*aor act ind*) κατέλαβον; (*aor mid-pass ind*) κατελήμφθην; (*pf act inf*) κατειληφέναι

καταλείπω leave (behind); cause to be left over

(*aor act ind*) κατέλειψα/κατέλ(ε)ιπον; (*pf mid-pass ptc*) καταλελειμμένος

καταπίνω swallow (up), gulp (down)

(*aor mid-pass subj*) καταποθῶ; (*aor act inf*) καταπιεῖν

καταφέρω bring/weigh down; bring against

(*aor act ind*) κατήνεγκα; (*aor mid-pass ptc*) κατενεχθείς

καταφθείρω destroy; corrupt

(*pf mid-pass ptc*) καταφθαρμένος

κατεργάζομαι do; produce, bring about; prepare

(*aor mid ind*) κατειργασάμην; (*pf mid-pass inf*) κατειργάσθαι

κατέρχομαι come/go down; arrive

(*aor act ind*) κατῆλθον

κατεσθίω devour, consume

(*aor act ind*) κατέφαγον; (*fut mid ind*) καταφάγομαι [there is no *fut act*]

κατέχω hold fast/to; possess; hold back, restrain, suppress

(*aor act ind*) κατέσχον; (*impf mid-pass ind*) κατειχόμην

καυχάομαι boast (about)

(*pres mid-pass ind 2sg*) καυχᾶσαι

κεράννυμι mix

(*aor act ind*) ἐκέρασα; (*pf mid-pass ptc*) κεκερασμένος

κερδαίνω gain

(*aor act ind*) ἐκέρδησα; (*fut act ind*) κερδήσω; (*aor act subj*) κερδάνω

κηρύσσω proclaim, announce

(*aor mid-pass ind*) ἐκηρύχθην; (*fut mid-pass ind*) κηρυχθήσομαι

κλαίω weep

(*aor act ind*) ἔκλαυσα; (*aor mid-pass ind*) ἐκλαύσθην;
(*fut act ind*) κλαύσω; (*fut mid-pass ind*) κλαυσθήσομαι

κλ(ε)ίνω (*trans act*) lay; bend, bow; (*intrans act*) decline, come to an end

(*pf act ind*) κέκλικα

κρεμάννυμι (*trans act*) make (something) hang; (*intrans mid*) hang

(*pres mid-pass ind*) κρέμαμαι; (*aor mid-pass subj 3sg*) κρεμασθῇ; (*aor act ptc nom masc pl*) κρεμάσαντες; (*aor mid-pass ptc gen pl*) κρεμασθέντων

κρίνω select, pass judgment, condemn, decide, consider

(*aor mid-pass ind*) ἐκρίθην; (*fut mid-pass ind*) κριθήσομαι; (*pf act ind*) κέκρικα; (*pf mid-pass ind*) κέκριμαι; (*plpf act ind*) κεκρίκειν

κρύπτω (*trans act*) hide (something); (*intrans mid*) hide (oneself), be hidden

(*aor mid-pass ind*) ἐκρύβην; (*pf mid-pass ptc*) κεκρυμμένος; (*aor mid-pass inf*) κρυβῆναι

Λ

λαγχάνω receive [as a portion], obtain [by lot]

(*aor act ind*) ἔλαχον

λαμβάνω take, receive

(*aor act ind*) ἔλαβον; (*fut mid ind*) λήμψομαι [there is no *fut act*]; (*pf act ind*) εἴληφα

λέγω say, speak

(*aor act ind*) εἶπον; (*aor mid-pass ind*) ἐρρέθην; (*fut act ind*) ἐρῶ; (*pf act ind*) εἴρηκα; (*aor mid-pass ptc*) ῥηθείς

Λύδδα Lydda

The *acc* Λύδδα can function as an *indecl* form.

Λύστρα Lystra

(*dat*) Λύστροις; (*acc*) Λύστραν

Μ

μανθάνω learn

(*aor act ind*) ἔμαθον; (*pf act ptc*) μεμαθηκώς

μέγας great, large

(*comp*) μείζων/μειζότερος; (*superl*) μέγιστος [rare; during the Hellenistic period, this was being replaced by the *comp*]

μέλας black; (*neut subst*) ink

The *gen sg* forms of the masculine, feminine, and neuter, respectively, are μέλανος, μελαίνης, μέλανος.

μέλλω be about to/going to

(*impf act ind*) ἔμελλον/ἤμελλον

μέν

The utterance introduced by μέν and the content that it anticipates provide relevant information about a preceding or presupposed topic. In certain contexts, the particle is similar to English's "on the one hand . . . ," though it is often preferable to leave it untranslated.

μεταβαίνω go, move

(*aor act ind*) μετέβην; (*fut mid ind*) μεταβήσομαι [there is no *fut act*]; (*aor act ptc*) μεταβάς

μεταλαμβάνω have/receive a share, partake

(*aor act ptc*) μεταλαβών; (*aor act inf*) μεταλαβεῖν

μεταστρέφω change, alter; distort, twist

(*aor mid-pass impv 3sg*) μεταστραφήτω

μετατρέπω turn (something) around; change (something)

(*aor mid-pass impv 3sg*) μετατραπήτω

μετέχω share, have a share in; partake of

(*aor act ind*) μετέσχον; (*pf act ind*) μετέσχηκα

μή not, lest

In most circumstances, μή negates non-*ind* verbs. It is also used in yes/no questions when a negative response is expected.

μήτι not

μήτι, like μή, is used in yes/no questions when a negative response is expected. It can also be collocated with εἰ to introduce an exceptive clause; hence, εἰ μήτι can be translated "except, unless."

μιαίνω stain, defile, taint

(*pf mid-pass ind*) μεμίαμμαι

μίγνυμι/μιγνύω mix, mingle

(*pf mid-pass ptc*) μεμιγμένος

μιμνήσκομαι/μιμνῄσκομαι remember; be mindful of

(*aor mid-pass ind*) ἐμνήσθην; (*fut mid-pass ind*) μνησθήσομαι

N

νέος new; young

(*comp*) νεώτερος

νοῦς mind; understanding, intellect; thought

(*dat sg*) νοΐ; (*acc sg*) νοῦν

Ξ

ξηραίνω (*mid*) become dry; wither

(*pf mid-pass ptc*) ἐξηραμμένος

O

οἶδα know, understand

This verb's lexical form, οἶδα, is the *pf act ind*. The other forms of this verb that are relevant for reading the NT are: (*plpf act ind*) ᾔδειν; (*fut act ind*) εἰδήσω; (*pf act impv 2pl*) ἴστε; (*pf act subj*) εἰδῶ; (*pf act ptc*) εἰδώς, εἰδυῖα, εἰδός; (*pf act inf*) εἰδέναι.

οἴομαι think, suppose, expect

(*pres act ind*) οἶμαι

ὀμνύω make an oath, swear

(*aor act ind*) ὤμοσα

ὄναρ dream

This word only occurs in the *nom* and *acc sg*.

ὀνίνημι (*mid*) have profit/benefit/delight

(*aor mid opt*) ὀναίμην

ὁράω (*trans act/mid*) see, perceive; (*intrans act*) look (at); (*intrans mid*) appear

(*aor act ind*) εἶδον; (*aor mid-pass ind*) ὤφθην; (*fut mid ind*) ὄψομαι [there is no *fut act*]; (*pf act ind*) ἑώρακα

οὐ no, not

οὐ negates *ind* verbs and is used in yes/no questions when an affirmative response is expected.

οὖν so, then, now [non-temporal], anyway, therefore

Like δέ, οὖν structures the discourse by explicitly segmenting distinct information units. οὖν has an additional constraint in that it marks a close continuative connection with some preceding material (whether immediate or not).

Π

παραγίνομαι come, arrive, be present

(*aor mid ind*) παρεγενόμην; (*aor mid-pass ind*) παρεγενήθην

παρακαλέω invite, implore; comfort; encourage

(*aor mid-pass ind*) παρεκλήθην; (*fut mid-pass ind*) παρακληθήσομαι; (*pf mid-pass ind*) παρακέκλημαι

παραλαμβάνω take (with/along), receive

(*aor act ind*) παρέλαβον; (*fut mid ind*) παραλήμψομαι [there is no *fut act*]; (*fut mid-pass ind*) παραλημφθήσομαι

παρεισέρχομαι come in (beside)

(*aor act ind*) παρεισῆλθον

παρεισφέρω apply (beside), bring to bear

(*aor act ptc nom masc pl*) παρεισενέγκαντες

παρέρχομαι pass by; pass [of time]; pass away, disappear; neglect, transgress

(*aor act ind*) παρῆλθον; (*fut mid ind*) παρελεύσομαι [there is no *fut act*]; (*pf act ind*) παρελήλυθα

παρέχω (*act*) bring about, furnish; present, provide; (*mid*) grant, show

(*aor act ind*) παρέσχον; (*aor act ptc*) παρασχών

παρίστημι (*trans*) put at one's disposal; present; (*intrans*) be present; come to

(*trans*): (*pres act*) παρίστημι; (*aor act*) παρέστησα; (*fut act*) παραστήσω

(*intrans*): (*root aor act*) παρέστην; (*fut mid*) παραστήσομαι; (*pf act*) παρέστηκα; (*plpf act*) παρειστήκειν

πάσχω suffer, endure

(*aor act ind*) ἔπαθον; (*pf act ind*) πέπονθα

πείθω (*act*) convince, persuade; (*mid*) obey, follow; be sure/convinced; (*pf act*) trust; (*pf act/mid-pass*) be certain

(*pf act ind*) πέποιθα

περιβάλλω (*trans act*) clothe, put on; (*trans mid*) clothe/put on oneself; (*intrans mid*) be wearing/clothed

(*pf mid-pass ptc*) περιβεβλημένος

περιέρχομαι go about

(*aor act ind*) περιῆλθον

περιζώννυμι/περιζωννύω (*act*) gird about; (*mid*) gird oneself

(*fut mid ind*) περιζώσομαι; (*aor mid ptc*) περιζωσάμενος;
(*pf mid-pass ptc*) περιεζωσμένος

περιπίπτω fall into, encounter

(*aor act subj*) περιπέσω

περισσεύω (*intrans*) abound (in), overflow;
(*trans*) cause (something) to abound, increase

(*aor act ind*) ἐπερίσσευσα

περιτέμνω circumcise

(*aor act ind*) περιέτεμον; (*aor mid-pass ind*) περιετμήθην;
(*pf mid-pass ptc*) περιτετμημένος

πίμπλημι fill, fulfill, complete

(*aor act ind*) ἔπλησα; (*aor mid-pass ind*) ἐπλήσθην;
(*fut mid-pass ind*) πλησθήσομαι

πίνω drink

(*aor act ind*) ἔπιον; (*fut mid ind*) πίομαι [there is no *fut act*];
(*pf act ind*) πέπωκα

πιπράσκω sell

(*pf act ind*) πέπρακα; (*aor mid-pass inf*) πραθῆναι

πίπτω fall, perish

(*aor act ind*) ἔπεσον; (*fut mid ind*) πεσοῦμαι [there is no *fut act*];
(*pf act ind*) πέπτωκα

πλάσσω form, mold

(*aor mid-pass ind*) ἐπλάσθην

πλήν nevertheless, but, only; (*prep +gen*) except

Like ἀλλά, πλήν is a corrective marker. Unlike ἀλλά, the correction that πλήν introduces is foregrounded relative to the material that came before the particle. This results in a sharper juxtaposition between what precedes and follows πλήν. Given this, πλήν is frequently used to cut off a themeline of the discourse and begin a new one.

ποιμαίνω shepherd, tend

(*fut act ind 3sg*) ποιμανῶ; (*aor act impv 2pl*) ποιμάνατε

πολύς much, many

(*comp*) πλείων, πλεῖον; (*superl*) πλεῖστος, πλείστη, πλεῖστον

πράσσω (*trans*) do, accomplish, perform; (*intrans*) act, behave

(*pf act ind*) πέπραχα; (*pf mid-pass ptc*) πεπραγμένος

προάγω (*trans*) lead/bring out; (*intrans*) go before, precede

(*aor act ind*) προήγαγον

προαμαρτάνω sin previously

(*pf act ptc*) προημαρτηκώς

προβαίνω move forward, advance

(*pf act ptc*) προβεβηκώς

προγινώσκω know beforehand

(*aor act ind*) προέγνων; (*pf mid-pass ptc*) προεγνωσμένος

προγράφω write befrehand/in advance

(*pf mid-pass ptc*) προεγραμμένος

προελπίζω hope beforehand/first

(*pf act ptc*) προηλπικώς

προέρχομαι go forward, advance; go ahead

(*aor act ind*) προῆλθον; (*fut mid ind*) προελεύσομαι [there is no *fut act*]

προλαμβάνω take/receive beforehand; catch, overtake, detect

(*aor act ind 3sg*) προέλαβεν; (*aor mid-pass subj 3sg*) προλημφθῇ

προοράω foresee; see previously

(*aor act ptc*) προϊδών; (*pf act ptc nom masc pl*) προεωρακότες

προπάσχω suffer previously/before

(*aor act ind*) προέπαθον

προσάγω bring forward/to [into someone's presence]

(*aor act ind*) προσήγαγον

προσέρχομαι come/go to, approach

(*aor act ind*) προσῆλθον; (*fut mid ind*) προσελεύσομαι [there is no *fut act*]; (*pf act ind*) προσελήλυθα

προσέχω look after, pay attention/attend to; devote/apply oneself to

(*pf act ind*) προσέσχηκα

προσκαλέω (*mid*) invite, call to, summon

(*pf mid-pass ind*) προσκέκλημαι

προσλαμβάνω (*mid*) take to oneself; receive, welcome; take aside; take, partake

(*aor mid ind*) προσελαβόμην

προσπίπτω fall down before/at the feet of; fall upon, strike against

(*aor act ind*) προσέπεσον

προστρέχω run to(ward)

(*aor act ptc nom masc sg*) προσδραμών

προσφέρω bring (to); offer

(*aor act ind*) προσήνεγκον/προσήνεγκα; (*pf act ind*) προσενήνοχα

πυνθάνομαι inquire, ask; learn [via inquiry]

(*aor mid ind*) ἐπυθόμην

Ρ

ῥαντίζω sprinkle; purify

(*aor act ind*) ἐ(ρ)ράντισα

ῥιζόω (*mid*) take root, (*pass*) be planted

(*pf mid-pass ptc*) ἐρριζωμένος

ῥύομαι save, rescue, deliver

(*aor mid ind*) ἐ(ρ)ρυσάμην

Σ

σάββατον Sabbath, week

The *pl* is sometimes used even when the referent is a single Sabbath day or a single week.

σβέννυμι extinguish, put out

(*aor act ind*) ἔσβεσα; (*fut act ind*) σβέσω

στηρίζω set, establish; strengthen/make more firm [inwardly]

(*aor act ind*) ἐστήριξα/ἐστήρισα; (*fut act ind*) στηρίξω;
(*pf mid-pass ind*) ἐστήριγμαι

στρέφω (*trans act*) turn; return; change; (*intrans mid*) turn (around); change

(*aor mid-pass ind*) ἐστράφην

στρωννύω/στρώννυμι spread/lay (something) out; equip, furnish

(*aor act ind*) ἔστρωσα; (*pf mid-pass ptc*) ἐστρωμένος

συγκαθίζω (*trans*) cause to sit down with; (*intrans*) sit down together

(*aor act ind*) συνεκάθισα

συγκλείω enclose, catch; confine

(*aor act ind*) συνέκλεισα

συγχέω/συγχύν(ν)ω (*trans act*) confuse, confound; stir up; (*intrans mid*) be confounded/confused

(*aor mid-pass ind 3sg*) συνεχύθη; (*impf act ind*) συνέχεον,
3sg συνέχυ(ν)νεν; (*pf mid-pass ptc nom fem sg*) συνκεχυμένη/συγκεχυμένη

συζωοποιέω make alive together with

(*aor act ind*) συνεζωοποίησα

συλλαμβάνω (*act*) capture, arrest; conceive; catch; (*mid*) assist, help; arrest

(*aor act ind*) συνέλαβον; (*fut mid ind*) συλλήμψομαι [there is no *fut act*]; (*pf act ind*) συνείληφα; (*aor mid-pass ptc acc masc sg*) συλλημφθέντα; (*aor mid-pass inf*) συλλημφθῆναι

συλλέγω collect, gather

(*aor act ind*) συνέλεξα

συμβαίνω (*impers*) it happens/comes about

(*pf act ind*) συμβέβηκα

συμβάλλω (*act*) confer, converse; meet; (*mid*) assist, help

(*aor act ind*) συνέβαλον; (*impf act ind*) συνέβαλλον

συμπαθέω sympathize with

(*aor act ind*) συνεπάθησα

συμπαραλαμβάνω take along with

(*aor act ptc*) συμπαραλαβών

συμφέρω (*impers*) it is beneficial/of advantage; it is better

(*aor act ptc*) συνενέγκας

συνάγω gather, bring together

(*aor act ind*) συνήγαγον/συνῆξα

συναποθνῄσκω die with

(*aor act ind*) συναπέθανον

συνεισέρχομαι enter/go into with

(*aor act ind*) συνεισῆλθον

συνέρχομαι come together with, gather; go/come with, travel together with

(*aor act ind*) συνῆλθον; (*plpf act ind*) συνεληλύθειν; (*pf act ptc*) συνεληλυθώς

συνέχω enclose, surround; hold, confine; constrain, affect

(*impf mid-pass ind*) συνειχόμην

συνθάπτω bury together (with)

(*aor mid-pass ind*) συνετάφην

συνίημι/συνίω understand, comprehend

(*aor act ind*) συνῆκα; (*fut act ind*) συνήσω; (*aor act impv 2pl*) σύνετε; (*aor act subj*) συνῶ

συντρίβω crush, shatter, break

(*pf mid-pass inf*) συντετρῖφθαι

συνυποκρίνομαι join in pretense

(*aor mid-pass ind 3pl*) συνυπεκρίθησαν

συσταυρόω crucify with

(*aor mid-pass ind*) συνεσταυρώθην; (*pf mid-pass ind*) συνεσταύρωμαι; (*aor mid-pass ptc*) συνσταυρωθείς <TH>

σφάζω slay, slaughter

(*aor act ind*) ἔσφαξα; (*aor mid-pass ind*) ἐσφάγην; (*fut act ind*) σφάξω; (*pf mid-pass ptc*) ἐσφαγμένος

T

ταράσσω agitate, disturb

(*aor mid-pass ind*) ἐταράχθην; (*pf mid-pass ind*) τετάραγμαι, *3sg* τετάρακται

τάσσω (*act*) order, arrange; determine, designate; (*mid*) agree upon, settle

(*pf mid-pass ind*) τέταγμαι

τίκτω give birth to, bear, [inanimate] produce

(*aor act ind*) ἔτεκον; (*fut mid ind*) τέξομαι [there is no *fut act*]

τρεῖς three

(*gen pl*) τριῶν, (*dat pl*) τρισίν, (*acc pl*) τρία

τρέχω run

(*aor act ind*) ἔδραμον

τυγχάνω happen upon, meet with, obtain, attain

(*aor act ind*) ἔτυχον; (*pf act ind*) τέτυχα; (*aor act opt 3sg*) τύχοι

Υ

ὑπομιμνῄσκω/ὑπομιμνήσκω (*trans act*) remind, bring up; (*intrans mid*) remember

(*aor act ind*) ὑπέμνησα; (*fut act ind*) ὑπομνήσω

ὑποτάσσω subject, subordinate

(*aor mid-pass ind*) ὑπετάγην; (*fut mid-pass ind*) ὑποταγήσομαι; (*pf mid-pass ptc*) ὑποτεταγμένος

ὑποφέρω endure

(*aor act ind*) ὑπήνεγκα

Φ

φέρω bring, take along, bear

(*aor act ind*) ἤνεγκα; (*fut act ind*) οἴσω

φεύγω flee; escape; avoid

(*aor act ind*) ἔφυγον; the *fut* is *mid* only.

φθείρω corrupt, ruin, destroy

(*fut mid-pass ind*) φθαρήσομαι; (*aor mid-pass subj*) φθαρῶ